Edited by Konstantin Butz and Christian Peters

Skateboard Studies

Koenig Books, London

Contents

ALOHA

Konstantin Butz and Christian Peters

Preface

A curved wooden ramp catapults a skateboarder onto the vertical space of a white wall. He hovers right between the marble floor and two framed pictures resembling mug shots of a man hanging above him. The skateboarder is wearing a white fencing suit that reads "ALOHA" in capitalized letters on his back. Next to him, another person in black sits on the floor and captures his maneuver with a camera. At first view, this scenario appears surreal. What is going on here? Where is this? What is this?

It becomes evident that the skating maneuver must be taking place in an exhibition space as soon as one realizes that the pictures on the wall are works by Andy Warhol. This has to be a museum. However, the skateboarder introduces an unexpected aspect into this institutional environment: instead of contemplatively looking at the artworks exhibited—as the accustomed museum visitor would normally do—the skateboarder maneuvers his body onto the wall with his four-wheeled device and thus performatively occupies and offers a new perspective, a new and versatile take on this spatial setting.

The protagonist we observe in this scene (or, more precisely: the protagonist in the photographic image that precedes this preface) is professional skateboarder and artist Mark Gonzales, who gained an international reputation as one of the pioneers of street skateboarding. The maneuver he executes took place at the Städtisches Museum Abteiberg in Mönchengladbach, Germany in 1998 and was part of a performance initiated by Gonzales and German artist Johannes Wohnseifer. Its title: *Backworlds/Forwords*.

Backworlds/Forwords raises a number of questions and thoughts that provide an ideal starting point for the introduction of this book. The performance presents skateboarding as the complex, challenging, creative, thought-provoking, and yet still very simple, playful, and immediate activity it has been for more than six decades now. Mark Gonzales's skateboard ride through a museum foregrounds the notion of bodily movement that pervades skateboarding as an essential trait and combines it with questions concerning space, architecture, media, art, economy, fashion, culture, history, identity, activism, authority, and creativity:

Who is this skateboarder? Where does he come from? What is his motivation? Is his performance a critique of the rather static and institutionalized museum space or is it art itself? Is his activity a contribution to an accepted cultural canon or does it represent a subcultural dissociation from an alleged norm? Is his vertical ride a trespassing upon established boundaries or a creative extension of available potentialities? Is his maneuver an adequate artistic expression for a museum? Is it a sport? Or is it a delinquency within a restricted social setting? Is the suit with the "ALOHA" message a fashion statement of individual style or a historical reference to skateboarding's connection to the Hawaiian culture of surfing? What do skateboarders usually wear? What follows from the fact that the protagonist in this performance is male? Is this moment representative for skateboarding or is it exceptional? What role does the photographer play in this setting? What medial image does capturing the performance in a photograph create? What would be different if it was filmed with a video camera? Where do skateboarders usually skate? What role does the city play in their activity? What kind of maneuvers do they perform? What reaction do they face?

Detached from the specific and yet exemplary setting of *Backworlds/Forwords*, *Skateboard Studies* tries to approach these and other questions regarding skateboarding from a variety of theoretical and methodological angles. Picking up on the performance title *Backworlds/Forwords* and its nuanced implications concerning a phenomenon that moves between the poles of physical *worlds* and discursive *words*, it offers comprehensive analyses of skateboarding as a material and cultural practice that has been the object of study for numerous international scholars over the last decades. While skateboarding continues to constitute the subject matter for a myriad number of books and magazines that mostly foreground its visual appeal by presenting it through images, photographs, and graphics in combination with shorter texts, background information, popular articles, retrospectives, and historical accounts,[1] there are hardly any publications that pay tribute to the growing number of academic contributions to this discourse. Since Iain Borden's groundbreaking book *Skateboarding, Space and the City* presented one of the first really serious and internationally received scholarly studies of the subject in 2001, a whole range of doctoral dissertations, master theses, and journal articles on skateboarding have followed and explored its cultural, social, historical, and material effects on an academic level integrating disciplines ranging from sociology, cultural studies, American studies, and gender studies to architecture, geography, history, art history, and sports science.[2] However, with the exception of the recently published anthology *Skateboarding: Subcultures, Sites and Shifts* (2016) edited by Australian scholar Kara-Jane Lombard, there are no collections that provide insight, let alone a condensed overview, of the scholarly work that has been done on skateboarding so far.

Skateboard Studies picks up on what Lombard's important contribution started. It tries to advance the discursive and theoretical engagement in the academic study of skateboarding without aiming at completeness. This book tries to offer different entryways into what its title stakes out as the comprehensive field of skateboard studies.[3] The term "skateboard studies,"

1 As examples of published accounts of skateboarding with a focus on photographs, images, and nonacademic texts, cf. Alv, Basile, and Trichet; Ausband and Sharp; Blümlein, Schmid, and Vogel; Brooke; Denike; Fitzpatrick; Giligan; Hoye; Leslie and Burgoyne; Marcus; Rose; Thrasher; Toole.

2 As examples of published dissertations and master theses on skateboarding, cf. Beal, *The Subculture of Skateboarding*; Butz, *Grinding California*; Friedel; Peters *Skateboarding*; Reinhart, *Wir wollten einfach*; Schweer; Vivoni, *Contesting Public Space*; Yochim.

however, is neither meant to define a clearly delineated set of scholarly assumptions nor does it postulate the emergence of a new academic discipline. It rather suggests a very open and flexible umbrella term uniting all kinds of disciplinary approaches interested in the impact of the skateboard and the accompanying activity of skateboarding as an almost ubiquitous phenomenon in today's urban environment.

The eleven essays presented in *Skateboard Studies* stem from different years and roughly cover the timespan from the beginning of the new millennium until today. Some of them have been previously published and others were specifically written for this volume. Some of them give broader overviews of different developments and evolutions in skateboarding while others focus on very specific and exemplary aspects. What they have in common is that they can all be read as both individual microstudies of phenomena, events, situations, and social settings somehow linked to the topic of skateboarding *and* as contributions to the heuristic academic endeavor that we associate with the notion of skateboard studies. As for the concrete selection of the texts we present in this volume, we followed a pragmatic approach: we asked those authors for contributions whose work has been extremely valuable and helpful in our own research activities. *Skateboard Studies* thus basically constitutes a compartment in the theoretical toolbox that accompanied us on our individual inquiries into the world of skateboarding. The contributing authors are all experts that apply their specific disciplinary backgrounds to the subject matter at hand. We recommend reading the essays collected in this book as exemplary insights into their respective expertise. All of them have extensively published on skateboarding and we strongly encourage our readers to consult these rich sources for further and deeper examinations.[4] We are aware that there are other established academics and promising young researchers out there who have already developed and are still working on their own takes on skateboarding; but as we mentioned above: *Skateboard Studies* does not claim completeness. At best, it

3 We are aware that the term "skateboard studies" might just as well (or should?) be introduced in the form of the gerund, i.e. skateboard*ing* studies, as this would emphasize the mobile, dynamic, and floating qualities that characterize the practice of movement on a wooden board with four wheels. The fact that we chose the shorter title *Skateboard Studies* for this book does not imply a mere focus on the skateboard as an object or product; *Skateboard Studies* refers to all aspects that constitute the practices and the cultures that evolve(d) around the skateboard and skateboarding.

4 As examples of other publications of the contributing authors of this book cf. Beal; Borden; Butz; Howell; Kusz; Peters; Reinhart; Schäfer; Vivoni; Yochim.

constitutes one of many possible starting points to trigger further complex, challenging, and ongoing discussions of skateboarding.

Since *Skateboard Studies* aims at a theoretical continuation and expansion of the already existent discourses around skateboarding, we deliberately decided to design our book as a reader, i.e. a book that particularly focuses on text. Not in contrast but as an addition to the manifold "coffee-table books" that deal with skateboarding and combine images, photographs, and texts, we opted for a smaller format that foregrounds a purely textual approach. Johannes Wohnseifer's photographs of Mark Gonzales in *Backworlds/Forwords* provide the only graphic contribution we chose to include in *Skateboard Studies*. They divert from the "usual" skateboard photography—if there is anything like that—in that they document a unique and inspiring skateboard performance in an exceptional space while capturing the versatile immediacy of active skateboarding in a characteristic snapshot aesthetic. Wohnseifer's photographs do not only constitute singular documents in the visual history of skateboarding; as brief visual intermezzi, they also help to mark the transitions between the different essays in this book and imply a concrete instruction for our readership:

Just as Mark Gonzales had to find and develop his own trajectory between the exhibition pieces of the museum, just as he brought his skills and his perspective to this new and unfamiliar context, the readers of *Skateboard Studies* are invited to freely *move* between its different texts. There is no definite choreography in skateboarding and there is none in this book. Consider the essays and their respective topics as skate spots that can be individually approached and require different interests and skills. You can read one after the other or you can dive right into the middle. You can revisit a certain text time and again or you can establish interconnections between various texts and turn them into your own smooth line. As the editors of this book we would be delighted if our collection of essays inspired you to come up with your own thoughts on skateboarding and its connections to critical academic analysis and other cultural practices.

The scholarly aspirations that motivate *Skateboard Studies* thereby do not postulate an insider status that considers itself authorized by some kind of alleged academic superiority. We know that many protagonists and activists involved in the various existing skateboard scenes and communities might—and often in fact do—react with a certain amount of skepticism if not contempt to analyses that academics conduct of "their" culture. We are aware that skateboarding in itself is not self-evidently tied to research projects at universities. First and foremost, it is a concrete activity and no scholarly approach can substitute the empirical knowledge of skateboarding gained through the act of skateboarding itself, i.e. the movement of your body with and on a skateboard. Nevertheless, the theoretical implications that follow from this movement and its discursive implementation in spatial, cultural, and social scenarios are eminently compatible with a whole variety of core questions posed in a variety of academic disciplines. Certainly, you do not need *Skateboard Studies* to practice skateboarding and, certainly, every active skateboarder individually occupies the status of an expert concerning the activity of skateboarding. However, as skateboarding can influence and touch upon so many aspects of our everyday life through its unique way of appropriating and relating to the urban environment, we are convinced that the theoretical reflections and discursive explorations it triggers are full of potential to alter the way we think and move.

Cologne,
Spring 2018

References and Further Reading

Alv, Pontus, Alexander Basile, and Bertrand Trichet. *Dirt Ollies: A Skateboard Trip to Mongolia*. Berlin: Bildschöne Bücher, 2007. Print.

Ausband, Ozzie and Sharp, William. *Back in the Day: The Rise of Skateboarding: Photographs 1975 - 1980*. Berkeley: Gingko Press, 2018. Print.

Beal, Becky. "Disqualifying the Official: An Exploration of Social Resistance Through the Subculture of Skateboarding." *Sociology of Sport Journal* 12.3 (1995): 252–67. Print.

Beal, Becky. *The Subculture of Skateboarding: Beyond Social Resistance*. Dissertation, University of Northern Colorado, 1992. Print.

Blümlein, Jürgen, Daniel Schmid, and Dirk Vogel. *Made for Skate: The Illustrated History of Skateboard Footwear.* Berkeley: Gingko Press, 2010. Print.

Blümlein, Jürgen and Dirk Vogel. *Skateboarding is not a Fashion.* Berkeley: Gingko Press, 2018. Print.

Borden, Iain. "Southbank Skateboarding, London and Urban Culture: The Undercroft, Hungerford Bridge and House of Vans." *Skateboarding: Subcultures, Sites and Shifts*. Ed. Kara-Jane Lombard. Abingdon: Routledge, 2015. 91–107. Print.

Borden, Iain. "The Spaces of Skateboarding." *Architect's Journal* 28 November (2014): 56–59. Print.

Brooke, Michael. *The Concrete Wave: The History of Skateboarding*. Toronto: Warwick Publishing, 2005. Print.

Butz, Konstantin. *Grinding California: Culture and Corporeality in American Skate Punk*. Bielefeld: Transcript, 2012. Print.

Butz, Konstantin. "The Authenticity of a T-Shirt: Ryan Gosling, Roddy Dangerblood, and the Rebellious Genealogy of Thrasher Magazine." *Rock Music Studies* 4.1 (2017). 47–56. Print.

Butz, Konstantin. "The Californian Safety Pin: Excerpts from a Journey to the Origins of Skate Punk." *HUCK Magazine* 25 (2011): 58–64. Print.

Denike, Bob (ed.). *Built to Grind: 25 Years of Hardcore Skateboarding*. San Francisco: High Speed Productions, 2004. Print.

Fitzpatrick, Jim. *Skateistan: The Tale of Skateboarding in Afghanistan*. Berlin: Skateistan, 2012. Print.

Friedel, Sophie. *The Art of Living Sideways: Skateboarding, Peace and Elicitive Conflict Transformation.* Wiesbaden: Springer, 2015. Print.

Giligan, Richard. *DIY. Underground Skateparks*. Munich: Prestel, 2012. High Speed Productions, 2004. Print.

Howell, Ocean. "Skatepark as Neoliberal Playground. Urban Governance, Recreation Space, and the Cultivation of Personal Responsibility." *Space and Culture* 11.4 (2008): 475–96. Print.

Howell, Ocean. "The Poetics of Security: Skateboarding, Urban Design, and the New Public Space." *Urban Action*. San Francisco State University, Urban Studies Department (2011): 64–86. Print.

Hoye, Jacob. *Boards: The Art + Design of the Skateboard*. Hombrechtikon: Edition Olms, 2003. Print.

Kusz, Kyle. *Revolt of the White Athlete: Race, Media and the Emergence of Extreme Athletes in America*. New York, et al.: Peter Lang, 2007. Print.

Kusz, Kyle. (2006). "Why be a 'Jackass'?: Media Images of Young White Men In and Out of Sport in New Millennium America." *Learning Culture Through Sport*. Eds. Sandra Spickard Prettyman and Brian Lampman. Lanham, MD: Rowman & Littlefield. 182–96. Print.

Leslie, Jeremy, and Patrick Burgoyne. *Surf/Skate/Snow Graphics*. London: Laurence King. 1997. Print.

Lombard, Kara-Jane, ed. *Skateboarding: Subcultures, Sites and Shifts*. Abingdon: Routledge, 2015. Print.

Marcus, Ben. *The Skateboard: The Good, the Rad, and the Gnarly*. Minneapolis: MVP Books, 2011. Print.

Peters, Christian. "Skateboarding als Stadt-Praxis. Zum Place-Making der Kölner Skateboarder." *Stadt, Land, Sport. Urbane und touristische Sporträume.* Eds. Hagen Wäsche and Tim Schmidt-Weichmann. Hamburg: Feldhaus Verlag, 2014. 34–44. Print.

Peters, Christian. *Skateboarding. Ethnographie einer urbanen Praxis*. Münster: Waxmann, 2016. Print.

Peters, Christian. "Skating the City. Feldforschung auf der Kölner Domplatte." *Feldforschung und Ethnographische Zugänge in der Sportpädagogik*. Ed. Tim Bindel. Aachen: Shaker, 2011. 144–57. Print.

Reinhart, Kai. 2010. *"Wir wollten einfach unser Ding machen." DDR-Sportler zwischen Fremdbestimmung und Selbstverwirklichung.* Frankfurt/M.: Campus, 2010. Print.

Reinhart, Kai. 2010. "'I ollied the Berlin Wall' – An Empirical and Theoretical Study on Skateboarding in Socialist East Germany (GDR)." *Stadion* 36 (2010): 157–76. Print.

Rose, Aaron (ed.). *Dysfunctional*. London: Booth-Clibborn Editions, 1999. Print.

Schäfer, Eckehart Velten. "Raum schaffen und Stadt machen: Body Spaces und Sportmobiliar in der Skateboard-Praktik." *Städtische Spielräume für Sport, Spiel und Bewegung*. Ed. Robin S. Kähler. Hamburg: Edition Czwalina, 2015. 69–78. Print.

Schäfer, Eckehart Velten. "Sport mit den Mitteln des Pop. Skateboard-Videos: Bewegungslernen, Vergemeinschaftung und Jugendmarketing." *Sport und Gesellschaft* 12.2 (2015): 149–70. Print.

Schweer, Sebastian. *Skateboarding zwischen urbaner Rebellion und neoliberalem Selbstentwurf*. Bielefeld: Transcript, 2014. Print.

Thrasher. *Skate and Destroy: 25 Years of Thrasher Magazine*. New York: Universe, 2006.

Toole, Nikki. *Skater*. Heidelberg: Kehrer, 2015. Print.

Vivoni, Francisco. *Contesting Public Space: Skateboarding, Urban Development, and the Politics of Play*. Dissertation, University of Illinois at Urbana-Champaign, 2010. Print.

Vivoni, Francisco. "Spots of Spatial Desire: Skateparks, Skateplazas, and Urban Politics." *Journal of Sport and Social Issues* 33.2 (2009): 130–49. Print.

Vivoni, Francisco. "Waxing Ledges: Built Environments, Alternative Sustainability, and the Chicago Skateboarding Scene." *Local Environment* 18.3 (2013): 350–53.

Yochim, Emily Chivers. *Skate Life: Re-Imagining White Masculinity*. Ann Arbor: University of Michigan Press, 2010. Print.

ululaau
HUIKALA

Iain Borden

Skateboarding and Public Space
A Brief History of 50 Years of Change

Skateboarding has always taken place in public. Although skate parks were highly favored during the late 1970s, and have become increasingly common again during the 2010s, it is in the beachside promenades, suburban streets, city sidewalks, plazas, and squares that skateboarding has been most persistently present. This essay traces the broad shift in these public and semi-public spaces over the last fifty years, noting how skateboarding practices, public perceptions, and urban policy have gradually moved from broad tolerance in the 1960s and 1970s, and then outright opposition in the 1990s and 2000s, into some more recent conciliatory negotiations and even creative partnerships.

Found Space

In the early 1960s, public skateboarding sites were located in surf-side Californian communities like Malibu, Santa Monica, Doheny, Huntington, and La Jolla, as well as Daytona Beach, Palm Beach, and Atlantic City on the American East Coast, and Oahu's North shore in Hawaii. Outside the US, other skateboarding centers included North Bondi and Manly Beach in Australia, and the surf towns of the UK's Cornwall and south Wales. In such venues, as Wentzle Ruml described skateboarding in Santa Monica, surfer-skateboarders "rode imaginary waves and blazed all over the city" (Marcus and Griggi 138).

After a massive downturn in popularity in the mid-1960s, skateboarding returned to the public realm with a vengeance in the mid-1970s, with suburban roads, school yards, drainage ditches, and swimming pools all being treated as what I have termed "found space" (Borden, *Skateboarding, Space and the City*)—places not intended for skateboarding but nonetheless appropriated by skaters, and often on a temporary or semi-illegal basis. Places like La Costa in North San Diego County quickly became a "Mecca for skateboarders from all over southern California" (Balma 13), allowing surfers to roll down asphalt paths as if these were ocean waves. In Australia, as shown in *The Ultimate Flex Machine* (dir. Jason Cameron, 1975), local skaters performed traverses, slides, and carves across the monumental slope of "The Spillway" in Victoria state, as well as at much smaller sites like roadside banks in Bellevue Hill, a suburb of Sydney. Other spots were even more demanding. Wallos, an extended rainwater ditch on Oahu, offered a mixture of steep banks and bowl-like interim stages, where overgrown vegetation, graffiti, and a semi-hidden location created a primeval skateboarding terrain. The overall effect was "akin to surfing consecutive big waves, a downhill run and a half-pipe combined. It was insane" (Weyland 221).

Public opinion on all these places was varied yet often critical. Indeed, the very first mention of skateboarding in the *Los Angeles Times*, on June 14, 1959, called for skaters to be outlawed in Pasadena. Soon afterwards, in the mid-1960s, skaters met with protests from the California Medical Association and legislative restrictions imposed by at least twenty American city councils, along with disapproving press reporting in publications like *Consumer Bulletin*, *Good Housekeeping*, the *Los Angeles Times*, the *New York Times*, the *Wall Street Journal*, and the *Washington Post*. Even more seriously, in 1964 Chris Villalobos, a fifteen-year-old Los Angeles skater, was shot dead by a neighbor annoyed by the sound of skateboarding ("Boy Killed" 3). Beyond the US, skateboarding on the Champs-Élysées in Paris was banned by police citing anti-roller skate laws, while the Canadian film *The Devil's Toy* (dir. Claude Jutra, 1966) showed Montreal skaters running from police, having their boards confiscated, and being penned into a flat roller skate rink. A deadpan voice-over, reminiscent of Jean-Luc Godard's dystopian *Alphaville* (1965), compared skateboarding to the terrors of guns, bombs, and the plague, being "a dread disease which needed only pavement in order to multiply and proliferate."

Yet it is important not to overstate such negative reactions. *The Devil's Toy* was, in fact, an ironic commentary on overly heavy-handed reactions to skateboarding, and did much to promote skateboarding as a healthy and independent activity. By the summer of 1965 skateboarding was fully established as a US-wide phenomenon, gaining national ABC "Wide World of Sports" television coverage for the National Skateboard Championships in Anaheim. Skateboarding also took center stage in the Academy Award-nominated and Palme d'Or-winning *Skaterdater* (dir. Noel Black, 1965), shown to audiences nationwide alongside the James Bond movie *Thunderball* (Green). The same year, a color cover of *Life* magazine sported Patti McGee from San Diego doing a handstand, and *Popular Mechanics* ran a five-page feature on "Skateboard Acrobatics" (Boykin and Grant); skate teams like Hobie, Jacks, Makaha, Palisades, Bayside, and Vita-Pakt were also well established, flying their riders around the US to exhibition events. McGee similarly gave demonstrations everywhere from Macy's in New York to department stores nationwide (Harms and Smith 323–4). Overseas, British Pathé news excitedly reported in 1964 on what they described as the new Australian pastime of "roller boarding," while France's *Pilote* (1965) and *Tintin* (1966) magazines both ran features. Furthermore, 1960s celebrities including Tom Jones in London, Clint Eastwood in Rome, Katharine Hepburn in Beverly Hills, John Lennon in the Bahamas, and even Snoopy the dog from the cartoon strip *Peanuts* were all depicted skateboarding, generating further public support.

Skateboarding might combine commercialism, professionalism, ambition, and even cynicism along with youthful exhilaration, movement, and pleasure.

During the 1970s, media attention continued this broadly affirmative tone. Documentary-style movies like *Super Session* (dir. Hal Jepsen, 1975), *Downhill Motion* (dir. Spyder Wills and Greg Weaver, 1975), *The Ultimate Flex Machine* (dir. Jason Cameron, 1975), *Freewheelin'* (dir. Scott Dittrich, 1976), *Magic Rolling Board* (dir. Jim Freeman and Greg Macgillivray, 1976), *Go For It* (dir. Paul Rapp, 1976), and *Hard Waves, Soft Wheels* (dir. Jim Plimton, 1977) all played to receptive surfer-skater audiences, while others, such as *Hot Wheels* (dir. Richard Gayer, 1978), *Spinn'in Wheels* (dir. Chris Carmichael, 1975), and *Skateboard Madness* (produced Hal Jepsen, dir. Julian Pena, 1980) even secured wider national distribution deals, often as support for mainstream movies. The widely watched 1978 BBC television documentary *Skateboard Kings* showed Jay Adams, Tony Alva, and other skaters on the search for the perfect Californian backyard pool, while the mainstream film release *Skateboard: The Movie*, (dir. George Gage, 1978) went beyond pure action footage to show how skateboarding might combine commercialism, professionalism, ambition, and even cynicism along with youthful exhilaration, movement, and pleasure.

Contestation

If benign acceptance and mild curiosity generally pervaded public reactions to skateboarding in the 1960s and 1970s, the next two decades saw substantial shifts in these attitudes. In the mid-1980s and into the 1990s, after the first wave of skate parks had come and gone, skateboarding began its seminal extension into what became known as "streetstyle" or, later, "street" skateboarding. Using the ollie as their primary tactic, street skaters rode up and over the curbs, ledges, planters, benches, stairs, rails, and other elements of urban public space. No longer situated among the detached villas and pools of undulating, semi-suburban, and surf-side landscapes, these skaters had moved into the downtown cores of cities worldwide. Furthermore, these new sites were no longer hidden away in suburbia, but were now fully visible in university campuses, urban squares, public institutions, national theatres, and commercial office plazas, as well as everyday roads, sidewalks, malls, and parking lots. In such places, skateboarding continued its thematic of appropriating found spaces, and so corresponded with theorist Michel de Certeau's notion of "foreign practices" which run counter to the "geometrical" or "geographical" space of panoptic city centers (de Certeau 93). Street skateboarding, then, helped unlock a hidden potential of cities; according to architect Anthony Bracali, it "energized many of these poorly conceived and under-utilized spaces with a new activity." Some of these new skate spots also acquired national and even international fame, including (among many others) places like MACBA (Barcelona), Kulturforum (Berlin), Jarmers Plads (Copenhagen), Yuexu Park (Guangdong), Hollywood High (Los Angeles), Hotel de Ville (Lyon), Plaza De Colón (Madrid), Flinders Street (Melbourne), Milano Centrale/MC (Milan), Brooklyn Banks (New York), Bercy (Paris), Embarcadero/EMB (San Francisco), Vale Anhangabau (São Paulo), Dongdaemun/Design Park (Seoul), People's Square (Shanghai), Deng Xiaoping Plaza (Shenzhen), and Pulaski Park (Washington, DC).

These new skate spots, however, have not been without their own challenges. Typically located in the very center of cities, amid places of work, tourism, retail, and leisure, these new venues were subject to much greater forces of power, commercialism, and general societal pressure than were the suburban skate spots of the 1960s and 1970s. Social space is always a matter of contestation (Lefebvre), and this fact was made extremely evident to skaters via innumerable anti-skateboarding bans, bylaws, fines, and even prosecutions. Furthermore, street skaters have been confronted by armies of killjoy knobs, blocks, and other protruding features being added to otherwise skateable surfaces, all aimed at preventing skaters' sliding, grinding, and rolling movements. By 2000, these devices were commonplace across urban squares and building frontages worldwide, and by 2015 the Californian company Skatestoppers, after which these devices are generically known, claimed to have introduced over one million devices in over ten thousand locations (www.skatestoppers.com). The SkateBlock company similarly offers eighteen different products, which, it proudly announces, "are 'on duty' 24 hours a day, 7 days a week, 365 days a year!" (www.block.com). More recently, in 2014 London witnessed the introduction of the "Camden bench," a complexly surfaced and specially coated seat deliberately designed to repel anyone wishing to linger, the homeless needing to lie down, street artists wanting to paint and, of course, anyone looking to skate. Here, skateboarding is caught up in the shift from the policing of specific individuals to the more general governance of "criminogenic" spaces, such as those town squares, bus stops, car parks, and late-night neighborhoods where crime is considered to be rifer (Lombard 481–82).

Even more problematic than skatestoppers has been the demolition or removal of skate spots from the public domain —a fate which has befallen many of the locations identified above. One of the most notorious examples of this process is Philadelphia's John F. Kennedy Plaza, aka Love Park, which has been examined in detail by Ocean Howell and Jeremy Nemeth. Originally devised by celebrated architect Edmund Bacon as a civic space, Love Park was opened in 1965, and during the 1990s and early 2000s became internationally renowned for its skateboardable terrain. Frequented by numerous locals as well as renowned professionals such as Brian Wenning, Matt Reason, Fred Gall, Ricky Oyola, Stevie Williams, and Josh Kalis, the skaters' presence helped keep the park safe from drug dealers and crime, and was even welcomed by neighboring business people. For example, investment banker Andrew Hohns viewed Love Park as "an international symbol of youth and vitality, an image Philadelphia desperately needs to project. It provides a generous amount of free publicity for the city, and generates a significant amount of tourism" (McHugh 111–12). In addition, Love Park's international reputation for street skating helped attract the 2001 and 2002 X Games, benefitting Philadelphia to the tune of $80 million (cf. Nemeth).

Nonetheless, citing $60,000 of damaged ledges and perceived dangers to other users, in 2000 a city ordinance was passed banning skateboarding; two years later the park was reconfigured with anti-skate measures such as new landscaping, intrusive planters, and wooden benches. Police patrols were reinforced by the threat of $300 fines and imprisonment. Despite the local skaters' counter-proposal to enhance the park's multi-use characteristics, support from the original architect Bacon, and even an offer by skate shoe manufacturer DC to pay $1 million toward maintenance costs, Love Park has remained off-limits to all but the most determined of skaters ever since.

And yet, even in this tale of dispossession and displacement, there are some positive signs. Significantly, much of the public debate around Love Park concerned its loss not only to skaters but to the city as a whole. In Richard Florida's influential *Rise of the Creative Class*, the accusation is made that favoring short-term business interests runs the risk of ignoring the younger creative generation, i.e. the workers, entrepreneurs, and future leaders of the very companies which modern cities are so keen to attract. As Florida commented about Love Park in 2002, such places "are very important to young people, an intrinsic part of their creative culture, part of their identity. To take the park away is to tell them that they are not valid. Big mistake" (quoted in Howell 35; also cf. Howell's essay in this book). Notably, in a 2003 online poll by *Philadelphia Daily News*, some 69% of responses favored skateboarding in Love Park (McHugh). Nor have such views been confined to Philadelphia; in the UK skateboarders have been interpreted as a positive presence in the streets of Newcastle and Gateshead, making the elderly feel safe, and even contributing to falls in crime and antisocial behavior (Jenson, Swords, and Jeffries).

One reason why the general public may support skaters is for the way the latter aid urban development. For example, Howell notes how the Love Park skaters acted as "shock troops of gentrification," part of a "creative class" which softened the presence of the homeless, inserted skate industry capital, and generally generated a hip urban image. Or as Oyola put it, "We made this place alive. It was just fuckin' drug dealers, dudes chillin' up there, fightin' each other all the time. We came here and we gave it life" (Howell 32, 40). Skaters in Hamilton (near Toronto) similarly acted as unwitting gentrifiers, rendering run-down neighborhoods more attractive to artists, professionals, and the affluent classes, and so helping Hamilton migrate from working-class steel town to creative and cultural hub (cf. Orpana).

Preservation

While Love Park was lost to Philadelphia skaters, other sites have enjoyed more positive outcomes. Perhaps most famously, this occurred at the Undercroft area of London's Southbank Centre, the Brutalist architecture and angled banks of which had been heavily skated since at least the mid-1970s as a kind of undercover skate park. During the 1980s and 1990s, as the new street skateboarding emerged, the Undercroft took on the character of an urban found space, and then subtly changed again in the mid-2000s when several skateable blocks were installed by Richard "Badger" Holland and the skateboard arts group The Side Effects of Urethane. At this juncture, murals and graffiti also started to appear, marking the Undercroft as a center not just for skaters but for the BMX riders, photographers, filmmakers, poets, dancers, and musicians who were increasingly drawn to the spot. As a result of all this rich history, the Undercroft achieved near mythic status in UK skateboarding, as a place where thousands learned their craft, from novices to professionals, and from hardcore locals to occasional visitors.

Given all this, it is unsurprising that large numbers of skaters and general public alike reacted extremely unfavorably to the Southbank Centre's suggestion in 2013 that, to help fund a massive improvement and redevelopment package for the arts buildings overhead, the Undercroft should be turned into retail units, with skaters being relocated to the adjacent Hungerford Bridge site. United mostly under the "Long Live Southbank" (LLSB) banner, the objectors mounted a skillful oppositional campaign under the headings of "You Can't Move History," "Preservation and Not Relocation," and "Construction Without Destruction." Widespread backing came from the skateboard community, academics like myself, musicians, artists, the general public, and politicians. Most importantly, after 150,000 people had signed a petition supporting the skaters and over 27,000 had opposed the Southbank Centre planning application, the Mayor of London, Boris Johnson, seized the sizeable political opportunity and declared the Undercroft as "part of the cultural fabric of London." Effectively vetoing the Southbank Centre's planning application, Johnson's pronouncement was a decisive moment (Brown). In January 2014, the Southbank Centre signed a Section 106 planning agreement with Lambeth borough council, effectively securing the Undercroft for skateboarding in perpetuity; a year later there was even talk of opening out the skate space to its much larger, original extent.

It is worth highlighting why so many nonskaters supported these London skaters. People from all over the city and wider world have enjoyed seeing the Undercroft's unique combination of skateboarding-against-concrete, of unruly disorder amidst increasing sanitization, and so witnessing a truly public space in action. Skateboarding here is "inspiring and uplifting," commented one member of the public. "It promotes all kind of values that we need in this society." Or as another noted, "take away the diversity of the Southbank and you will kill the charm" (Long Live Southbank). Even the conservatively minded newspaper *The Times* proclaimed that destroying the skate space to provide retail outlets would amount to "cultural vandalism" (Purves).

This is important stuff, and transcends the immediate needs of skateboarding to speak to a larger question as to the kinds of public spaces we desire today. As David Harvey has noted, the right to the city "is not merely a right of access to what the property speculators and state planners define, but an active right to make the city different, to shape it more in accord with our heart's desire, and to re-make ourselves thereby in a different image" (Harvey 940). In concert with Harvey, skateboarding at the Undercroft suggests that public spaces can be culturally richer than typical shopping malls or high streets, where predictable coffee outlets, branded shops, and chain restaurants abound. Above all, it suggests that we most enjoy cities and buildings when they both comfort and challenge us, when they provide us with things which we both expect and cannot anticipate. Skateboarding at the Undercroft is, then, one small yet vital part of this process.

Nor is this an isolated example, with other instances of skateboard space preservation also now emerging. Preeminent here is the "Rom" skate park in Essex, UK. First constructed in 1978 by Adrian Rolt and G-Force, it was this skate park which in 2013 I recommended to English Heritage, then the UK's national body for the historic preservation of architecture. After English Heritage subsequently underlined Rom's historic interest as deriving from being the best preserved of the early UK skate parks, from the technical aspects of its concrete construction, and from its standing as a skateboarding and youth cultural icon, Rom was granted Grade II listing status in September 2014—the first skate park in Europe to be accorded this status (cf. English Heritage).

Significantly, Rom's preservation order met with considerable media attention, including substantial news coverage by the BBC, ITV, and *The Times*, and an extended article by myself in *The Guardian* extolling the skate park's steeped history, beguiling charms, and obdurate survival (cf. Borden, "Pipe Dreams"). As government minister Ed Vaizey commented of Rom's listing, this "highlights how the UK's unique heritage reflects all parts of our culture and history" (*BBC News*), and clearly skateboarding was now an integral part of that official, pluralistic narrative.

This kind of acceptance of skateboarding as an intrinsic part of urban culture and heritage is also discernible elsewhere in other countries. In Montreal, a concrete entrance tunnel within the 1976 Olympics complex was appropriated post-games by local skaters. The Big O, as the squashed-oval and whistle-shaped tunnel is commonly known, became the city's most revered skate spot, whose tight transitions, punctured roof, and short side walls created an idiosyncratic and challenging terrain. By 2006, the commemorative *Pipe Fiends* publication was calling its graffiti-covered walls a "skateboarding sanctuary" and a piece of "true punk essence" (cf. Tison and Welsh).

Significantly, many Montreal skaters also referred to the Big O's central place in the city's wider urban heritage. "The energy that the Pipe has generated over the years has spread worldwide," stated Barry Walsh. "Let's hope the city opens its eyes and decides to preserve the infamous Pipe as a heritage landmark." As a result of these views, when in 2011 the pipe faced demolition due to construction work on Montreal Impact's soccer stadium, the skaters decided to do something to protect their hallowed ground. Unlike the skaters of London's Undercroft, however, the Montreal skaters decided not to mount outright opposition but instead to work with the authorities to have the tunnel relocated to an adjacent position, some thirty meters away. Reopened in 2013, the relocation of the Big O was celebrated as a victory for local skateboarders, Montreal Impact, and the city alike, and is seen as a new chapter in the ongoing history of skateboarding in the city ("Big O Rebirth").

In Tampa Bay, USA, the skate park in the Perry Harvey Sr. Park, commonly known as the "Bro Bowl," has also been subject to a similar process of protection and relocation. Originally designed by Joel Jackson and constructed in 1978, the Bro Bowl consists of a gentle snake run leading to a dish-like bowl and low-level bumps. Although less innovative than the commercial skate parks then being built around the world, the Bro Bowl was nonetheless a welcome open-access facility devoid of fees, safety gear regulations, or other constraints. Indeed, over subsequent decades the Bro Bowl became renowned for encouraging relaxed and creative skateboarding, and a community-oriented "common ground where people of different backgrounds, gender, and ethnicity could coexist through brotherhood" (Snyder 610–13).

In 2013, however, the city proposed demolishing the skate park as part of wider alterations to the surrounding park. After many years of contestation, locals such as Shannon Bruffett and Craig Snyder succeeded in getting the Bro Bowl placed on the National Register of Historic Places. This helped ensure that, even though the original Bro Bowl was demolished in June 2015, it was first accurately laser-scanned by the University of South Florida, enabling a duplicate to be reconstructed nearby in the park later the same year. Like the Undercroft, Rom skate park, and Big O pipe, the Bro Bowl has thus raised similar issues regarding the architectural heritage value of early skate parks and skate spots, as well as the community value of skateboarding to skaters and nonskaters alike. And although the final result in Tampa Bay, as duplication rather than outright protection, may not be to everyone's liking, the very fact that the city has agreed to maintain a skate park, as well as replicating the original Bro Bowl's design, shows that skateboarding and skate parks are now firmly established as part of social and architectural history.

Terrain Vague

Also running counter to skatestoppers and other anti-skateboarding practices are a small yet gradually increasing number of public spaces where skateboarding has actually been encouraged, either explicitly or implicitly. The resulting sites are a version of what architect Ignasi de Solà-Morales has called "terrain vague": empty spaces in which architecture acts not with aggressive power or abstract reason but with "attention to continuity of the flows, the energies, the rhythms established by the passing of time and the loss of limits" (Solà-Morales). More pragmatically, architect Anthony Bracali has argued for the positive impact of skateboarding in such public spaces. "Skateboarding is an activity which contributes to the variety, vitality and security of outdoor public spaces," states Bracali. "Skateboarders are tourists, consumers and participants in the arts, culture and economy of cities. Skateboarders extend the hours of the use of public spaces. Many non-skateboarders are attracted to spaces where people skateboard, just to watch the activity" (Bracali).

One variation of this theme is the Bracali-designed Paine's Park. Following the controversial banning of skateboarding from "Love Park," this $4.5 million facility for street-based skateboarding was opened in 2013 in a nearby waterside park, next to the Philadelphia Museum of Art. Designed by Bracali with local skaters, and financed by the Franklin's Paine Skatepark Fund, it offers 2.5 acres with brick banks, handrails, stone ledges, stairs and blocks, and even benches rescued from Love Park. As Bracali explains, the main idea was for a skateable space that looked unlike a skate park, "a great public space that just happened to be a skate park," thus merging different uses and so allowing the space to be "more usable and sustainable over time" (Clark and Hyland).

Similar considerations for an open public terrain suitable for skateboarding also lie behind the 2013 design for the Hungerford Bridge skateable space, as proposed by myself, Richard Holland, architect Søren Nordal Enevoldsen of SNE Architects, and local skaters for the Southbank Centre. Mooted as a potential replacement for—or addition to—the renowned nearby Undercroft skate space, this unrealized design incorporates high quality public space whose various ledges, stairs, banks, rails and other features are also attuned for skateboarding. With a projected total cost of £2–3 million (including significant new roofing and surrounding architectural modifications), materials for Hungerford Bridge's skateable areas are not the ultra-smooth concrete of skate parks, but the same sorts of everyday paving slabs, granite, and brick found in a typical urban space. Above all, nothing is provided *only* for skateboarding; everything has at the very least a dual function, hence seeking to integrate skaters, BMX riders, street artists, and members of the general public into an accessible and welcoming space, all nestling under a protective illuminated roof.

Some skaters have rejected the Hungerford Bridge design on the *a priori* grounds that, as street skaters often prefer appropriating existing architecture rather than using purpose-designed skate parks, it is impossible to deliberately design architecture which is directed at street skaters yet still attractive to them. Still others, however, take the opposite view, and according to one local skater, the Hungerford Bridge design had the potential to provide "a true street-skateboarding spot" which "builds on the Undercroft's street heritage whilst providing the right flow and openness" (Borden and Holland). Support for this view comes from numerous other places worldwide where skateboard-friendly design has been successfully implemented into urban spaces and buildings. Not least here is the Undercroft itself, where the original 1960s architects' preference for providing open space for indeterminate uses may not have expressly targeted skateboarding but certainly allowed for its possibility. Even more tellingly, the Undercroft features used most extensively today—the skateable blocks first installed by Holland and others in the mid-2000s—were indeed provided expressly for skateboarding, thus making the Undercroft into a complex amalgam of raw found space, delightfully accidental functionality and deliberately skate-focused interventions. In late 2015, several other purpose-designed features, including a quarter pipe and new blocks, were also added to the Undercroft by the Southbank Centre at the bequest of local skaters.

Skaters often prefer appropriating existing architecture rather than using purpose-designed skate parks.

Other places are even more subtle in the way they attract skaters. For example, at the stealth-skateable Auditoria Park in Barcelona, designed by Foreign Office Architects, innumerable walls, banks, and ramps tempt skaters with curving transitions and long runs, as do the curved banks and handrails of the Phaeno Science Centre in Wolfsburg, designed by Zaha Hadid Architects (2005). At the $700 million Opera House in Oslo (2008), architects Snøhetta even consulted skateboarders regarding textures, materials, and skateable areas; parts of the building and surroundings are consequently arranged with marble ledges, curbs, bench-like blocks, and railings (cf. Borden, "The Spaces of Skateboarding").

As Snøhetta's actions in Oslo and these other examples all suggest, it is perfectly possible to design public spaces suitable for skateboarding. Sometimes the results are quite skate park-like, as at Ursulines Square in Brussels (2005), where the skate collective Brusk installed a bowl (repainted annually) and other transitions, gradually merging skate-oriented into multipurpose and nonskate functions. More understated is the Landhausplatz (LHP) public plaza in Innsbruck (2011), designed by LAAC Architekten and Stiefel Kramer Architecture, where an undulating surface of flats, banks, ledges, plateaus, and blocks accommodates a new mélange of urban activities suitable for pedestrians, skateboarders, and BMX riders alike (cf. Ritter, Treichl, and Wedekind). Yet another example of a skate-friendly terrain vague is the mixed-use Rabalder Parken (2012) in Roskilde, Denmark, by Enevoldsen and SNE Architects. Here, an existing 9-meter-wide and 440-meter-long rainwater system has been inventively repurposed for skateboarding, trampolining, barbecues, and other activities, thus recalling the drainage ditches appropriated by American skaters in the 1960s and 1970s.

Even purpose-designed skate parks can adopt equivalent tactics. Designed by Metrobox Architekten, the linear Kap 686 skate park (2011) in Cologne plays subtle games, weaving skaterly lines and obstacles among pedestrians and geometric landscaping ("Kap 686 Skate Park"), as does a proposed 18,000-square-feet under-bridge skate park in Wilmington, Delaware, where Grindline's streetscape design (2015) allows for a crisscrossing of skaters, cyclists, and pedestrians. At the small, 1,200-square-meter Lemvig skate park in Denmark (2013), designed by Glifberg+Lykke and Effekt, the undulating route and varying bank heights of a gentle snake run are included alongside a basketball area, sandpit, and other park features. The overall effect is of a subtly integrated harborside landscape, a place where skateboarding coexists with other pleasurable pursuits. Similarly inventive is the proposed "skatepath" in Omokoroa, New Zealand, where in 2015 a community skate group and Rich Landscapes designed a loop and figure-of-eight circuit around a local park, around which various "skate dot" ledges, banks, taco corners, pump bumps, rails, and other skateable features are placed ("Omokoroa's Eco-Friendly Skate Path"). The aim here is less to provide a traditional, stand-alone skate park and more to integrate skateboarding *within* a park-like setting, while also meeting community and environmental goals.

Regeneration and Tourism

If these kinds of progressive designs are largely aimed at local neighborhoods and communities, other skate-related developments within the urban realm have more commercial intentions at heart. As Lee Bofkin notes, cities which support street artists like Above, Banksy, SpY, and Vhils are more able to develop their unique urban identities, to engage with local communities, and to attract tourists (Bofkin 6–8). Skateboarding, too can be part of this kind of process, helping places to enrich, express, and promote their own culture.

One of the earliest examples of this process was the "Extreme Park" skate park (2002) in Louisville, Kentucky, opened partly to satisfy local skaters but also to attract new visitors to the city. Louisville Metro Government's four-thousand-square-meter facility cost \$2 million, and its layout, as originally conceived by skate park designers Wormhoudt, boasted a street course, vert ramp, several bowls, large full-pipe, and floodlit 24/7 opening. The booster intention was successful, and as mayor David Armstrong explained, Louisville consequently "gained a reputation of no longer being a sleepy little southern town but became an exciting, youthful extreme town" ("Final designs on Louisville Extreme Park"). A \$2.2 million reconfiguration was subsequently undertaken by Wormhoudt in 2014–15, including a new flow bowl and full-pipe, the latter sporting dramatic upper perforations.

Even more ambitious is "SMP" skate park (2005) in New Jiangwan City on the edge of Shanghai. Named after its principal backers, sports clothing company SMP, it covers 13,700 square meters of rideable terrain and includes the "Mondo Bowl"—the world's largest concrete bowl (1,415 square meters) for skateboarding—plus seating for five thousand spectators. Designed by Australia's Convic Design and built by Chengtou Construction at a cost of over \$26 million, SMP is also the world's most expensive skate park, and has even been used for the promotion of off-road Range Rover vehicles. Similarly ostentatious and constructed primarily for tourism is the 5,760-square-meter Black Pearl skate park (2005) in the Cayman Islands, while the

Streetdome skate park (2014) in Haderslev, Denmark, provides a massive indoor-outdoor $5.5 million facility spanning 4,500 square meters. Designed by skating pro Rune Glifberg along with Ebbe Lykke and CEBRA architects, and constructed by American skate park builders Grindline, it boasts a grass-domed weatherproof arena, as well as provision for kayaking, music, parkour, and climbing. This "cultural and experiential powerhouse" acts as a "facilitator" where "urban sport, street culture and youthful souls all meet together" (Streetdome).

Just as grandiose and quite possibly unique in skateboarding history is the world's first multistory skate park, the five-level "Urban Sports Park" in Folkestone, UK, (2018). Here, skateboarding is integrated within highly ambitious plans by the Roger De Haan Charitable Trust to transform a relatively run-down town into a creative, dynamic, and sustainable environment. The skate park building—designed by Guy Hollaway Architects and Maverick, with additional design input from myself—consequently comprises an extraordinary intersection of semitransparent outer skin, fluid interconnecting rideable surfaces, and significant community facilities.

If tourism and regeneration lie behind the Louisville, Cayman Islands, Haderslev, and Folkestone projects, more overtly commercial aims are apparent at the House of Vans in London (2014). Occupying 2,500 square meters of railway arches, House of Vans is a highly unusual combination of a free-access skate bowl and street course alongside art, music, and film facilities. Operating as a continuous advertisement for its multi-billion-dollar backer, the House of Vans's broad artistic and social net is cast wide, the carefully nuanced design (by Tim Greatorex, Pete Hellicar, and Mark Churchill) and program of activities being clearly generous to the wider skate community. All this stands in knowing contrast to the corporate annexation and media spectacularization of skateboarding for which Nike SB, the X Games, and Street League Skateboarding, among others, have been criticized.

House of Vans, then, marks a shift in the outright opposition between, on the one hand, the authentic, real, street-level, and unfunded (as many skaters commonly perceive skateboarding) and, on the other hand, the inauthentic, mediatized, controlled, and commercial (companies, sponsors, marketers); understood within the wider context of Vans and skateboarding, House of Vans is an example of what Lawrence Lessig has termed a "hybrid" economy, operating simultaneously as a commercial economy for financial gain *and* as a sharing economy for collaborative and collective benefit. In short, House of Vans shows how the commercial, spectacular, and controlled might marry with the authentic, performative, and disorderly.

Social Enterprise

Skateboarding can also integrate into the public realm in ways that are more than just spatial and economic; social and cultural dimensions are also being increasingly explored, and particularly through a number of initiatives which might be loosely gathered under the heading of social enterprise.

One of the most successful and best-known of these projects is the skateboard-based school Skateistan in Kabul, Afghanistan. Oliver Percovich, the Australian skater who founded Skateistan in 2008 and is now its executive director, has explained how—after many decades of civil war as well as Soviet, Communist, Taliban, NATO, and local rule—the children who make up 70% of the Muslim population of Afghanistan often have only roadsides on which to play, with girls in particular being banned from such activities as riding bicycles or flying kites. But the girls are allowed to skateboard—hence Skateistan's efforts to teach boys and girls alike to skateboard alongside an educational arts-based curriculum ranging from world cultures, human rights, and environmental studies to nutrition, hygiene, and storytelling (cf. Fitzpatrick).

The aim here is to break the cycles of violence, desperation, and poverty to which Kabul youth are only too commonly accustomed, and instead to build confidence and other skills. "When it comes down to it, kids just want to be kids," explains Percovich. "Skateboarding provides that because it's fun and challenging. It lets them forget their problems for a moment. Once kids are hooked on skateboarding, so much more is possible, especially in the classroom. Skateboarding itself teaches important life skills, like creativity and problem solving" (Borden, "The New Skate City").

Keen to avoid charges of cultural imperialism and imposing Western skateboarding on Kabul children, Skateistan provides knowledge and social skills; as Paul O'Connor notes, change at Skateistan ultimately comes not from skateboarding per se but from the bodies of the Kabul skaters, such that "skateboarding is in multiple ways a vehicle for transformation but not the driving force" (O'Connor 38). In this context, Skateistan's most significant success lies beyond skateboarding itself, through its three main programs—"Skate and Create," "Back to School," and "Youth Leadership"—which together teach the kids about health and nutrition, operate arts, computing, and environmental workshops, and hold Dari language, math, and Quranic study sessions, as well as help children develop qualities of confidence, courage, self-esteem, and trust. Working, learning, and playing with each other, the children also find themselves developing friendships between those of Pashtun, Hazara, Tajik, and Uzbek ethnicity, as well as recognizing gender-based equality—one of the first things the boys have to learn is that the girls have as much right to skate. "Even in the most desolate of situations," explains Lukas Feireiss, "skateboarding, as a performative instrument for transformation, teaches the children of Skateistan not to accept the city and therefore society as it is, but to create their own city, their own spaces, and their own futures. In its essence, the power of skateboarding in Afghanistan is about what it symbolizes: the freedom of movement and the empowerment of the individual beyond all restrictions and conventions" (Fitzpatrick 191). These achievements are substantial and profound, helping to do no less than, in the words of Skateistan volunteer Sophie Friedel, "build peace" (Friedel 59). In 2013, Skateistan was included in *Global Journal*'s list of "Top 100 NGOs," the same year it reached 850 youths weekly with 40–50% female participation in all activities. Many pro skaters have visited and supported Skateistan, including Cairo Foster, Maysam Faraj, Tony Hawk, Louisa Menke, Kenny Reed, and Jamie Thomas, while Black Box, Fallen, IOU Ramps, Route One, Skateroom, Spitfire, Theeve, TSG, and Zero are among the many skate companies to provide support, as are Architecture for Humanity along with the Canadian, Danish, Finnish, German, Norwegian, Swiss, and US governments, the Kabul municipality, and the Afghan National Olympic Committee. As a result of this worldwide backing, by 2015 Skateistan had been able to spread its operation beyond Kabul, setting up facilities in the northern Afghan city of Mazar-e-Sharif, in Phnom Penh in Cambodia, and most recently in the Maboneng precinct of Johannesburg, South Africa.

Sometimes inspired by Skateistan, and sometimes just pursuing their own path, are numerous other social enterprises which use skateboarding for similar aims. Since 2008, Board Rescue has provided skate equipment to low-income kids and at-risk youth in the US, with the idea that skateboarding teaches children the lesson that healthy exercise, determination, practice, and commitment can lead to positive results. During the 2010s, other community-oriented projects—like Ride-It, Salemboards, and Stoked Mentoring in the USA, Cuba Skate in Cuba, EthiopiaSkate, and Megabiskate in Ethiopia, Skate-aid and Skatepal in Palestine, 7Hills skate park in Amman, Jordan, Engineers Without Boarders and Outlangish in Cape Town, and Indigo Skate Camp in South Africa, Skate Style in Cambodia, and Bedouins in Tunisia—have all deployed skateboarding to build social capital and counter such deep-rooted issues as alcohol and drug abuse, unemployment, poverty, violence, religious intolerance, ethnic and gender prejudices, and poor access to education.

One particularly focused initiative is A.Skate, which provides lessons for skaters with autism, as well as raising awareness about this condition generally and so addressing related problems of lowered self-esteem, heightened anxiety, truancy, depression, and suicide (www.askate.org). Also in America, the All Nations Skate Project, Stronghold Society, and Wounded Knee "4-Directions" skate parks have similarly engaged with issues of violence, drugs, alcohol, and suicide among Native youth ("Skate Life on an Indian Reservation"); some support has come here from Jeff Ament of US rock band Pearl Jam, who has also helped fund several skate parks in other less privileged neighborhoods (Nieratko). In the same way, Forks skate park in Winnipeg, Canada, runs skate camps and film/photography workshops for underprivileged young people, and is co-located with the world's first Human Rights Museum (Daniello), while the "Holystoked" skate park in Bangalore, India, was constructed by a local and international skater collective, as was the "Pura Pura" skate park in La Paz, Bolivia (Mehring). The German-based organizations Make Life Skate Life and Skate-Aid have been involved in several of these schemes, as has Nick Smith's Indian-focused Advaita (www.makelifeskatelife.org; www.skate-aid.com; www.weareadvaita.com).

In all of these projects, skateboarding is part of an answer to complex social conditions, where both the act of skateboarding itself, and the avenues it can lead toward and help open up, are of equal value. Undoubtedly, many public attitudes toward skateboarding in our cities today are still regressive and exclusionary, and can even be downright hostile. But, as this brief history shows, such attitudes are far from being either necessary or all pervasive. Instead, we are beginning to see public attitudes move beyond the mild curiosity of the 1960s and 1970s, and through the oppositional stances of the 1980s onwards, into a world where many of the more enlightened urban citizens, designers, officials, and managers can see the value of skateboarding as an integral part of the public realm. This process of transformation is very far from being complete, but there are many hopeful signs.

Skateboarding is part of an answer to complex social conditions.

Acknowledgements
Financial support for this essay was provided by the Architecture Research Fund (ARF) of the Bartlett School of Architecture, UCL. Some details of this essay are drawn from Iain Borden, *Skateboarding and the City: A Complete History* (London: Bloomsbury, 2019) and from Iain Borden, "Southbank Skateboarding, London and Urban Culture: The Undercroft, Hungerford Bridge and House of Vans." *Skateboarding: Subcultures, Sites and Shifts*. Ed. Kara-Jane Lombard. Abingdon: Routledge, 2015. 91–107.

References

Balma, Larry. *Tracker: Forty Years of Skateboard History.* Oceanside: Foundry Press, 2015. Print.

"Big O Rebirth." *YouTube* uploaded by Eternal Skate Films, August 31, 2013, www.youtube.com/watch?v=feRrG34LWY4.

Bofkin, Lee. *Concrete Canvas: How Street Art Is Changing the Way Our Cities Look*. London: Cassell, 2014. Print.

Borden, Iain. "Pipe Dreams: Rom Skatepark." *The Guardian*, November 1, 2014: 36–7. Print.

Borden, Iain. *Skateboarding, Space and the City: Architecture and the Body.* Oxford: Berg, 2001. Print.

Borden, Iain. "The New Skate City: How Skateboarders Are Joining the Urban Mainstream." *The Guardian*, April 20, 2015, www.gu.com/p/46yh7/stw. Accessed December 16, 2017.

Borden, Iain. "The Spaces of Skateboarding." *The Architects' Journal*, November 28, 2014: 56–9. Print.

Borden, Iain, and Richard Holland. "Evaluation of the Hungerford Bridge Skate Space." Report, Southbank Centre Planning Application #13/05522/FUL, London Borough of Lambeth. November 26, 2013.

"Boy Killed by Shot After Skateboards Anger Man." *Los Angeles Times*, September 1, 1964: 3. Print.

Boykin, John, and Bob Grant. "Skateboard Acrobatics." *Popular Mechanics*, July (1965): 81–5. Print.

Bracali, Anthony. "Thanks, Le Corbusier (from the Skateboarders)." www.anthonybracali.com. Accessed July 11, 2015.

British Pathé. "Gremlins and Sandies in New Craze." 1964. www.britishpathe.com. Accessed December 16, 2017.

Brown, Mark. "Southbank Skate Park Must Stay, Says Boris Johnson." *The Guardian* January 15, 2014, www.theguardian.com. Accessed January 15, 2014.

Certeau, Michel de. *The Practice of Everyday Life*. Berkeley: University of California Press, 1984. Print.

Clark, Katie, and Tim Hyland. "Q&A with Drexel Alum Tony Bracali." *Drexel Now*, May 21, 2013, http://drexel.edu/now/archive/2013/May/Tony-Bracali-Paines-Park. Accessed December 16, 2017.

Daniello, Frank. "The Plaza at the Forks, Winnipeg." *Concrete Skateboarding*, March (2007), 53–63. Print.

English Heritage. "Case Name: London Sporting Buildings: The Rom Skatepark, London Borough of Havering. Case Number: 1416690." Advice report, July 21, 2014.

"Final Designs on Louisville Extreme Park Being Fine-Tuned." *The Courier-Journal*, October 29, 2013, www.courier-journal.com. Accessed October 29, 2013.

Fitzpatrick, Jim, ed. *Skateistan: The Tale of Skateboarding in Afghanistan*. Berlin: Skateistan, 2012. Print.

Friedel, Sophie. *The Art of Living Sideways: Skateboarding, Peace and Elicitive Conflict Transformation.* Berlin: Springer Verlag, 2015. Print.

Green, Nick. "Cast of Acclaimed 1965 Skateboarding Film 'Skaterdater' Reunite." *Daily Breeze*, June 28, 2015, www.dailybreeze.com. Accessed June 28, 2015.

Harms, Jonathan, and Jack Smith, eds. *The Skateboarder's Journal: Lives on Board 1949–2009.* Morro Bay: Morro Skateboard Group, 2009. Print.

Harvey, David. "The Right to the City." *International Journal of Urban and Regional Research* 27.4 (2013): 939–41. Print.

Howell, Ocean. "The 'Creative Class' and the Gentrifying City: Skateboarding in Philadelphia's Love Park." *Journal of Architectural Education* 59.2 (2005): 32–42. Print.

Jenson, Adam, Jon Swords, and Michael Jeffries. "The Accidental Youth Club: Skateboarding in Newcastle-Gateshead." *Journal of Urban Design* 17.3 (2012): 371–88. Print.

"Kap 686 Skate Park/Metrobox Architekten." *Arch Daily*, September 1, 2011, www.archdaily.com. Accessed September 1, 2011.

Lefebvre, Henri. *The Production of Space*. Oxford: Blackwell, 1991. Print.

"Le roll'surf: acrobaties pour une planche à roulettes." *Tintin* 916 (1966): 12–13. Print.

"Le roll'surf: un sport acrobatique." *Pilote* 316 (1965): 46–7. Print.

Lessig, Lawrence. *Remix: Making Art and Commerce Thrive in the Hybrid Economy*. New York: Penguin Press, 2008. Print.

Lombard, Kara-Jane. "Skate and Create/Skate and Destroy: The Commercial and Governmental Incorporation of Skateboarding." *Continuum* 24.4 (2010): 475–88. Print.

"London Rom Skatepark Given Listed Status." BBC News, October 29, 2014, www.bbc.co.uk/news/uk-england-london-29801513. Accessed October 29, 2014.

Long Live Southbank. "Southbank Undercroft: Cultural & Heritage Assessment Report." London: Long Live Southbank, September 2014. Print.

Marcus, Ben, and Lucia Daniella Griggi. *The Skateboard: The Good, the Rad, and the Gnarly. An Illustrated History*. Minneapolis: MVP Books, 2011. Print.

McHugh, Kevin. "Authority, Politics and Love." *No Comply: Skateboarding Speaks on Authority*. Eds. Chris Long and Travis Jensen. Ventura County Star: FunNotFame, 2006. 105–14. Print.

Mehring, Jonathan. *Skate the World*. Washington: National Geographic, 2015. Print.

Nemeth, Jeremy. "Conflict, Exclusion, Relocation: Skateboarding and Public Space." *Journal of Urban Design* 11.3 (2006): 297–318. Print.

Nieratko, Chris. "Pearl Jam's Bassist Has Personally Funded More Than a Dozen Skateboard Parks in the Midwest." *Vice*, August 24, 2015, www.vice.com. Accessed August 24, 2015.

O'Connor, Paul. "Skateboard Philanthropy: Inclusion and Prefigurative Politics." *Skateboarding: Subcultures, Sites and Shifts*. Ed. Kara-Jane Lombard. Abingdon: Routledge, 2016. 30–43. Print.

"Omokoroa's Eco-Friendly Skate Path." *Sun Live,* February 23, 2015, www.sunlive.co.nz. Accessed February 23, 2015.

Orpana, Simon. "Steep Transitions: Spatial-Temporal Incorporation, Beasley Skate Park, and Subcultural Politics in the Gentrifying City." *Skateboarding: Subcultures, Sites and Shifts*. Ed. Kara-Jane Lombard. Abingdon: Routledge, 2016. 152–68. Print.

Purves, Libby. "Let These Skaters Swoop and Crash and Rattle." *The Times*, May 13, 2013, www.thetimes.co.uk. Accessed May 13, 2013.

Ritter, Arnon, Marina Treichl, and Claudia Wedekind, eds. *Auszeichnung des Landes Tirol* für *Neues Bauen 2012*. Innsbruck: Culture Department Tyrol, 2012. Print.

"Skate Life on an Indian Reservation – Skate or Die." *YouTube*, uploaded by Red Bull, March 28, 2013, www.youtubo.com/watch?v=SYRINJZ7qWLI

Snyder, Craig B. *A Secret History of the Ollie. Vol 1: The 1970s*. Delray Beach, FL: Black Salt Press, 2015. Print.

Solà-Morales, Ignasi de. "Terrain Vague." *Center 14: On Landscape Urbanism*. Ed. Dean Almy. Austin: Center for American Architecture and Design, 2007. 104–13. Print.

Streetdome. 2015, http://streetdome.dk. Accessed October 10, 2015.

Tison, Marc, and Barry Walsh. *Pipe Fiends: A Visual Overdose of Canada's Most Infamous Skate Spot*. Montreal: Media MudScout, 2006. Print.

Weyland, Jocko. *The Answer Is Never: A Skateboarder's History of the World*. London: Century, 2002. Print.

World About Us: Skateboard Kings. Dir. Horace Ové. BBC Two, 1978. Film.

Eckehart Velten Schäfer

From Record to Ritual *Outlines of an "Effective History" of Skateboarding*

Translated by Moritz Ingwersen

The history of skateboarding evidently knows a number of phases. Skateboarders from 1975 look and move in different ways to those from 1985, 1995, or 2005. How can these differences be systematized? And what relation does skateboarding hold to the history of sports and the culture of the second half of the twentieth century? In order to answer these questions, it is first necessary to accurately characterize the forms of practice. This will facilitate an understanding not only of the relations between them but also of the dynamics by which practices are time and again induced to undergo a process of transformation. Secondly, skateboarding needs to be analyzed as a "technology of the self" (cf. Foucault, "Technologies"). What do its routines do to the skateboarders? Which behavior patterns, attitudes, and self-images does their practice lead them to internalize? To address both dimensions, this essay offers a praxeological subject analysis (cf. Alkemeyer). It operates "beyond methodological holism and individualism" (Moebius 136) and comprehends the social as a texture of practices, while proposing praxis as "the primary generic social thing" (Schatzki, "Introduction" 1). A social praxis is thus a serial enactment of a "spatially dispersed nexus of doings and sayings" (Schatzki, *Social Practices* 89).

How can a particular practice be reconstructed? One might turn to the instruments offered by Shove, Pantzar, and Watson. They isolate three classes of "elements" and characterize social practices as "active integrations of *material*, *competence* and *meaning*" (Shove, Pantzar, and Watson 24; my emphasis). As "recognizable conjunction of elements" or "practice-as-entity," a practice is perpetuated if the links between its elements are retained in "countless recurrent enactments" of a "practice-as-performance" (7). With Hebdige, this condition of stability can be called a "homology": a "symbolic fit between the values and lifestyles of a group, its subjective experiences, and the [...] forms it uses to express or reinforce its focal concerns" (Hebdige 113). If, however, an element changes, that is, if new material appears, if competencies take a leap, or meanings are shifted, all elements, as well as the practice-as-entity, change accordingly. And if the links between elements—the homology—fade away and a practice fails to offer sufficient "internal reward" or loses its "symbolic or normative anchoring" (Shove, Watson, and Pantzar 75), the practice disappears. With this model, we are able to describe not only the transformations of skateboarding, but also the waves of popularity that characterize its history: more than once skateboarding has "died"—in the USA, as happened in the late 1960s, at the end of the 1970s, and most recently in the early 1990s—only to return reinvigorated and transformed.

A history of collaborating or conflicting elements and the *effects* that manifest between them speaks to Foucault's notion of *genealogy* as "'effective' history" (Foucault, "Nietzsche, Genealogy, History" 88). A genealogical approach remains skeptical toward the belief in a coherent development of an identical historical core. Instead, it uncovers the "subtle, singular and subindividual marks" that intersect and interlink in complex constellations and become the catalyst of ever-new consolidations and dissolutions (81). Effective history is not a "contemplation of distances and heights"; it "shortens its vision to those things nearest" (89). It disassembles the compact into components, underlines discontinuities, and exposes events in their interdependence with a multiplicity of heterogeneous influences. In this sense, genealogy requires "a vast accumulation of source material" (76). This is not what can be offered in this short essay. Instead, I will propose a model for the arrangement of such material.

What then are "those things nearest?" By "competence," Shove, Pantzar, and Watson mean "skill, know-how, and technique" (14), "multiple forms of understanding and practical knowledgeability" (23). Materials are "objects, infrastructures, tools, hardware and the body itself" (23) and "the stuff of which objects are made" (14). To simplify, according to this model, meaning encompasses everything that turns practice into sense—from symbolic representation that renders practice recognizable on the one hand, to the motivation of its participants on the other. Shove, Pantzar, and Watson speak of "teleoaffective structures," according to Schatzki (Schatzki, *Social Practices* 89), and include "projects, tasks, purposes, beliefs, emotions and moods" (Shove, Pantzar, and Watson 24).

This classification is an *analytic strategy*, not a *substantive* differentiation. Especially with regard to sportive practices, competencies cannot be separated from what has been proposed as meaning: competencies—the movements—are motives and goals embodied. In this essay, I will consider as competencies the generations of skateboard maneuvers and their "sense"—that is, practical knowledge as well as the teleoaffective structures it encapsulates. As materials, I will primarily regard the artifacts used as terrain; video technologies, without doubt of immense relevance for this practice, will be disregarded. As meanings, I will examine the representations that ascribe "sense" to the practice—in the form of graphics on skateboards or in various versions of the figure of the "skateboarder" showcased in skateboard media. Social identity along the axes of gender, race, and class is from this perspective a "subcategory of meaning" (Alkemeyer 45).[1] Following this pattern, I will begin by reconstructing four historical forms of practice. My conclusion will point toward possible connections and resonances between the results of this analysis and the history of sport and (Western) societies in the second half of the twentieth century.

1 All quotations that do not stem from English publications have been translated by Moritz Ingwersen.

2 This number can be partly explained by noting that skateboards distributed via toy stores in the 1960s were very low-priced, so that even small defects or damages merited the purchase of an entirely new board.

1. "A Sport of *Control*": The "Sixties Paradigm" of Skateboarding

The point of departure is a nowadays forgotten formation of skateboarding: the period from approximately 1960 until the late 1970s. This phase, which the skateboarder Stacy Peralta calls the "sixties paradigm of skateboarding" (*Dogtown and Z-Boys*, 00:49:12) can be divided into two waves of popularity: a first boom culminates in the middle of the 1960s, a second builds up roughly ten years later and subsides around 1980. Both waves are associated with staggering numbers: approximately fifty million skateboards were reportedly sold between 1962 and 1967 (Krosigk 16);[2] in 1978 a trade magazine for sports facilities expects six million skateboarders in West Germany alone in the near future (Tietz, "Skateboard" 513). This era is of particular interest, because the practice at the time differed significantly from what was later to be known as skateboarding.

It makes sense to begin the reconstruction of these differences at the level of the maneuvers. In the 1960s and 1970s skateboarding consists of the "disciplines" of high jump, broad jump, freestyle, and racing. The slight misnomer "freestyle" is dominated by a canon of movements set down in training manuals. Alongside wheelies or 360ies, movements with an origin in gymnastics that can or must be practiced *without* a skateboard dictate the repertoire: strength exercises such as the L-Sit or the V-Sit or the balance exercise "christie," as well as handstand rides (cf. Stauder 61, 62). Downhill racing experimented with aerodynamic positions (Davidson and Klein 51) and the supreme discipline of slalom was based on rhythmic turns that resemble the choreography of alpine skiing.

What is the "sense" of these movements? Which teleoaffective structures do they embody? As early as 1965, the first issue of *Quarterly Skateboarder* speculates about Olympia and classifies the "athletic discipline" in between skiing and surfing. "It's similar in many ways to surfing and to skiing, not only in maneuvers and techniques [...]." In contrast to surfing, skateboarding was seen as a "more 'measurable' sport [...] and therefore lends itself more to competition: In the slalom there is no question as to who the winner is [...]. Flatland [...] performance will be a matter of judgement but at least the asphalt isn't moving—everyone gets an equal opportunity." Skateboarding was considered "a sport of skill" and "a sport of control." The task was "up to you to see that skateboarding does not become a sport of rebels and radicals. It's a sport for young sportsmen" (quoted in Brooke 33). Of course, the latter also expressed a desire. But it seems that initially the sport format did indeed prevail. Triggered by the development of polyurethane wheels, which radically improved the ride comfort (46f.), the second boom of the "sixties paradigm" in 1973 was also marked by "a real drive to establish and legitimize skateboarding as a sport with defined rules, associations, and competitions" (Porter, Pos. 101). The body techniques imported from skiing, gymnastics, roller- and ice-skating carry with them corresponding motifs—teleoaffective structures of control and sportsmanship that can be categorized with the help of a typology offered by Roger Caillois (12ff.). He distinguishes between four game characteristics: *agon* (competition), *mimicry* (simulation), *ilinx* (vertigo, adrenaline rush) and *alea* (chance, hazard). These move between the poles of *ludus* (reglementation, organization) and *paidia* ("childish" improvisation, spontaneous joy). Classical sport—and early skateboarding—is thus ludic *agon*.

Skateboarding was considered "a sport of skill" and "a sport of control."

This teleoaffective structure is an effect of the elements. The material—the artifacts that serve as terrain—does also have a ludic impetus. While surfaces for freestyle are easy to find, downhill, for instance, requires a significant effort: "Best suited are [...] exposed terrains surrounded by unfenced meadows," a German skateboarding book specifies (Stauder 31), "therefore the [...] search for a suitable training ground can be time-consuming." In order to reach these locations, it is necessary to have a car, and attendants need to secure the course. Advice on how to mark slalom routes can be found in skateboarding books (Stauder 118). Moreover, commercial skate parks[3] have existed since the 1960s and increased in number throughout the 1970s. Strictly regulated, they were envisioned as sites for family excursions, offering leisure activities for accompanying parents. One of the most ambitious projects of this kind was the skate park in Montebello, California which featured timekeeping facilities and even a surface lift for skateboarders.

Representations of the practice remain similarly conventional. Up until the late 1970s, boards of leading manufacturers such as G&S or Logan are imprinted with plain-colored, "serious" logos (cf. Cliver 86, 96): they are supposed to be sports equipment. Pop songs about skateboarding paint an equally harmless picture. Their sound is a mixture of "all mainstream music styles" (Hofmeister 89). The German chartbuster "Skateboard-Uh-ah-ah" by the artist Benny promotes an image of skaters as friendly teenagers, who are diligent about their homework and ignore their loitering schoolmates. From today's perspective, the representation of gender is especially notable: skateboarding books of the 1970s are nearly balanced in their display of women and men (cf. Davidson and Klein), which feeds into a narrative of the decade as the "golden days" of female participation (Porter, pos. 255). By contrast, representations of people of color are virtually nonexistent. An effective history is able to trace this "white," but weakly gendered middle-class mentality, not only in its representations but also in its elements: in the kinesthetic kinship or "family resemblance" (Alkemeyer and Schmidt 83) between the practice of skateboarding and sports such as skiing and gymnastics, which to this day continue to be predominantly white-coded, and spatial settings that are tailored to family activities.

3 Little research has been conducted on the skate parks of the 1960s. In reference to 1966, the skateboarder Paul Fisher mentions a "new skatepark in Orange County that was one of the first parks of its kind," the "most striking feature" of which was a "large blue concrete hill that had waves from top to bottom and side to side that created the image of low undulating moguls" (quoted in Brooke 32). In the late 1970s two generations of skate parks emerged in rapid succession. The first facilities follow a "linear" design and correspond with the "sixties paradigm" of skateboard manoeuvres (Borden 59). The slightly more recent parks are already adapted to the contemporaneous rise of vertical skateboarding in empty swimming pools.

2. *"Aggressive"* Skateboarding: The Ages of Vert

The first "death" of skateboarding in the mid-1960s finds its cause in "internal rewards"—in the long run, clay wheels curb the fun. Yet, why does the second wave of the "sixties paradigm" in the late 1970s disappear? Secondary sources frequently seek reasons in US insurance policies: almost all of the commercial skate parks that flourished in the second half of the 1970s were forced to close by the 1980s because they were unable to find an insurance provider (Borden 175). This is how skateboarding returns in a different shape in the early 1980s. Leading into the early 1990s, a second wave (or third, in the US) builds up. In 1989 a German professional magazine for green spaces estimates the number of skateboarders at eighteen million in the U.S. and two million in England (Tietz, "Planung und Ausbau" 690). Other estimates arrive at a global number of two to three million in 1988 (Seewaldt 21). In numbers, the 1980s "wave" turns out shallower than its predecessor(s).

Culturally, however, it was significantly more incisive. The graphic embellishments of skateboards are now elaborate, mostly multicolored, and function as "subcultural" totems. Motifs like the "Dogtown Cross"—a tombstone inscribed with the words "dog" and "town" intersecting at the "o"—and the graphic designs of Powell-Peralta or Zorlac, displaying monsters and skeletons akin to the aesthetics of punk, hardcore, and metal, are typical (cf. Cliver 187f, 258f). A significant change is also notable in musical representations: as a typical example of "skate rock" after 1980, we might turn to The Faction, whose most popular anthem is entitled "Skate and Destroy" and whose bassist Steve Caballero is also a skateboard star. What emerges is a cross section of skateboarding and music that culminates in formations like Jody Foster's Army (JFA) who sell records and skateboards. Whereas the skateboarding of the "sixties paradigm" was still a sport, it has now become a subculture.

The most noticeable marker of this subculturalization is a new representation of race, class, and gender. Skateboarding remains predominantly "white"; yet Kusz's postulation of a white backlash along a reading of the documentary film *Dogtown and Z-Boys* appears exaggerated (cf. Kusz). In fact, the practice becomes selectively accessible to people of color: stars such as Christian Hosoi, Lester Kasai, Steve Caballero, Ray Rodriguez, or Eddie Elguerra have an Asian or Hispanic background; African-American protagonists like Steve Steadham remain an exception.[4] The masculinization of meanings also emerges: women are almost exclusively relegated to the role of an admiring audience. Porter notes a new "attitude towards female participation": "With the emergence of punk, the emphasis for skateboarding seemed to shift towards being [...] a proof of masculinity" (Porter, Pos. 259). Women, according to Porter, "were intimidated by the frat club mentality" that began to spread (Pos. 264). Effective history reconstructs such a "mentality" or "attitude" by "focusing on the interdependencies between bodily behavior and mental phenomena" (Schmidt 59). So, attention is shifted to the competencies. Based on the so-called Dogtown-style (cf. *Dogtown and Z-Boys*), a new set of maneuvers is formed in the late 1970s that survives the practice's 1980s death: a repetitive acceleration in between facing inclined slopes that allows for a play on the edge. "Vertical skateboarding" is based on bodily techniques that are borrowed from surfing but rapidly develops a pattern of movement that has no precedent. It is thus centered on the *invention* of movements: "It was something instinctive," skateboarder Tony Alva recalls about the advent of "airs": "Either you made it or you ended up on the bottom of the pool [...] It happened by total spontaneous combustion. Then we realized that there was an endless array of things we could do" (quoted in Vivoni 93f.).

In Caillois's terminology, vertical skateboarding emerges as *paidia*, as permanent experiment in which *agon* recedes in the shadow of *ilinx* and *alea*. Under the influence of audiovisual media, the teleoaffective structure of vertical skateboarding is no longer aligned with an objectively measurable performance but with a veritable embodiment of this posture. The practice is no longer geared toward results but toward styles of movement. This already becomes apparent in the names given to maneuvers. While the L-Sit or V-Sit of the "sixties paradigm" are matter-of-fact descriptions, a term like "grind" for the chafing slide of the axle on the curb connotes an attitude. Other names for maneuvers highlight that the practice is no longer kinesthetically related to a sport but to the musical and physical stylistics of punk and hardcore. There is a maneuver called "rock 'n' roll" and one called "pogo"—and as in the mosh pit dance, the second is an exaggeration of the first. It is possible to give this teleoaffective structure of *paidia*, *ilinx*, and *alea* a name. The skateboarder Nathan Pratt is not the only one to speak of "*aggressive* skating" to characterize this style (Brooke 57, my emphasis).

In these style-oriented movements, skateboarding constitutes itself as a "subculture." The kinship with a style of music popular among white, Hispanic, and Asian young people, but only few African-American youths, is indicative of its *selective* opening toward people of color. And if the motif of *aggression*

4 In fact, some representations are openly racist toward African-Americans. In an acted scene of a 1989 Santa Cruz video, for instance, a white man is sentenced to death for skateboarding while a black murderer only receives five years in jail (Butz 191). Only a few years later these types of depictions would have been unimaginable.

inherent to these movements is to be understood as a central feature of "hegemonic masculinity in sport" (Beal, "Alternative Masculinity" 207), the masculinization of the practice of skateboarding becomes apparent. This bodily-mental pattern is not only constitutive of a "live fast and die young" attitude that flirts with underclass motifs and excludes women. It also links up with the prevailing female habitus of the time, which associates defensive and closed bodily postures with the "moral posture and restraint appropriate for women" (Bourdieu 55).

Due to the abovementioned closures of skate parks around 1980, this specifically masculine subculturalization of meanings and competencies takes place on a very specific terrain: in drained swimming pools. Their use is precarious and illegal; it forges "conspiratorial communities" and has a gender-selective effect: female skateboarders frequently claim to prefer legitimate, organized, "often adult supervised spaces" (Atencio, Beal, and Wilson 6). The *paidia* mode of vertical skateboarding constitutes itself less in the legal status of the pools than in its surfaces: if the surface is the "material substrate" of skateboarding-oriented planning (Läpple 193), it will support the skate praxis. But it will also standardize and "ludicize" because it can be assumed that it resembles the surface of other skateboard artifacts. However, if a surface is *not* meant for skating, it compels the creative conquest of its own unsuitability via an experimental *paidia*. Since surfaces that are not meant for skating vary immensely, particular performances of the practice at different sites are difficult to compare; the affinity of the practice toward the classical *agon* therefore decreases.

This is how the plural in the heading is justified: regarding the surfaces of vertical terrains we can speak of *two* ages of vertical skateboarding. The experimentalist and hazard-oriented phase of its invention between the mid-1970s and the early 1980s hinges on "discovered" pools. However, "vert" celebrates its triumph on half-pipes—functional architectures that comprise elements of pools and full pipes (Schäfer 70f). These are invariably found at legitimate locations and on their surfaces, optimized for skateboarding and virtually standardized, the practice shows a tendency to return to "measurability." In 1992 *Thrasher* writes that in the middle of the 1980s everything revolved around "how high you could go, or how many handplant variations you could flap" (Dirtball 28). Improved protective gear and smoother curves relativize the *paidia-ilinx-alea* orientation. Maneuvers can now be practiced in incremental steps and aborted in controlled "bails," which mitigates the hazard motif considerably. In the wake of this development, a new canon of four groups of movements—airs, handplants, footplants, and liptricks—is established that follows a more or less clearly articulated hierarchy: most skateboarders would agree that, for instance, a frontside handplant is more difficult to do than a regular one. Thus, by the end of the 1980s, the teleoaffective structure of the practice is moving in the direction of a "ludic *ilinx*" while *agon* too has its comeback in skateboarding.

3. *Artistic Thugness:* The Era of Street

In the early 1990s vertical skateboarding initially disappears almost entirely; the practice suffers yet another "death." In hindsight, *Thrasher* diagnoses "vert's inaccessibility to the urban lifestyle": "Where in the city will you find public ramps? Nowhere except for Australia and Europe" (Dirtball 28). Yet in those places too, vert is "dying." First, the appearance of an initially androgynously coded techno culture introduces a movement-oriented youth scene with which skateboarding never manages to connect. Second, the homology between "subcultural" meanings and the subtly re-sportified competencies and materials crumbles: it no longer feels particularly "rebellious" to pilgrimage to half-pipes with rigid opening hours equipped with boards packed up in "session bags." Third, the emergence of "street skateboarding" begins to offer an attractive alternative that soon provides the foundation for a new "wave." Approximately 4.5 million active skateboarders exist in the US in the mid-1990s (Howell 476). In the 1996 study *Jung sein in Deutschland* (Being Young in Germany) 3.5 percent of youths identify themselves with the "skateboard scene" (Heinzlmaier 23). In 1998, the youth market study *Icon Kids & Youth* identifies 16% of teenagers between the ages of twelve and seventeen as "fans" of skateboarding (24). While these statistics leave open how many of these "fans" actively skate, they highlight the significant role that the practice is again about to assume.

The reason for the popularity of this new type of skateboarding even among youths who do not actively participate lies in its terrain. The practice leaves the secluded half-pipes and appropriates the city as playground. It thereby returns to illegitimate locations. Especially in the US this leads to demonization, as municipal policies of zero tolerance toward the deviant use of public space emerge and draconian measures are invoked to ban skateboarders from the inner cities. As a result, the identification with an outlaw sensibility is reinforced and later even academically ratified. In this sense, skateboarding begins to be interpreted as a "resistance to the spatial and representational regulation of Los Angeles" (cf. Flutsy).

Furthermore, the habitualized space practice of street skateboarding indicates another modification of its teleoaffective structure. It undermines the principle of *ludus* and *agon*, which had been rehabilitated in later half-pipe skateboarding in two ways. Firstly, street skateboarding emerges as a specific anti-discipline that opposes the spatial and temporal constraints of competitive settings. Beal's oft-cited claim of a "resistance" in skateboarding is founded on her observations at a street contest in 1991 (Beal, "Disqualifying the Official" 258f.) where many participants refuse to only use the course in defined groups and time windows and respond to their disqualification for rule violation with boycott. Beal does not reflect on the *specificity* of the situation—at vert contests a few years earlier such observations could hardly have been made because the half-pipe teaches that it can only be used by one person at a time. Still, Beal's observation is typical: similar conflicts occur at a German championship in Rüdesheim and even end in a scuffle. Secondly, the surfaces of the artifacts—stairs, handrails, planters, benches, curbs, ledges, etc.—are at odds with the ludic *agon* that was reinstalled in late vertical skateboarding. The spots show a greater variation than even "discovered" pools. One local scene might be specialized in curbs, another in stairs—which is the 'better' scene? "Contests suck," writes *Thrasher* in 1992: "How is it possible to judge something that *comes from the soul*? Where can you find qualified and unbiased observers to tabulate an *art form*? How can you process a large amount of skaters in a limited amount

The practice leaves the secluded half-pipes and appropriates the city as playground.

of space so they can best demonstrate their *creative talents*?" ("Contests suck" 38, my emphasis)

Just a few years earlier, such a self-confident claim of an "artistic" skateboard subject would have been hard to find. It has its background in space practices that transform mundane architectures into stages. This skateboarding as "art" is represented in a new generation of graphic designs that depart from the hardcore/punk/metal aesthetics of skull and bones. A good example are the graphics of Marc McKee, who designs lewd comic motifs that play with allusions to the symbols of pop and consumer culture as well as pinup themes (Tseng and McKee 35). While many vertical skateboarders were also musicians, the 1990s bring about an overlap between street skateboarding and street art—personified by, for instance, the skateboarder, graphic designer, and painter Andy Howell (cf. Howell and Greeven) or street art pioneer Shepard Fairey, who built his first stencils while he was working in a skate shop (Reinecke 56).

Furthermore, these "street" aesthetics become apparent in a convergence with hip-hop that includes both music and fashion. Motifs of the "ghettos" shine through in the *Thrasher* claim that "some of the greatest street skateboarders have come from the worst parts of town and know the true meaning of street life" (Dirtball 28). Motifs of the "artist" are accompanied by the image of the "thug." Brayton analyzes such a representation of street skateboarding as a clichéd, hypermasculine, and exaggerated "performance of 'blackness'": "Essentialized black style takes up residence in the rebellious white body" (Brayton 365). In street skateboarding, Brayton writes, "whiteness" appears as "something to be rejected" (368) while "blackness is reduced to a univocal expression of 'thug resistance'" (368). It is fair to argue that, after 1990, skateboarding turns into a culture of "wigger" and "wanksta" (cf. Kitwana). However, the practice does indeed acquire more "color." Next to Daewon Song, who comes from an Asian background, a lot of the protagonists are African-American, such as Shiloh Greathouse, Ray Barbee, Jovontae Turner, Ron Chatman, and many others.

The invasion of the street is made possible by the street ollie, a jump triggered by kicking the tail end of the board. This skill emerges in the vertical walls of the late 1970s, is transferred to the horizontal plane in the freestyle of the 1980s, and popularized in the 1990s. It turns handrails, planters, etc. into potential terrains and thereby renders the cityscape three-dimensional. In yet another playful and experimental mode of movement, canonic vert maneuvers—including grinds and board slides—as well as freestyle techniques such as manuals, wheelies, flips, and varials[5] are transformed into a multiplicity of combinations of tricks that render direct comparisons impossible: "The tricks became ever more complex and technical [...] The goal was to demonstrate increasingly difficult maneuvers whose kick flip variations were oftentimes impossible to follow" (Hälbich 63). With their multiple twists and changes in rhythm, these patterns of movement show a clear affinity to hip-hop. Street skateboarding is *paidia* game with the sense of *mimicry*, the creative imitation of familiar movements on unfamiliar terrains. Initially, these movements have little in common with the "aggressive" vertical skateboarding. Following Schwier, who compares the bundle of "practice [*Handlungspraxis*], dress code, behavior pattern, and music" typical of street skateboarding with the "'black' style'" of basketball (17f.),[6] the teleoaffective structure of this pattern of movement can be paraphrased as "coolness."

5 Manuals or wheelies denote riding on two wheels. Flips are rotations of the board along the longitudinal axis; varials are rotations along the transversal axis.

6 What is referred to here is the choreographed and aestheticized style of African-American basketball players that appears during the 1980s. It became popular with the show team Harlem Globetrotters and at the same time began to shape the emergent street ball practice. (Also cf. Schmidt 74f.).

Deflating the notions of "aggression" and "competition," street skateboarding takes on two of the central features of "hegemonic masculinity in sport" (Beal, "Alternative Masculinity" 207). The fact that the practice remains linked to accentuated masculine ascriptions has to do with the terrain: the "street" is a gendered space. Since the nineteenth century, patriarchal curfews have in a long-ranging "internalization of norms" transformed into a "self-marginalization of women in public space" (Ruhne 191). These "spaces of fear" —places without social control, dilapidated squares, downtown areas at night, car parks (23) —are spaces in which street spots can be found. In this sense street skateboarding reaffirms the masculinization that has already been associated with pool skateboarding. At the same time, it is precisely this *boyishness* that allows female skateboarders to disassociate themselves from dominant gender norms (cf. Kelly, Pomerantz, and Currie).

4. Between *Stunt* Skating and Longboard Cruising

With the exception of a slight decline in the aftermaths of 9/11 and the Dot-com bubble, no further "deaths" of skateboarding have been registered since the mid-1990s. Rather, skateboarding ascends to the level of a mass phenomenon, at least in the US: estimates arrive at the figure of twelve million active skateboarders in 2005 (Howell 476). In this context, another stealthy reconfiguration begins to occur around 2000. This caesura is primarily rooted in a new mass medialization of the practice via formats such as the ESPN X Games, which delineate a new highly competitive and sport-oriented form of skateboarding. Since 2003, their most visible signs have been the "mega ramps," structures that recall ski jumping hills and the "big-air" architectures in snowboarding. In contrast to the half-pipe, the mega ramp does not reference "found" terrain but is a mathematically charted architecture designed for the production of spectacular movements. As in the motorcycle stunts of an Evel Knievel, the terrain in the case of the mega ramp precedes the movement. These material arrangements make skateboarding into an "extreme sport"—both in its movements, which could be characterized in Caillois's terms as ludic, even *mathematical*, hazard, and also in its meanings: the X Games and similar formats transplant skateboarding from the metaphorical "ghetto" into the sport arena, transport it from teenage spaces into the living rooms of the "white" middle class, and position it alongside practices like motocross freestyle from which street skaters of the early 1990s would have kept a safe distance. What is more, events like the X Games or Street League Skateboarding (SLS) necessitate the invention of instruments that render skateboarding the subject of "exact" measurement. Software such as *Instant Score Experience* that ascribes each maneuver a score in real time promotes competition tactics that have long been foreign to the practice. Now, depending on their score, riders can specifically "calculate whether they want to perform an easy but safe trick [...] or a risky but highly remunerative one" (Schweer 118).

Due to its enormous presence, this TV mega-skateboarding has an appeal that exceeds far beyond its limited circle of participants. On the one hand, the "growth" experienced by street skateboarding since the 2000s is hard to miss. A "trend towards stunts" emerges, a hazard skateboarding that sets itself apart from the rather minute and technical street praxis of the early 1990s. This segment of the practice witnesses the rise of the slur "abd": anyone aspiring to fame was not to be seen on photos or videos performing a maneuver that had "already been done." Atencio, Beal, and Wilson observe a gender-hierarchical "street habitus" among street skateboarders after 2000 that is based on a "distinction of risk" (Atencio, Beal, and Wilson 14). On the other hand, the reframing of the practice as an accepted sport also contributes to a boom of precisely the "ramp skateboarding"[7] which, according to Atencio, Beal, and Wilson is regarded as "suburban" and "feminine" among risk skaters (14). Finally, its metaphorical "de-ghettoization" encourages a new urban planning perspective on the practice. While skateboarding was considered a signal of urban decline in the era of zero tolerance, the practice is now viewed positively under the new mantra of *talent, technology, and tolerance* (Schäfer 75f). In the East German city of Halle (Saale), for instance, the construction of a skate park in a depopulated housing area was expected to bring about a sociocultural vivification (Schäfer 76). With the reform of the hazardous sports legislation around the millennial turn, political obstacles begin to fall in the US at least: users of skate parks are no longer able to litigate for compensation (Howell 491).

7 Obviously this does not refer to mega- but to mini- and quarter ramps in skate parks.

Not least because of this exception from the standards common in the US, Howell describes this new generation of skate parks, in contrast to the playgrounds of the *progressive era*, as "neoliberal playgrounds." According to him, the facilities, which in many states were funded by their users or by sponsors they were obliged to find, contributed to a habitualization of "neoliberal" concepts of ownership. "Skaters 'own' their parks because they are responsible for a significant portion of the funding, whereas playgrounds were funded exclusively with public moneys. Skaters own their parks because they manage, police, design, and even build these parks" (491). Whereas the playgrounds of the progressive era were supervised by trained adults, the new principle is "supervision is self-supervision" (491). The same hardly applies in Western Europe. Here public funding is the standard, and comparable personal injury claims are uncommon, especially in light of the fact that all users have health insurance. Following the claim of positive correlation between legitimate skateboard facilities and female participation, this boom of *public* skate parks could contribute to a more gender-inclusive orientation of the practice on both sides of the Atlantic Ocean. Atencio, Beal, and Wilson emphasize, moreover, that especially *commercial*, "supervised skate parks," which sometimes offer exclusive sessions for women, have a "'positive' and 'empowering'" effect in this regard. Oftentimes these opportunities are framed in "corporate social contexts" and are designed to foster "the development of a broad consumer base" (15). It is therefore safe to conclude that the meaning of the practice as "proof of masculinity" that went along with the "subculturalization" of the 1970s, tends to be revoked with the commercialization after 2000.

New competencies and meanings are eventually also tied to the mass revival of longboards since approximately 2010, which might be interpreted as a response to mega- and risk-skateboarding. Since their structural design rules out the execution of an ollie, they rid skateboarders of the possibility as well as the social pressure to perform risky maneuvers of street skateboarding. Even though longboards can on their part be used for dangerous downhill rides, they seem to bring about new forms of skateboarding beyond a distinction of risk in their urban use. At least in Germany, longboards are apparently much more attractive to women than regular skateboards. This might possibly contribute to a partly polemical dismissal of longboards in parts of the culture that identifies as "hardcore" (Taylor).

5. Postmodern Sports

This essay is closer to a literature-backed theory than to a source-saturated genealogy. Nonetheless, it illustrates that an effective history approach that draws from Foucault and Schatzki as well as Shove, Pantzar, and Watson is indeed suitable for writing a history of skateboarding and other social and cultural practices. This method allows for a fruitful integration of the frequently isolated or insufficiently linked dimensions of bodily movements and embodied "mentality," of spatial praxis and material culture, and of formative symbolic representation in literature about (not only) skateboarding. In this manner, four formations of skateboarding can be systematically distinguished. The reconfigurations that can be gleaned from these formations are contingent: if, for instance, California had not been afflicted by a drought and economic crisis in the mid-1970s, it would not have been possible to find that many pools that could have served as the sites for the invention of vertical skateboarding. If the practice had not all but "died" around 1980, it might have retained a racing version, as in the case of snowboarding, that could have long since turned Olympic.

So how does this effective history of skateboarding relate to the history of the sport and culture of Western societies in the second half of the twentieth century? The classical modern sport takes form in a trajectory "from ritual to record": in a long series of reconfigurations that culminate in secularity, equal opportunities, role specialization, rationalization, bureaucratization, and the principle of the record, physical exercise, and games are divested of their ritual contexts (Guttmann 25f.). Under the 1960s paradigm, downhill, slalom, freestyle, as well as high and broad jump skateboarding all satisfy the criteria of a sport. With vertical and street skateboarding, however, the practice has since the late 1970s transformed into an unprecedented ritual of (sub-)cultural affiliation. With the emergence of formats like X Games or SLS, specific segments of the practice drift back into sport. Yet, cutbacks become apparent with respect to bureaucratization and record-orientation. Given that the traditional sport system—for instance, the Olympic Games—has in recent years begun to integrate skateboard-related practices such as half-pipe choreographies on skis and snowboards as well as—in 2016—skateboarding itself, and since the representation of multiple athletic disciplines has been undergoing radical changes, one might argue that the practice has in turn contributed to the modification of the classical domain of organized competitive sports.

If we consider sport as a technology of the self through which normalized subjects come to form themselves and which thereby contributes to the constitution of social order, skateboarding appears as a prime example of a specifically "postmodern" sport. Meters, grams, seconds, goals, or points, the anchors of the classical modern sport, are replaced by aesthetic horizons as the "sense" of the game. Postmodern sport is no longer concerned about community in ways that center on bureaucratic mediation and are structured around local and regional clubs and association, but through the appeal to transnational, informal, and yet structured communities of style (cf. Stern). The daily routines of skateboarding are not an exercise in *discipline* as the quantifiable perfection of given movements within potentially scientific training arrangements, but rather a practice of creativity in the combination and invention of movements. In this sense, skateboarding can roughly be interpreted as an athletic enactment of precisely that "creativity dispositif" (Reckwitz, *Die Erfindung der Kreativität* 49ff.) that began to challenge the Fordist culture of Western societies in the second half of the twentieth century and has helped to install the new hegemony of a "creative subject" (Reckwitz, *Das hybride Subjekt* 75). Let it be understood, however, that this is not to say that subjects of skateboarding invariably and by all accounts have to be conformist prototypes of a post-Fordist subjectivity.

References

Alkemeyer, Thomas, and Rober Schmidt. "Habitus und Selbst. Zur Irritation der körperlichen Hexis in der populären Kultur." *Aufs Spiel gesetzte Körper. Aufführungen des Sozialen in Sport und populärer Kultur*. Eds. Thomas Alkemeyer and Bernhard Boschert et al. Konstanz: UVK, 2003. 77–102. Print.

Alkemeyer, Thomas. "Subjektivierung in sozialen Praktiken. Umrisse einer praxeologischen Analytik." *Selbstbildungen. Soziale und kulturelle Praktiken der Subjektivierung*. Eds. Thomas Alkemeyer, Gunilla Budde, and Dagmar Freist. Bielefeld: Transcript, 2013. 33–68. Print.

Atencio, Matthew, Becky Beal, and Charlene Wilson (2009). "The Distinction of Risk: Urban Skateboarding, Street Habitus and the Construction of Hierarchical Gender Relations." *Qualitative Research in Sport, Exercise and Health* 1.1 (2009): 3–20. Print.

Beal, Becky. "Disqualifying the official: an exploration of social resistance through the subculture of skateboarding." *Sociology of Sport Journal* 12.3 (1995): 252–67. Print.

Beal, Becky. "Alternative Masculinity and its Effects on Gender Relations in the Subculture of Skateboarding." *Journal of Sport Behaviour* 19.3 (1996): 204–20. Print.

Borden, Iain. *Skateboarding, Space and the City: Architecture and the Body*. Oxford/ New York: Berg, 2003.

Bourdieu, Pierre. *Die männliche Herrschaft*. Frankfurt (Main): Suhrkamp, 1995.

Brayton, Sean. "'Black-Lash': Revisiting the 'White Negro' Through Skateboarding." *Sociology of Sport Journal* 22.3 (2005): 356–72. Print.

Brooke, Michael. *The Concrete Wave: The History of Skateboarding*. Toronto: Warwick Publishing, 2005. Print.

Butz, Konstantin. *Grinding California: Culture and Corporeality in American Skate Punk*. Bielefeld: Transcript, 2012. Print.

Caillois, Roger. *Man, Play and Games*. Urbana, IL and Chicago, IL: University of Illinois Press, 2001.

Chiu, Chihsin. "Contestation and Conformity: Street and Park Skateboarding in New York City Public Space" *Space and Culture* 12.1 (2009): 25–42. Print.

Cliver, Sean. *The Disposable Skateboard Bible*. Berkeley, CA: Gingko Press, 2009. Print.

"Contests Suck." *Thrasher* 4 (1992): 38–43. Print.

Davidson, Ben, and Fritz Klein. *Skateboard. Sport und Spaß mit dem Rollerbrett*. Oldenburg/ Hamburg: Stalling, 1976. Print.

Dirtball, Dick. "Who Killed Vert?" *Thrasher* 3 (1992): 26–33. Print.

Dogtown and Z-Boys. Dir. Stacy Peralta. Sony Pictures Classics, 2001. DVD.

Flutsy, Steven. "Thrashing Downtown: Play as Resistance to the Spatial and Representational Regulation of Los Angeles." *Cities* 17.2 (2000): 149–58. Print.

Foucault, Michel (1984 [1971]). "Nietzsche, Genealogy, History." *The Foucault Reader*. Ed. Paul Rabinow. New York: Pantheon Books, 1984. 76–100. Print.

Foucault, Michel. "Technologies of the Self." *Technologies of the Self: A Seminar with Michel Foucault*. Eds. Luther H. Martin, Huck Gutman, and Patrick H. Hutton. Amherst, MA: University of Massachusetts Press, 1988. 16–50. Print.

Guttmann, Allen. *Vom Ritual zum Rekord. Das Wesen des modernen Sports*. Schorndorf: Hofmann, 1979. Print.

Hälbich, Felix. *Die Geschichte des Skateboarding. Von den Anfängen bis heute*. Hamburg: Diplomica, 2008. Print.

Hebdige, Dick. *Subculture. The Meaning of Style*. London: Methuen, 1979. Print.

Heinzlmaier, Bernhard (1999). "Jugendszenen. Szeneanalyse als neue Grundlage für das Jugendmarketing." *Jugendmarketing. Setzen Sie ihre Produkte in Szene* Eds. Bernhard Heinzlmaier, Beate Großegger, and Manfred Zentner. Vienna/ Frankfurt (Main): Wirtschaftsverlag Carl Ueberreuter 1999. 15–35. Print.

Hofmeister, Florian. "Skateboard Dancin': The History of Skate Rock Part II." *Boardstein* 12 (2001): 86–89. Print.

Howell, Andy, and Amely Greeven. *Skateboarding, Art & Life*. La Jolla, CA: Untitled Publishing, 2005. Print.

Howell, Ocean. "Skatepark as Neoliberal Playground: Urban Governance, Recreation Space, and the Cultivation of Personal Responsibility." *Space and Culture* 11.4 (2008): 475–96. Print.

Kelly, Deirdre M., Shauna Pomerantz, and Dawn Currie, D. "Skater Girlhood and Emphasized Femininity: 'You can't land an ollie properly in heels.'" *Gender and Education* 17.3 (2005): 129–48. Print.

Kitwana, Bakari. *Why White Kids Love Hip-Hop: Wankstas, Wiggers, Wannabees, and the New Reality of Race in America*. New York: Basic Civitas Books, 2005. Print.

Krosigk, Holger von. *Alles* über *Skateboarding. History, Basics, Tricks, Material*. Hamburg: Tropen, 2009. Print.

Kusz, Kyle. *Revolt of the White Athlete: Race, Media and the Emergence of Extreme Athletes in America*. New York: Peter Lang, 2007. Print.

Läpple, Dieter. "Essay über den Raum." *Stadt und Raum. Soziologische Analysen*. Eds. Hartmut Häußermann, et al. Pfaffenweiler: Centaurus, 1992. 157–207. Print.

Moebius, Stephan. (2010): *Kultur*. Bielefeld: Transcript, 2010. Print.

Porter, Natalie. *The History of Women in Skateboarding*. Kindle Edition, 2014. Ebook.

Reckwitz, Andreas. *Das hybride Subjekt. Eine Theorie der Subjektkulturen von der bürgerlichen Moderne zur Postmoderne*. Weilerswist: Velbrück, 2010. Print.

Reckwitz, Andreas. *Die Erfindung der Kreativität. Zum Prozess gesellschaftlicher* Ästhetisierung. Berlin: Suhrkamp, 2012. Print.

Reinecke, Julia. *Street Art. Eine Subkultur zwischen Kunst und Kommerz*. Bielefeld: Transcript, 2012. Print.

Ruhne, Renate. *Raum Macht Geschlecht. Zur Soziologie eines Wirkungsgefüges am Beispiel von (Un)Sicherheiten im* öffentlichen *Raum*. Wiesbaden: VS Verlag, 2011. Print.

Schäfer, Eckehart Velten. “Raum schaffen und Stadt machen: Body Spaces und Sportmobiliar in der Skateboard-Praktik.” *Städtische Spielräume für Sport, Spiel und Bewegung*. Ed. Robin S. Kähler. Hamburg: Edition Czwalina, 2015. 69–78. Print.

Schatzki, Theodore R. *Social Practices: A Wittgensteinian Approach to Human Activity and the Social*. Cambridge: Cambridge University Press, 1996. Print.

Schatzki, Theodore R. “Introduction. Practice Theory.” *The Practice Turn in Contemporary Theory*. Eds. Theodore R. Schatzki, Karin Knorr Cetina, and Eike von Savigny. London/ New York: Routledge, 2001. 1–14. Print.

Schmidt, Robert. *Pop - Sport - Kultur. Praxisformen körperlicher Aufführungen*. Konstanz: UVK, 2002. Print.

Schmidt, Robert. *Soziologie der Praktiken. Konzeptionelle Studien und empirische Analysen*. Berlin: Suhrkamp, 2012. Print.

Schweer, Sebastian. *Skateboarding. Zwischen urbaner Rebellion und neoliberalem Selbstentwurf*. Bielefeld: Transcript, 2014.

Schwier, Jürgen. “Stile und Codes bewegungsorientierter Jugendkulturen.” *Jugend - Sport - Kultur: Zeichen und Codes jugendlicher Sportszenen*. Ed. Jürgen Schwier. Hamburg: Edition Czwalina, 1998. 9–29. Print.

Seewaldt, Christian. *Alles* über *Skateboarding*. Münster: Monster Verlag, 1990. Print.

Shove, Elizabeth, Mika Pantzar, and Matt Watson. *The Dynamics of Social Practice: Everyday Life and How It Changes*. Los Angeles/ London: Sage, 2012. Print.

Stauder, Hannes. *Skateboard Fahren. Für Anfänger und Fortgeschrittene*. Munich: Nymphenburger, 1977. Print.

Stern, Martin. *Stil-Kulturen: Performative Konstellationen von Technik, Spiel und Risiko in neuen Sportpraktiken*. Bielefeld: Transcript, 2010. Print.

Taylor, Blair. “Longboards sind Wrongboards.” *Jungle World* 33 (2015), https://jungle.world/artikel/2015/33/longboards-sind-wrongboards. Accessed January 1, 2016.

Tietz, Helmut. (1978). “Skateboard - eine junge Sportdisziplin. Skateparks - ein neuer Sportanlagentyp.” *sb: Internationale Fachzeitschrift für Sportstätten und Freizeitanlagen* 5 (1978): 513–14. Print.

Tietz, Helmut. “Planung und Ausbau von Skateboard-Anlagen.” *Neue Landschaft* 34 (1989): 690–97. Print.

Tseng, Winston, and Mark McKee. *Warning: The Art of Marc McKee*. New York: Mark Batty Publisher, 2011. Print.

Vivoni, Francisco. *Contesting Public Space: Skateboarding, Urban Development and the Politics of Play*. Dissertation, University of Illinois at Urbana-Champaign, 2010. Print.

Yochim, Emily Chivers. *Skate Life: Re-Imagining White Masculinity*. Ann Arbor: University of Michigan Press, 2010. Print.

Kyle W. Kusz

The Next Progression *Centering Race and Ethnicity in Skateboarding Studies*

In this essay, I encourage skateboarding researchers to put the sociological and cultural analysis of race, racisms, and the reproduction of white normativity at the center of their investigations. Such work can take the form of examining such phenomena as: the racial dynamics of the sociohistorical contexts and lived experiences of skaters; the racial norms and relations of local skating scenes or specific skate parks; the racial politics of the styles, performances, and identities of participants and professionals; or the representations of race in skateboarding media, whether niche, mainstream, or new media. To be sure, some scholars have already ably begun this critical work (Atencio and Beal; Atencio, Beal, and Yochim; Brayton; Butz; Yochim; Kusz, "Interrogating"). But, more will need to follow—and even go further—if skateboarding studies are to be read and deemed meaningful for racial scholars who have never experienced the joys of the board. Cultural shifts in racial and ethnic participation within skateboarding and shifts in race relations beyond demand that the next wave of skateboarding studies examine more closely the complex and complicated ways that skateboarding cultures function as contested racial terrains that both reproduce structural inequalities of race while also enabling social possibilities that can expand freedom for people of color and facilitate struggles for racial justice.

As a scholar trained in cultural studies, I invite the next generation of skateboarding researchers to use the methods of articulation and conjunctural analysis, because they allow the development of deep, detailed understandings of the ways that skateboarding cultures, texts, performances, and social relations are always already constituted by, and constitutive of, the social, political, cultural, and economic forces and conditions of specific historical conjunctures (King, "Methodological"). Cultural studies analyses informed by semiotics also allow one to unpack the cultural histories of ideas and chains of signification that silently inform the cultural meanings given to skateboarding cultures and the commercial and social identities of skaters. Such work is especially important given the way racial meanings are often coded and mystified in our post-racial moment. Another aim of cultural studies work is to make sense of the complex, complicated, and even contradictory ways that everyday and popular cultures—especially sporting cultures like skateboarding—are regularly politicized and are always already terrains produced out of, and productive of, relations of power embedded in local and broader sociocultural histories. As sport studies scholar Michael Silk puts it: "at the heart of this project [critical sport research that matters] is a need to unpack the [...] instances of inequality, inequities, and power imbalances [...] to challenge and disrupt any forms of social injustice" (13). Using a cultural studies approach to the study of skateboarding cultures is advantageous because it is open to using any and all theories and research methods drawn from numerous disciplines (such as, but not limited to: cultural studies, sociology, cultural anthropology, sport studies, literary criticism, geography, economics, history, American studies, urban studies, gender studies, and ethnic studies) to make sense of the varied and dynamic ways cultures are produced, experienced, mediated, and/or consumed in and through historically specific cultural, social, economic, and political forces and conditions.

To study the cultural politics of race, racism, and white privilege in skateboarding, I urge skateboarding scholars to immerse themselves in the literatures of critical race theory (CRT) and critical whiteness studies (CWS). In particular, I recommend reading: Bonilla-Silva; Davy; DuBois; Dyer; Dyson; Feagin; Ferber; Haney Lopez; Hill Collins; hooks; Irving; Lipsitz; Roediger; Savran; Shome; and Weigman, for these writings can be very helpful in the development and sharpening of one's racial consciousness. Their work will allow one to learn the fundamental assumptions and concepts of these analytic perspectives and to get up to speed on the present state of contemporary racial analysis in and beyond sports. In sport studies, one can get a good primer on concepts useful to studying the racial dynamics of sport and physical cultures from reading the work of: Coakley; Carrington; Birrell; Cole; Douglas; King and Leonard; King, Leonard, and Kusz; McDonald; Miller and Wiggins; and Newman, to name just a few. These literatures provide a variety of approaches to studying the cultural politics of race that can enable researchers to recognize the ways in which race, racism, and white supremacy organize the social worlds, lived cultures, and cultural representations of skateboarding wherever they are produced and practiced. Ideally, such racial analysis should proceed by using an intersectional approach (Hill Collins) that seeks to understand how racial meanings in skateboarding cultures and media always intersect with, and are saturated by (Davy), social class, gender, age, ethnicity, nationality, and sexual identity.

Using cultural studies methods and engaging with CRT and CWS should also enable researchers to avoid producing static, stereotypical, and monolithic interpretations of the racial dynamics and politics of skateboarding culture(s). Instead, they should allow the development of novel, thickly described, theoretically grounded, and vibrantly historicized analyses that illuminate the varied, locally inflected, and culturally specific ways that skateboarding cultures are always already racialized and participate in broader racial forces and conditions. Omi and Winant's concept of "racial formation" can be particularly useful because it emphasizes the fluidity of the racial meanings and power relations in culture and society, understanding them to always be products of changing material, social, economic, political, and cultural forces and conditions. Omi and Winant's concept gives primacy to the fact that racial ideas, racisms, and racial power relations are always in flux, constantly changing like the shifting color panels of a kaleidoscope whose combination of colors (i.e. specific historical articulations of race and racism) change slightly with each turn even though it is made up of the same palette of racial ideologies, stereotypes, racial histories, and structures of white supremacy and colonialism. When applied to skateboarding, Omi and Winant's concept of racial formations compels skateboarding researchers to see skateboarding cultures as dialectically constituted in relation to the racial discourses and politics that circulate in any given historical moment and social place.

I also urge skateboarding researchers to more closely detail how skateboarding cultures, communities, and cultural representations are produced out of the residues of the deeper racial histories of local places and national contexts. To do so will require engaging with studies of the histories of racially oppressed populations. Some have rightly criticized the 1990s wave of CWS for having the unintended effect of producing a field of racial scholarship dominated by white researchers who too often did not substantively engage with, and/or acknowledge their debt to, at least one hundred years of racial scholarship ably produced by people of color that continues to this day. As someone whose scholarship certainly exemplified this mishap, but who has since immersed himself more deeply into American racial history centered on African-American experiences and engaged with more contemporary racial analyses of anti-black racism and state violence against black and brown bodies, I can attest that theoretical training in CRT and CWS alone is not adequate enough to produce the sort of deep, meaningful, and historically informed racial analysis of various sporting cultures that skateboarding studies needs at this time. Considering the overwhelming whiteness of the participants of many skateboarding cultures and the unspoken white normativity of most mainstream cultural representations of skateboarding (at least in the United States, even today), racial analyses of skateboard-

Skateboarding cultures are always already racialized and participate in broader racial forces and conditions.

ing cultures where people of color are absent or underrepresented should aim to expose "the deep entanglements of white power today with historic forms of white supremacy" (King and Leonard 17). Such work should also excavate and explain how the cultural meanings of skateboarding in a given space and time are products of, and help to produce, the web of dominant, emergent, and residual racial discourses that constitute the popular/dominant culture in any historical moment (cf. Williams).

To be more concrete, following skateboarding's more prominent cultural and corporatized presence in the global sports media landscape (and in some national sport mediascapes like the US) since the advent of the X Games, skateboarding can no longer be uncomplicatedly theorized as a sporting subculture authentically opposed to, or resistive of, mainstream sports or society (if it ever truly existed in that way). Instead, researchers should contemplate how the residue of this former subcultural identity is strategically mobilized, whether by multinational companies who seek to profit from its sign values of youthful "cool" and rebelliousness, or by skaters, particularly white male skaters, in their own processes of racial identity formation in an attempt to fabricate an imagined difference from white, middle-class culture and society (cf. Yochim). Daniel Traber's insightful analysis of the contradictory racial politics of the efforts of white Los Angeles punks to construct themselves as a "white minority" in the 1980s offers a model of critical racial analysis of whiteness that would be quite useful to those studying the racial politics of the identity formation of far too many white skateboarders over the past twenty years (cf. Traber).

Putting race at the center of research on skateboarding would mean beginning scholarly investigations with questions like: How are skateboarding spaces racialized? What sorts of racial performances are authorized and made normative in specific, local skateboarding spaces? And what sorts of racial performances are still not possible? To what extent are skateboarding spaces being made more racially inclusive (and what exactly would that mean?) and how are they still largely governed by ways of being and knowing the world oriented by and around white norms, values, and ideologies? And what meanings about race, particularly about blackness and Latinness are produced in mainstream and niche skateboarding media spaces? What is the relationship between the policing of white bodies and space through skateboarding and the policing of black and brown bodies and space in the age of mass incarceration? What sorts of relationships exist between local skateboarding cultures and social movements for racial justice? What sorts of relationships exist between local skateboarding scenes and more retrogressive and reactionary racial actors and movements?

In what follows, I want to sketch out a few ideas on what this sort of deeper analysis of the racial politics of skateboarding might look like for a couple of skateboarding texts I have found interesting. First, I want to revisit a racial analysis of the award-winning documentary, *Dogtown and Z-Boys*, I produced years ago. Then, I want to conclude by offering some brief, passing ideas about what I see as some fruitful topics for future projects ripe for racial analysis by scholars who focus their work on skateboarding media.

***Dogtown* Redux**

Previously, in my book, *Revolt of the White Athlete*, I critically analyzed the racial politics of the skateboarding documentary *Dogtown and Z-Boys* (Kusz, "Interrogating," Kusz, *Revolt*). Admittedly, I came across the film by chance. But when I first watched it, I found it fascinating on many levels. First, I read it as unintentionally offering a captivating origin story for the extreme sports-media-cultural industry that was rapidly expanding in the late 1990s. Second, the film's representations of white masculinity exemplified a broader trend in the 1990s of whites attempting to distance themselves from white privilege that was central to my research at the time. But it was only after reading film reviews by white American film critics that I felt compelled to critically analyze the film's racial politics in order to try to make sense of how nonskaters could so easily connect with the stories and identities of the Z-Boys (Kusz, "Interrogating"). Many of the film critics, like myself, had never set foot on a skateboard, yet they expressed a surprisingly uncomplicated affection for, and connection with, these youthful Peter Pan board performers. That a nostalgic skateboarding film would appeal to nonskaters suggested there was something beyond skateboarding drawing them to the narrative. I believed that, in large part, it had to do with how the film offered a representation of white masculinity that embraced living on the social margins and presented itself as authentically lacking social privileges.

Consistent with a cultural studies view, I first contextualized the film's representations of white masculinity as a product of the racial formation of late 1990s America, a time that Cameron McCarthy identified as "the era of the Multicultural" (McCarthy). Whiteness and white privilege were being explicitly made visible and undergoing critique in American culture in an almost unprecedented way. This new awareness of white privilege left many white people feeling anxious, alienated, and even angry. The new visibility of whiteness, with its concomitant exposition of continued patterns of racial inequalities, called into question their beliefs—formed from popular racial narratives of the day—that the United States, in the post-civil rights era, was free of systemic racial discrimination and equal opportunities existed for all regardless of race. This was especially true for whites who imagined themselves as not living a "privileged" life. But this critique was further complicated by globalization, deindustrialization, and neoliberalism, macroeconomic forces that were creating more economic instability and uncertainty not just for working-class people of color, but increasingly also for whites (even though, as a group, white Americans still fared better economically relative to African Americans and Latino/as). In response, some whites attempted to manage their relationship to the privileges of whiteness by trying to minimize or disavow it completely, whether through the stories they told about themselves, or the ways they performed their cultural identities. This was the era when Nirvana, Pearl Jam, SubPop, and the Seattle sound emerged; the time when grunge—a music and style fronted by white men performing a working-class aesthetic—was not so coincidentally embraced and commodified in the American mainstream. The year before *Dogtown* was released, the all-white male post-punk band Green Day produced the song "I want to be the minority," which spent five weeks at the top of the Top 40. It was a time when "white trash" gained new currency in our popular cultural lexicon.

Additionally, it was the moment when ESPN and its corporate advertisers manufactured a new sport formation—extreme sports. This sport formation—which facilitated the mainstreaming of skateboarding—featured a legion of young white men, many of whom wore grunge clothing styles and wouldn't have looked out of place at a Nirvana or Green Day concert. So, within this context, I read the rapid emergence, commodification, and formation of the extreme sports media complex as the sporting analogue of this broader white reaction to the incremental de-centering of whiteness brought about by the multicultural era in American popular culture. And the appearance of *Dogtown and Z-Boys*, its surprising popularity with nonskaters, and the subsequent transformation of the documentary into a 2005 Hollywood film, *Lords of Dogtown*, seemed to largely confirm my interpretation that mainstream white America, at the turn of the twenty-first century, had an appetite for authentic stories of white difference and marginality (cf. Kusz, *Revolt*).

Turning to the film itself, I was fascinated by the racial logics that organized the *Dogtown* narrative even though race and ethnicity were rarely explicitly mentioned. The film abided by, and showcased, the logics of post-racial ideology that were hegemonic at the time. It offered an American story of a youthful white-led brotherhood where racial, ethnic (and even gender) difference was visible, but went unremarked, and did not seem to materially matter. *Dogtown* was discursively oriented by a white racial frame, as indicated by the way white people were firmly centered in the film, race was not a central focus, and the US's messy history of racial violence and oppression was elided. Drawing heavily on the work of Yudice; Savran; Robinson; and Wiegman, I sought to show how the film's representations of whiteness and the film's post-racial logics proved useful to the maintenance of white normativity in the multicultural era.

Although I didn't make this interpretation years ago, it is now apparent that the language of revolution, constant progression, and endless innovation, so popular within core skateboarding communities—and instrumental in the construction of the Z-Boys' identity and their story in the documentary—has, since the film's release, become widely appropriated in American promotional culture by a cosmopolitan class of business elites who have used it as a means to spread neoliberal ideology and to rationalize their own capitalization on the creative destruction that has taken place over the past few decades. Through his study of skate park construction in urban spaces in the United States, Howell has shown how neoliberal ideologies, relations, and ways of life are being spread and normalized through the construction of skateboarding spaces (cf. Howell). But, Howell's incredibly insightful analysis, I would argue, could be critically enhanced by substantively addressing the racial dimensions, implications, and politics of the neoliberal aspects of skate park construction in these local communities.

Another part of the film that grabbed my attention when I first watched it that I have not written about before was the opening scene of *Dogtown*. The scene is an amazing piece of filmmaking. It begins with a shot of the earth taken from outer space. Next, in one seemingly continuous shot, viewers descend down from outer space, through the Earth's stratosphere, to focus first on the US, then California, before finally zeroing in on the area of Dogtown in Santa Monica. During this amazingly seamless visual, a voiceover from iconoclastic Hollywood actor Sean Penn explains that Venice Beach, California, and Dogtown are endpoints of the intersection of Route 66 and the US project of Manifest Destiny. While the reference to Route 66 and the use of Penn as narrator were rather obvious ways of articulating the Z-Boys with a sanitized version of youthful white male rebellion, I found the articulation of Dogtown and the Z-Boys with Manifest Destiny much more interesting. For me, it emphasized, again, how the Z-Boys' story was framed through a particular whitewashed version of American history; a view of American history constructed and imagined from the perspective of white American conquistadors. The positive and optimistic representation of Dogtown as an endpoint/product of Manifest Destiny implicitly assumes that the Z-Boys' tale would be consumed by a prideful, ideologically white American subject who lives comfortably as a result of this history of American national expansion and who displays little racial consciousness or understanding of how this representation of American history would create dissonance or tension for nonwhite Americans. It is a view that shows little awareness, empathy, regret, or connection to those Americans of Mexican and/or Native American heritages whose relatives' lands and livelihoods were conquered and stolen through this

The Z-Boys' story was framed through a particular whitewashed version of American history.

colonial/imperial project. It is a view that contemplates the history of Manifest Destiny only from the perspective of those who benefited from it, rather than from those for whom it is a more complicated, tension filled, and perhaps even familial story of dispossession and cultural imperialism. This peculiar linking of the story of the Z-Boys with Manifest Destiny as a way of introducing the group to the film's audience reveals how the Z-Boys' story is built on a contradiction; on one hand, the Z-Boys' story has currency with contemporary American audiences who have not ridden a skateboard because it features a performance of seemingly authentic white antiestablishment rebellion, white difference, and marginality (from suburban normativity). Yet, when one uses a lens informed by CRT and CWS, one cannot *not see* how anchoring the Z-Boys' story in the history of Manifest Destiny—an unavoidably racialized tale of white American imperialism, exploitation, and state violence—defuses the Z-Boys' putative form of white rebellious difference of any real potential threat and reveals how this performance of white marginality is paradoxically complicit with the maintenance of white normativity and the market expansions of neoliberal capitalism in turn-of-the-twenty-first-century America. As with so many other young white rebel figures, the Z-Boys prove to be without any other cause than reproducing white supremacy through the reaffirmation of white normativity in a different edgy guise.

The racial paradoxes produced by the post-racial, colorblind frame that filmmaker, former Z-Boy, and successful skateboarding media entrepreneur Stacy Peralta used to tell the story of the Z-Boys are also fascinating to examine with CRT and CWS lenses. Even though Peralta partially relies on the ethnic differences of some of the Z-Boys members (Jeff Ho, Tony Alva, Peggy Oki) to construct the group's collective identity of white difference and marginality, the colorblind frame that organizes the film's narrative largely mutes any deep, substantive discussion of the racial and ethnic roots of the Z-Boys, or differences that exist within the group. Perhaps the one notable exception is a superficial aside midway through the film by Skip Engblom where he conveys, in a disturbingly fetishized way, his admiration for vato car culture and sexual preference for big-haired Latinas rather than blonde-haired girls. Engblom's comments—which go unchallenged in the film—reveal the racial lie upon which colorblindness and post-racial ideology is founded. The film's racially colorblind, post-racial, and seemingly inclusive logics work to keep white male figures at the center both within the camera frame and behind the camera in the construction of the Z-Boys' story (which undoubtedly could be told differently if the film was centered on Alva's, Ho's, or Oki's perspectives rather than Peralta's). At the same time, *Dogtown*'s post-racial logics are grounded in, and reinforce, essentialized and stereotypical ideas about Latinos that render invisible the complexities of social life for the Latin and Hispanic diasporas that live in southern California.

Reexamining *Dogtown* (and my own analyses of the film) today in the context of the thinly disguised racial hysteria of Trump's disaffected whites (many of whom gave life to the Tea Party and Birther movements during the early years of the Obama presidency), fueled by conservative news outlets like Fox News and Breitbart, and the emergence of the Black Lives Matter movement in response to the murders of numerous unarmed young black men and women by police and white vigilantes also sheds new light on the racial politics that inform the film. When watching the film within this racial context, it is hard for me not to read the scenes of a number of the white male Z-Boys waxing nostalgic about, and taking humorous pride in, terrorizing old women on public buses and destroying rich people's swimming pools in order to give birth to vertical skateboarding as deeply problematic. The same goes for the film's sentimental depiction of Jay Adams. Unknowingly, both of these parts of the film signify the ontological gulf that exists between the social realities experienced by young white men relative to young black and brown men in the US today. At the same time, they unknowingly evince how white privilege is a sociocultural force that really does materially matter in contemporary America.

To delve further into the racial politics of the film's depiction of Adams, late in the film, Peralta interrupts the collective narrative of the Z-Boys to go into depth about Adams' personal story. Jay is cast as a boyish skateboarding whiz that skated, in part, to overcome his father's abandonment. He is also portrayed as having been exploited by the skateboarding industry. At the time he was interviewed for the film, Jay was incarcerated for repeated drug offenses. Yet, his incarceration is given little more than passing mention. Instead, Peralta uses

Neil Young's song "Old Man" to establish a sentimental relation between Adams and the viewer. Numerous shots show Adams not as an adult, but as a bright eyed, blonde-haired young boy. Race is never explicitly mentioned in these scenes and it doesn't need to be because the strong association of whiteness with innocence that pervades American culture silently displaces Adams's status as a felon, while it generates sympathy for a white boy seemingly destined for greatness if only he would have been given the right support. Of course, this depiction of Adams—the abandoned and exploited white boy wonder—makes it nearly impossible, especially for whites who largely interpret American social life through deracialized frames of rugged individualism, to recognize the existence of systemic white male privilege in Adams's story. But imagine for a second if Jay Adams was African American. Would his story still be constructed to induce empathy and humanize him? Or would it more likely be cast through racial stereotypes, heavy-handed moralistic commentary about personal responsibility, absent black fathers, and unstable black families largely absent of empathy and understanding? As the recent spate of American police and white vigilante shootings of black and brown people reveal—the choice of the epistemological frame one uses to see people and the color of our skin can mean the difference between life and death.

White privilege is a sociocultural force that really does materially matter in contemporary America.

So then, when read with a lens informed by CRT and CWS, the racial representations of *Dogtown and Z-Boys* evince a socially conservative racial epistemology prominent in late 1990s/early 2000s US media culture that is still with us today—one organized by post-racial ideology that denies that race matters in post-civil rights America even as it contradictorily recognizes white marginality, difference, and supposed lack of privilege, and breathes new life into essentialist and stereotypical ideas about race and ethnicity. In other words, what seemed on the surface, at least to me, to be a nostalgic mythology about a group of radical, rebellious young white men with putative authentic street cred who created a sporting/cultural revolution was simultaneously a story white American audiences could find pleasure in for reasons unrelated to skateboarding, but central to the dynamic racial politics of the day.

New Lines

So then, it is clear that one can't make the same sort of arguments about the racial terrain of professional skateboarding or skateboarding media in 2018 as one could in late 1990s America. This is due, in part, to social and cultural shifts that have taken place within skateboarding over the past two decades. For example, more people of color participate in the professional ranks today and at grassroots levels in skateboarding cultures across the world. Indeed, skateboarding is now entrenched within a global circuit of cultural industries and has a footprint of locations that expand beyond Global North sites (Wheaton). These empirical changes in racial and ethnic participation rates of skateboarding, the new racial and ethnic contexts in which skateboarding is being practiced, and the broader social and racial contexts in which skateboarding cultures are formed necessitate more robust analyses of the ways skateboarding articulates with contemporary racial formations and deeper racial histories.

But racial analyses of skateboarding must also change because the moral and political grounds of the times in which we live have also shifted in ways that skateboarding researchers can only ignore at their own risk as a scholarly community. Expanding income and wealth inequality, the increased visibility of the violence and exploitation of the American incarceration state (and its agents) against black and brown bodies, new intranational and international flows of migration creating new perceptions of cultural citizenship (not to mention the flows of refugees due to war), and the increased militarization of everyday life produced from the global war on terror demand that skateboarding scholars make sense of the ways that skateboarding cultures are implicated in these contexts. Recent signs carried at Black Lives Matter protests in the United States make plain the criticism that could be levied against skateboarding studies (indeed of any academic field) if it does not investigate the racial dimensions of its subject: "white silence is violence."

To be sure, some recent skateboarding research has already carved a line for others to follow. These scholars have been looking into the ways various skateboarding cultures and communities articulate with racially progressive and retrogressive social movements; how skateboarders use and reimagine space and place racially; how skateboarding is racially marketed and mediated; and how skateboarding has functioned as a neoliberal project and as a vehicle for the naturalization of neoliberal values and logics (Atencio and Beal; Atencio, Beal, and Yochim; and Howell). In reading this work, it is encouraging to see that these studies have largely avoided uncritically celebrating superficial forms of racial inclusivity and instead have demonstrated a sharp and incisive eye on the subtle ways that racial inequalities are being reproduced through the racist, colonizing, and neoliberal aspects of a number of global and local skateboarding projects. In particular, the work of Atencio and Beal, and Yochim stands out as exemplary for how they have critically mapped and interrogated a number of new articulations between skateboarding and race. Another study coauthored with Yochim, Atencio, and Beal shows how efforts to expand skateboarding as a market in the mid-2000s included the creation of "skurban" racialized masculinities in the context of "neoliberal multiculturalism." In each of their analyses, Atencio and Beal have been careful to emphasize how new racialized skateboarding masculinities—that too often are read as racially progressive because they are more inclusive of people of color—actually reinscribe and reinforce racial ideologies and discourses that maintain white normativity in skateboarding spaces, as well as attempt to carve out some new racial possibilities.

Finally, as someone who has focused my own research on illuminating how particular white masculinities in contemporary mainstream sports media (films, journalism, and television shows) articulate with retrogressive racial and gender politics to reproduce the hegemony of white patriarchy through new discursive logics and narratives, I am surprised by the absence of critical scholarly analysis of the skateboarding celebrities of Tony Hawk, Shaun White, and/or Rob Dyrdek, especially of the racial meanings of their white masculinities and entrepreneurial projects. Insofar as I can tell, no one has examined how media stories about these skateboarding celebrities and their entrepreneurial projects serve as popular sites where neoliberal values, ideologies, ways of knowing, and ways of being are being naturalized and normalized in American popular culture and how they are being articulated with particular racial visions, relations, and power relations. And no one has examined the racial politics that organize their neoliberal entrepreneurial work and the performances of white masculinity that figure into and complement their neoliberal projects. For example, narrative analysis of Tony Hawk's two autobiographies, *Hawk: Occupation: Skateboarder* (Hawk and Mortimer) and *How Did I Get Here? – The Ascent of an Unlikely CEO* (Hawk and Hawk) and/or a conjunctural analysis of the social, cultural, political, and economic forces and conditions that enabled Hawk to build his skateboarding empire seem to be great analytical projects for the next generation of skateboarding scholars.

And perhaps even more than Hawk, Rob Dyrdek's celebrity and skateboarding entrepreneurialism seems deserving of critical scholarly attention for a variety of reasons. First, Dyrdek has filled the void left by Hawk's retreat from the limelight to enjoy the biggest media presence of any skateboarder in American culture today. He has enjoyed a successful run on MTV over the past decade through the shows: *Rob & Big*, *The Fantasy Factory*, and *Ridiculousness*. In particular, Dyrdek's first show, *Rob & Big*, seems so ripe for deep and critical racial analysis in order to excavate how the "odd couple" relationship/friendship between Rob and "Big Black" (aka Chris Boykins), as he is referred to in the show, revives plantation (Montez de Oca) and minstrel relations and logics that are alarming and offensive when one disrupts the white racial frame that organizes the show's representations of race and sees through the show's pretense of cross-racial friendship and fraternal high jinks.

But it also appears that Dyrdek aspires to take Hawk's template of transforming himself from a pro skateboarder into a skateboarding entrepreneur to a whole new level. Not only has Dyrdek evolved from suburban skateboarder into a skateboarding entrepreneur, but he is now working to become a neoliberal empire builder. His personal transformation, and the particular social conditions of the past decade that have enabled it, are worthy of critical sociocultural analysis. Today, Dyrdek's enterprises range from reality media production to sport celebritydom to brand management to merchandising to sport league administration and venture capitalism (Dyrdek), each of which originally sprung from, but are not now limited to, skateboarding. Investigating Dyrdek's story of transformation from pro skateboarder to a burgeoning entrepreneurial media mogul who transcends skateboarding, particularly as it has been mediated through several of his MTV television shows and DC skateboarding videos, seems like a fertile project that could allow one to investigate and explain how some of the most important macro-level social forces and conditions of our time intersect with and have enabled Dyrdek's emergence and expanding cultural presence in the present: the cultural workings and economic inequities of neoliberal capitalism, the opportunities enabled within the post-network era of televisual media, the reproduction of white patriarchy in times of rapid social, economic, and technological change, and the complicated contours of the reassertion of white supremacy and anti-black racism in the Obama era. Like Foer's book *How Soccer Explains the World* or Cole's examination of the racial meanings of Michael Jordan's celebrity in 1980s America, a scholarly investigation of Dyrdek's celebrity, media content, and complicated entrepreneurialism promises a project that could illuminate how skateboarding studies too can offer a unique vantage point on our contemporary social world writ large. Yet, to date, Dyrdek and his shows seem to have warranted only passing mentions rather than deep, historicized analysis (cf. Yochim).

Skateboarding studies can offer a unique vantage point on our contemporary social world writ large.

By way of conclusion, from my vantage point, it seems to be an exciting time for the fledgling field of skateboarding studies. The publication of this anthology evinces that it is a time pregnant with new possibilities for scholarly work on skateboarding. But in order for these potentials to be realized it is imperative that the next generation of skateboarding scholars carve out new lines of inquiry that decenter the kinds of insider and participant standpoints that organized the first generation of skateboarding studies and largely ignored or minimized the racial dimensions of skateboarding cultures. Those principally aracial viewpoints should be set aside in favor of more deeply contextualized, historically based, and richly theorized racial modes of analysis informed by CRT and CWS. They would also be wise to engage with forward-looking racial theories emerging from new social movements like Black Lives Matter. As a community that has long valued perpetual progression, I look forward to reading and learning from the next wave of research that skateboarding's intelligentsia produces.

References

Atencio, Matthew, and Becky Beal. "Beautiful Losers: The Symbolic Exhibition and Legitimization of Outsider Masculinity." *Sport in Society* 14.1 (2011): 1–16. Print.

Atencio, Matthew, Becky Beal, and Emily Chivers Yochim. "'It Ain't Just Black Kids and White Kids': The Representation and Reproduction of Authentic 'Skurban' Masculinities." *Sociology of Sport Journal* 30 (2013): 153–72. Print.

Birrell, Susan. "Racial Relations Theories and Sport: Suggestions for a More Critical Analysis." *Sociology of Sport Journal* 6 (1989): 212–27. Print.

Bonilla-Silva, Eduardo. *Racism Without Racists: Color-Blind Racism and the Persistence of Racial Inequality in America*. Lanham, MD: Rowman & Littlefield, 2006. Print.

Brayton, Sean. "Black-lash: Revisiting the 'White Negro' Through Skateboarding." *Sociology of Sport Journal* 22.3 (2005): 356–72. Print.

Butz, Konstantin. *Grinding California: Culture and Corporeality in American Skate Punk*. Bielefeld: Transcript, 2012. Print.

Carrington, Ben. "Introduction: Race/Nation/Sport." *Leisure Studies* 23.1 (2004): 1–3. Print.

Coakley, Jay. *Sport in Society: Issues and Controversies*. New York: McGraw-Hill, 2015. Print.

Cole, Cheryl L. "American Jordan: P.L.A.Y., Consensus, and Punishment." *Sociology of Sport Journal* 13 (1996): 366–97. Print.

Davy, Kate. "Outing Whiteness: A Feminist/Lesbian Project." *Theatre Journal* 47.2 (1995): 189–205. Print.

Douglas, Delia. "Forget Me...Not: Marion Jones and the Politics of Punishment." *Journal of Sport and Social Issues* 38.1 (2014): 3–22. Print.

DuBois, W. E. Burghardt. *The Souls of Black Folks*. Mineola, NY: Dover Thrift Edition, 1994. Print.

Dyer, Richard. *White: Essays on Race and Culture*. New York: Routledge, 1997. Print.

Dyrdek, Rob. www.robdyrdek.com. Accessed August 18, 2016.

Dyson, Michael Eric. *The Michael Eric Dyson Reader*. New York: Basic Civitas, 2004. Print.

Duncombe, Stephen, and Maxwell Tremblay, eds. *White Riot: Punk Rock and the Politics of Race*. London: Verso, 2011. Print.

Feagin, Joe. *The White Racial Frame: Centuries of Framing and Counter-Framing*. New York: Routledge, 2009. Print.

Ferber, Abby. *White Man Falling: Race, Gender, and White Supremacy*. Lanham, MD: Rowman & Littlefield, 1998. Print.

Foer, Franklin. *How Soccer Explains the World*. New York: Harper, 2004. Print.

Haney Lopez, Ian. *Dog-Whistle Politics: How Coded Racial Appeals Have Reinvented Racism and Wrecked the Middle Class*. New York: Oxford University Press, 2014. Print.

Hawk, Tony, and Hawk, Pat. *How I Became a CEO: The Ascent of an Unlikely CEO*. Hoboken, NJ: Wiley, 2010. Print.

Hawk, Tony, and Sean Mortimer. *Hawk: Occupation: Skateboarder*. New York: Harper Entertainment, 2001. Print.

Hill Collins, Patricia. *Black Feminist Thought: Knowledge, Consciousness, and the Politics of Empowerment*. New York: Routledge, 2008, Print.

hooks, bell. *Black Looks: Race and Representation*. Boston, MA: South End Press, 1992. Print.

Howell, Ocean. "Skatepark as Neoliberal Playground: Urban Governance, Recreation Space, and the Cultivation of Personal Responsibility." *Space and Culture* 11.4 (2008): 475–96. Print.

Irving, Debby. *Waking Up White, and Finding Myself in the Story of Race*. Chicago, IL: Elephant Room Press, 2014. Print.

King, C. Richard, and David Leonard. *Beyond Hate: White Power and Popular Culture*. Burlington, VT: Ashgate, 2014. Print.

King, C. Richard, and David Leonard, eds. *Visual Economies of/In Motion*. New York: Peter Lang, 2006. Print.

King, C. Richard, David Leonard, and Kyle Kusz. "White Power and Sport: An Introduction." *Journal of Sport and Social Issues* 31.1 (2007): 3–10. Print.

King, Samantha. "Methodological contingencies in Sport Studies." *Qualitative Methods in Sport Studies*. Eds. David Andrews, David Mason, and Michael Silk. New York: Sage, 2005. 21–38. Print.

Kusz, Kyle. "Interrogating the Politics of White Particularity in *Dogtown and Z-Boys*." *Visual Economies of/in Motion: Sport and Film*. Eds. C. Richard King and David Leonard. New York: Peter Lang, 2006. 135–63. Print.

Kusz, Kyle. *Revolt of the White Athlete: Race, Media and the Emergence of Extreme Athletes in America*. New York: Peter Lang, 2007. Print.

Lipsitz, George. *The Possessive Investment in Whiteness: How White People Profit from Identity Politics*. Philadelphia, PA: Temple University Press, 1998. Print.

McCarthy, Cameron. "Living with Anxiety: Race and Renarration of Public Life." *White reign: Deploying whiteness in America*. Eds. Joe Kincheloe, Shirley Steinberg, Nelson Rodriguez, and Ronald Chennault. New York: St. Martin's Press, 1998. 329–41. Print.

McDonald, Mary. "Thinking Through Sport, Analyzing Whiteness." *Journal of Multicultural Discourses* 7.3 (2012): 235–41. Print.

Miller, Peter, and David Wiggins, eds. *Sport and the Color Line: Black Athletes and Race Relations in Twentieth Century America.* New York: Routledge, 2004. Print.

Montez de Oca, Jeffrey. "White Domestic Goddess on a Postmodern Plantation: Charity and Commodity Racism in The Blind Side." *Sociology of Sport Journal* 29 (2012): 131–50. Print.

Newman, Joshua. "Army of Whiteness? Colonel Reb and the Sporting South's Cultural and Corporate Symbolic." *Journal of Sport and Social Issues* 31.4 (2007): 315–39. Print.

Omi, Michael, and Howard Winant. *Racial Formation in the United States*. New York: Routledge, 1994. Print.

Painter, Irvin. *The History of White People*. New York: W.W. Norton & Co., 2010. Print.

Robinson, Sally. *Marked Men: White Masculinity in Crisis*. New York: Columbia University Press, 2000. Print.

Roediger, David. *The Wages of Whiteness: Race and the Making of the AmericanWorking Class.* New York: Verso, 2007. Print.

Savran, David. *Taking It Like a Man: White Masculinity, Masochism and Contemporary American Culture*. Princeton, NJ: Princeton University Press, 1998. Print.

Shome, Raka. "Race and Popular Cinema: The Rhetorical Strategies of Whiteness in *City of Joy*." *Communication Quarterly* 44.4 (1996): 502–18. Print.

Silk, Michael. *The Cultural Politics of Post-9/11 American Sport: Power, Pedagogy, and the Popular*. New York: Routledge, 2012. Print.

Traber, Daniel S. "L.A.'s 'White Minority': Punk and the Contradictions of Self-Marginalization." *White Riot: Punk Rock and the Politics of Race*. Eds. Stephen Duncombe and Maxwell Tremblay. Verso: Brooklyn, NY, 2011. Print.

Wiegman, Robyn. "Whiteness Studies and the Paradox of Particularity." *boundary 2* 26.3 (1999): 115–50. Print.

Williams, Raymond. *Marxism and Literature*. New York: Oxford University Press, 1977. Print.

Wheaton, Belinda. *The Cultural Politics of Lifestyle Sports*. New York: Routledge, 2013. Print.

Yochim, Emily Chivers. *Skate Life: Re-imagining White Masculinity*. Ann Arbor, MI: University of Michigan Press, 2010. Print.

Yudice, George. "Neither Impugning Nor Disavowing Whiteness Does a Viable Politics Make: The Limits of Identity Politics." *After Political Correctness: The Humanities and Society in the 1990s*. Eds. C. Newfield and R. Strickland. Boulder, CO: Westview Press, 1995. 255–85. Print.

Konstantin Butz

Backyard Drifters *Mobility and Skate Punk in Suburban Southern California*[1]

> Only when conditions directly related to literal movement are firmly grasped will it be possible fully to understand the metaphorical movements: between center and periphery; faith and skepticism; order and chaos; exteriority and interiority. Almost every one of these metaphorical movements will be understood, on analysis, to involve some kinds of physical movement as well. (Greenblatt et al. 250)

Introduction

"And remember: No skateboarding until you've done your homework!" These are the words that introduce the theme of the 1986 music video for the song "Possessed to Skate" by Venice Beach hardcore punk band Suicidal Tendencies (referred to below as "Possessed"). A middle-aged father, ironically played by Timothy Leary, admonishes his son thus before he goes on vacation with his wife. As the parents depart in their minivan, the viewer catches a glimpse of the neighborhood: a suburb in Southern California. The son waves goodbye to his parents while standing in front of their home, a typical "McMansion," surrounded by almost identical single-family houses, palm trees, and wide streets, before reluctantly starting to do his homework. When, out of frustration over his math assignment, he touches a wheel of his skateboard and starts to spin it absentmindedly, suddenly distorted guitar chords can be heard. A burning pentagram appears on his exercise book, and after a few shots of the neatly decorated living room and the luxurious swimming pool in the backyard, a group of skateboarders enter the house, headed by Suicidal Tendencies' lead singer Mike Muir, who kicks in the door and shouts: "Let's skate!" The skateboarders literally start to tear the place apart, skate on the furniture, and spray-paint the walls. The homeowners' son joins the gang in destroying the house's furnishings and in performing various maneuvers on their skateboards. The swimming pool is drained and turned into a makeshift skate park as well as a stage for a concert by Suicidal Tendencies. The video ends with the parents' return and their shock at finding their home destroyed.

The video presents a condensed account of the "corresponding cultures" of skateboarding and of hardcore punk, which can be subsumed under the term "skate punk."[2] In the video, punk rock and skateboarding turn an apparently average teenager against his middle-class home and into an "outcast of society," as the lyrics of "Possessed to Skate" suggest. A few chords and a skateboard seem to be enough to disrupt the orderliness of a wealthy Californian neighborhood: parental and educational authority is disregarded, math assignments are put aside, paintings are torn from the walls and are replaced by graffiti, and the living room and the swimming pool are reappropriated for skateboarding. The pool's significance for the plot is obvious from its prominent position in the video's *mise-en-scène*: As a "saturated symbol of luxury," the swimming pool stands for the family's upper middle-class affiliation; its reappropriation by

1 This essay was first published in *Pirates, Drifters, Fugitives: Figures of Mobility in the US and Beyond. Eds. Heike Paul, Alexandra Ganser, Katharina Gerund. Heidelberg: Winter, 2012. 175–94.* [The editors]

2 I use Emily Yochim Chivers' concept of "corresponding cultures" to avoid the ambiguous term "subculture." Whereas the term "subculture" implies a strict separation from an alleged "mainstream" culture, Chivers explains that "[c]onstantly in motion, a corresponding culture is a group organized around a particular lifestyle or activity that interacts with various levels of media—niche, mainstream, and local—and variously agrees or disagrees with those media's espoused ideas" (5). The verb form of "corresponding" suggests a constant movement which does not only "bridge a false [and static] dichotomy between 'subculture' and 'mainstream'" but also perfectly works for my inquiries about the interplay, i.e. the correspondence, between skateboarding and hardcore punk (3).

teenage skate punks thus represents a direct attack on the values of suburban prosperity (Halberstam 81). The pool is sonically "under attack" by the punk band playing next to it and by the skateboarders scratching its concrete surface. The homeowners' version of the American Dream is assaulted by virtually everything that happens in the music video. Its protagonists rebel against the domesticity associated with a suburban lifestyle and try to escape it through physical movement. Rebellion in this music video is ultimately articulated through the movement of the body. The tranquility of middle-class life is disrupted by the bodily movement of rebelling skate punks, and although they do not actually leave the suburban locale, they try to escape the constraints of this conservative environment.

In what follows I will explicate to what extent skate punk provides an opportunity for teenagers of the American middle class to "bodily" distance themselves from their social background and from middle-class normativity. I will approach the skate punk's body as a bearer of cultural as well as material mobility. The notions of movement and mobility that pervade the depiction of skate punks in "Possessed" can be analyzed with reference to what has recently been termed the "mobility turn," and subsequently "mobility studies" (cf. Urry; Greenblatt et al.). I will seek to illuminate both the contradictory aspects of skate punk as a rebellious activity dominated by white middle-class males and the critical potential of skate punks physically engaging with Southern California's suburban landscape. I will investigate how mobility constitutes the basis for the corporeal contestation of a conservative environment that secures the privileges of white middle-class America while simultaneously enforcing conformity: how do skate punks deploy cultural and physical mobility? What role does the body play in their allegedly rebellious acts? Is their rebellion credible? In what way does their culture depart from "mainstream" values and to what extent do they unwittingly reproduce those values?

Bodies, Movement, and Politics

Since movement and mobility are linked to the body, it is necessary to start out with a closer look at the connection between them. In their 2007 anthology *Beyond the Body Proper*, Margaret Lock and Judith Farquhar begin with the notion of the "lived body" (1). "To make bodies a topic for anthropological, humanistic, sociological, and historical research," they explain, "is to ask how human life can be and has been constructed, imagined, subjectively known—in short, lived" (2). They do not see lived bodies as proper entities, but "as contingent formations of space, time, and materiality, [which] have begun to be comprehended as assemblages of practices, discourses, images, institutional arrangements, and specific places and projects" (1). Opposing "the impossible poles of a Cartesian social science," they suggest a more flexible approach (15). Whereas Descartes thought that "we perceive bodies only by the understanding which is in us, and not by the imagination, or the senses, and that we do not perceive them through seeing them or touching them, but only because we conceive them in thought" (33), Lock and Farquhar's notion of lived bodies escapes this mind/body split:

> Rather than taking (apparently) empirical bodies and (apparently) interior experience as a starting point (this is, we think, the central limitation of many phenomenological approaches), comparative scholarship in anthropology, history, and the humanities shows that the problem of the body can be read from many kinds of discourses, mundane practices, technologies, and relational networks. The bodies that come into being within these collective formations are social, political, subjective, objective, discursive, narrative, and material all at once. They are also culturally and historically specific, while at the same time mutable, offering many challenges to both scholarship and the everyday politics of a world compressed in time and space. (9)

If bodies come into being within "collective formations" that range from the discursive to the material, it is impossible to speak of "the body" as a single and finite entity. Rather, "bodies" should be approached in the plural. In "The Mobilities Paradigm," John Urry also argues against fixity and adds the notion of performance to create a flexible approach to bodies and their entanglement in movement:

> Bodies are not fixed and given but involves [sic] performances especially to fold notions of movement, nature,

> taste and desire, into and through the body. Bodies navigate backwards and forwards between directly sensing the external world as they move bodily in and through it, and discursively mediated sensescapes that signify social taste and distinction, ideology and meaning. The body especially senses as it *moves*. It is endowed with kinaesthetics, the sixth sense that informs one what the body is doing in space through the sensations of movement registered in its joints, muscles, tendons and so on. Especially important in that sense of movement, the "mechanics of space," is that of touch, of the feet on the pavement or the mountain path, the hands on a rock-face or the steering wheel. (48)

Urry's insistence on the importance of movement reverberates with his essay's question how bodily movement mediates a rebellious momentum in skate punk culture. It relates movement, or what Urry calls the "mechanics of space" (48) to the touch of pavements, mountains, rocks, and steering wheels. Feet on a skateboard, a hand on a microphone, bodies touching in front of a concert stage—all these examples are analogous to Urry's. The fact that skateboarding and hardcore punk both rely on movement in its various meanings—to skateboard is literally to move on a wooden board with four wheels, and hardcore punk involves the "movement" of chords, dancing, and touring—proves that these phenomena constitute valuable examples that, through their relation to movement and the body, incorporate discursive as well as material ramifications in a moment of allegedly rebellious mobility.

Lock and Farquhar state that although "some philosophers have done much to overcome these invidious classifications, perhaps no writing in modern Western languages can entirely escape the persistent dualism of body and mind. It is this dyad that serious thinking about collective, material human life [...] must work to overcome" (111). Urry provides a useful step in that direction. Although the navigation between an assumed "external world" and "discursively mediated sensescapes" seems to reinstall a binary between the realm of corporal materiality and the realm of thought, the strict division between the two is done away with through the notion of movement. According to Urry, the body "senses as it *moves*"—be it in sensescapes or be it in the external world. He shifts the focus from a Cartesian bipolarity to a circular flux that merges these opposites through movement. Whereas bipolarity suggests rigidity, movement implies flexibility; thus, the ideas of thought (or "discursively mediated sensescapes") and materiality (or "the external world") are folded into each other.

This assumption enhances the conception of the body as involved in a "political field," a term from Michel Foucault's *Discipline and Punish* (28). Foucault explains that "power relations have an immediate hold upon [the body]; they invest it, mark it, train it, torture it, force it to carry out tasks, to perform ceremonies, to emit signs," which, in his view, composes a "political investment of the body" (25). While it is still possible to speak of a politically motivated struggle which characterizes the forces that constitute the body, Foucault points out to what extent this relationship is bound to the body's "economic use" (25–26). He adds that

> it is largely as a force of production that the body is invested with relations of power and domination; but, on the other hand, its constitution as labor power is possible only if it is caught up in a system of subjection (in which need is also a political instrument meticulously prepared, calculated, and used); the body becomes a useful force only if it is both a productive body and a subjected body. (26)

Foucault suggests that resistance against a system informed by economic modes of production and consumption can be articulated through bodily activism. If the body is constituted through political power that seeks to subject the body to "economic terms of utility" as well as "political terms of obedience," then, so it seems, the bodily investment in *dis*utility and *dis*obedience mark ways of rebellious counterengagement (138). Skate punk clearly embraces such an approach, given its sympathy for (if not direct affiliation with) anarchism and skate culture's disdain for its capitalist co-optation (cf. Brooke 95; Macleod 128; Weyland 28).

Bodies, Postmodernism, and Capitalism

Foucault's notion of a body's "economic use," i.e. its "constitution as labor power" (25–26), is applied to the postmodern consumer culture of 1980s California in Donald M. Lowe's monograph *The Body in Late Capitalist USA*. Lowe expounds the problems of "embodied existence in a world where all aspects of our lives, the environment we live in, and everything in between, have become means, or signifiers, of exchange value" (Lowe 15). While cautioning against a "fall back on the body as an individual identity, subjectivity, private self, or any other autonomous, stable, unitary entity" (175), Lowe uses his conception of the body referent to delineate its entanglement in the material realm of "space/time" as well as the sociohistorical field of "the construction and satisfaction of needs" (174). He acknowledges the body's uniqueness as an "embodied being-in-the-world" (174–75), i.e. a "lived body" whose materiality is "constructed and realized within social practices to satisfy changing needs" (1), and simultaneously avoids reducing it to an essentialist entity able to escape the postmodern "politics of decoding and recoding" (175). Thus, Lowe's work builds upon Foucault's argument about the disciplining powers that organize the economic use of the body and applies it to the late-capitalist USA. While Foucault asks for the "mode of investment of the body [that] is necessary and adequate for the functioning of a capitalist society like ours" (*Power/Knowledge* 58), Lowe pursues the question of active resistance. He explains that "[r]esistance is the negation of, i.e., the active opposition to, capital" (175). His study refers back to the idea of the body as the nexus of activism against the social constraints of capitalist society. He is no longer concerned with the modes that are required for capitalist society to function but with the investment that disrupts it.

An analysis of skate punk can build on Lowe's conception of resistance:

> Resistance as counter-practice must seize and recode issues of bodily needs which the hegemony of exchangist practices have provoked. It must be founded on class/gender/race differences, not because they are essential, but because capital accumulation exploits all these differentials. Resistance must be discursively coherent and plausi-

> ble, yet transgressive against existing discourses, in order to mobilize different groups and sorts of peoples. It must take into account the weight of cybernetic systems, which favor the established power. And it must be semiotically sophisticated in its counter-practices. Otherwise, it can mount no effective opposition to capital's combination and recombination of structural, discursive, systematic, and semiotic practices. (176)

According to Lowe, an effective critique of capitalism is bound to bodily needs and their multilayered entanglement in the differentiating categories of race, gender, and class. An analysis of a youth cultural phenomenon in postmodern California needs to incorporate these categories in order to examine their role in bodily mediation: if race, gender, and class are deployed to organize capitalist society, then they consequently need to be taken into account by a rebellion against society. In the case of California skate punk, it is important to complement the triad of race, gender, and class with the notion of space, i.e. the site-specific characteristics of suburban Southern California, since it constitutes the environment in which the cultures of skateboarding and punk first merged.

With the concept of intersectionality, these differentiating variables can be approached critically[3] "as signifying the complex, irreducible, varied, and variable effects which ensue when multiple axis [sic] of differentiation—economic, political, cultural, psychic, subjective, and experiential—intersect in historically specific contexts" (Brah and Phoenix 76): the concept helps to identify space, race, gender, and class within skate punk culture as axes of differentiation. They literally intersect in the specific context of 1980s Southern California where they function as affective elements of the lived body. Being entangled in categories of privilege, i.e. white middle-class masculinity, the protagonists of "Possessed" try to overcome these categories of differentiation in an act of rebellion against the society producing them:[4] their bodily movement is a means of resisting these categories imposed by the mainstream.

3 For seminal work on intersectionality cf. e.g. Crenshaw; Collins.

4 The claim that all hardcore punks or skate punks in California have a white middle-class background is questionable. The fact that members of Suicidal Tendencies have a Latino background only constitutes one example of diversity within (skate) punk culture. However, the main protagonists in "Possessed" are all middle-class whites.

"Possessed to Skate:" An Intersectional Analysis of Skate Punk

Dewar MacLeod, in his essay "'Social Distortion': The Rise of Suburban Punk Rock in Los Angeles," explores the emergence of Californian hardcore punk, an important component of skate punk culture. He describes hardcore punk as a subculture that "opposed fundamentally that mass culture which [the participants] sat at the center of in suburbia" (129). He illustrates this statement by quoting from the liner notes of an early hardcore punk compilation:

> Fuck Authority. I hate war and I hate big business and I'm glad that other people feel the same way. Isn't it great that not *all* teenagers are sucking bongs on the way to play Pac-Man at some sick zoo of a shopping mall? (quoted in MacLeod 128)

MacLeod not only characterizes suburbia as a consumption-oriented site of capitalist exchange—represented by the shopping mall—but simultaneously evokes the postmodern notion of hyperreality through the quotation's reference to a computer game (Pac-Man) that took center stage in teenagers' lives. His conception of 1980s suburbia can help inform the analysis of "Possessed."

The shots of a suburban environment in the opening sequence of the video locate the song within the culture of suburban hardcore punk. The scenario can be interpreted as a citation of the front cover of the 1978 seven-inch record *Out of Vogue* by the band Middle Class[5] from Santa Ana, Orange County. The record's "front cover photo depicts a mundane Southern Californian suburban scene" and focuses on "two young girls [that] stand in the middle of a street, surrounded and almost dwarfed by the still life of a housing tract with Big Wheels, a basketball backboard, and a VW bus in a driveway" (MacLeod 126–27). The image and the setting of the video do not entirely match, but they certainly depict basically interchangeable representations of a prosperous middle-class neighborhood. MacLeod refers to *Out of Vogue* as the "first suburban punk rock record" and thus helps to locate "Possessed" within youth culture and its ties to Californian suburbia via its deployment of suburban imagery (126).[6] In addition to *Out of Vogue* he mentions the seven-inch record *Nervous Breakdown* by Hermosa Beach's Black Flag, published in the same year. "With these two singles," MacLeod states, "hardcore was born" (127). The fact that Black Flag "developed an especially rabid following among young surfers and skateboarders from Southern California's beach towns" anticipates the correspondence of punk music and skateboarding that is manifest in "Possessed" (Moore 53). The video not only references the geographical origin of American hardcore music in suburbia but also the interconnections with skateboard culture that reach back to the first recordings of the genre in 1978.[7] MacLeod emphasizes the importance of suburbia for hardcore:

> Setting its protest solidly in American suburbia, hardcore removed the working class and artistic connotations from punk. While suburbia had always been essential to punk, as the place to leave and destroy, now suburbia was subject to attack from within. (127)

This claim again suggests how suburbia, as a category of intersectional differentiation, is implicated in skate punk. It seems crucial that the homeowners' son in "Possessed" remains within the suburban environment while his parents go on vacation. Enmeshed in the discourse of tourism—symbolically signified by the Hawaiian shirts they wear—the parents appear to hold the most mobile position within the narrative: they are free to leave while their son must stay behind and is faced with the boredom and bleakness of suburbia, which the video presents as a space of ultimate immobility. Whereas the parents enjoy the mobility that their middle-class prosperity provides, their son is faced with the fact that "[l]ife in the suburbs [is] limited and dull to young people who [are] anxious to experiment and explore the world" (Sobin 80). Rebelling against a site where "the local movie house, bowling alley, or pizza place is expected to take up the slack and energies of the adolescent" thus seems to be

5 The name of the band ironically references its members' social background.

6 Additionally, the scenario appears to be an almost exact reiteration of the TV documentary "We Destroy the Family – Punks vs. Parents" that was aired on Los Angeles's KABC in 1982 and presented the suburban punk scene as a dangerous threat to American family life. The documentary introduces a middle-class couple whose son and daughter turned from high school football star and cheerleader into punks. Their home matches the style of the single-family house in the video by Suicidal Tendencies, and even the minivan in the driveway matches the model depicted in "Possessed."

7 Parts of the lyrics for the song "Wasted" from the *Nervous Breakdown* seven inch read as follows: "I was so wasted / I was a hippie / I was a burnout / I was a dropout I was out of my head / I was a surfer / I had a skateboard / I was so heavy man, I lived on the strand" (Black Flag). It is evident that from its beginning in 1978, the hardcore movement was closely connected to the Californian beach, surf, and skateboard cultures.

centered on matters of mobility (85). In "Possessed," the skateboard provides the only opportunity for the "backyard drifters" to move despite restrictive middle-class surroundings.

The negotiation of suburbia in "Possessed" heavily depends on the role of the parents; their authority is imposed at the very beginning by the father's instructions to his son, and the parents' return at the end of the video completes the framing of the narrative and symbolically captures the restrictive mechanisms to which the son is subjected. It becomes evident that the parents' mobility and motorized movement is very different from their son's skateboarding, because their mobility as tourists is implicated in modes of capitalist exchange mechanisms. The portable TV they carry with them appears as crucial evidence of the fact that they do not try to escape the postmodern, mass-mediated consumer culture of suburbia, but on the contrary travel precisely within this discourse. The parents, and by implication, suburbia in general are thus framed within a "Bourgeois Utopia" that is "based on the economic structure and cultural values of the Anglo-American bourgeoisie" for which "the home [was] more sacred [...] than any place of worship" (Fishman 24, 21). Although suburban family life began to change with the beginning of the 1970s (cf. Baldassare viii), the video foregrounds the privileged prosperous suburbs of Southern California. To counter the fixity of suburbia, the skate punks deploy not only physical movement (i.e. skateboarding), but also redefine their status as affluent white middle-class suburbanites in regard to the discursive fields of race and class.

Steven Blush's statement that "[t]he first HC [hardcore] bands came out of suburban LA beach towns, probably 'cause there they lived as close to The American Dream as you could get" underlines the privileged surroundings that hardcore punk emerged from as "a full-on white suburbanite rebellion" (Blush 13; Mugger quoted in Mullen and Spitz 193). It is possible to read the self-fashioning of suburban hardcore punks as a form of "playing dress 'down'—a version of symbolic capital acquisition in the economy of youth culture" that deploys dichotomous racial and class signifiers in order to produce oppositions to an alleged American mainstream (Traber 53). As "whiteness is configured as the subject position of the center" and associated with the suburb, it appears logical that white suburban teenagers who want to rebel against the environment they live in try to do so by refusing that subject position (43). Traber explains that the middle class experiences "mobility as an unspoken birthright"; he thus sees social decline within the discursive realm of race and class signification as providing an important antibourgeois component for hardcore punks (45).

Analyzed through the lens of intersectionality, it becomes evident that the narrative of "Possessed" is informed by this dynamic of physical movement and discursive mobility in suburbia and its reference to race, class, and gender aspects. The disruption of the suburban home's order is enacted through male skateboarders who on the one hand reappropriate the furniture and swimming pool of the house for their purposes; Borden suggests that

> [b]y focusing only on certain elements (ledges, walls, banks, rails) of the building, skateboarders deny architecture's existence as a discrete three-dimensional indivisible thing, knowable only as totality, and treat it instead as a set of *floating*, detached, physical elements isolated from each other. (145, my emphasis)

The skaters' treatment of architecture as "floating" elements suggests that they perceive it as, or indeed turn it into something that literally is *mobile*. On the other hand, they also replace the suburban symbols of prosperity with markers of urban decay and attributes of lower-class marginality. Traber describes a scene from the 1980 documentary *The Decline of Western Civilization* by Penelope Spheeris, in which Black Flag is portrayed in "a room brimming with signifiers of extreme poverty" that include "decrepit furniture" and "walls covered with spray-painted band names and profane slogans" (35). The fact that Traber reads these attributes as signifiers of poverty helps explain that what appears as the total destruction of the house's living room in "Possessed" actually constitutes a quotation of existing images of punk self-fashioning, through which the protagonists are positioned in a discourse of urban poverty. Punk graffiti calls attention to "the dreadful landscape of decaying urban America" (Lewis 87), a specter which had haunted middle-class suburbanites since the beginning of the 1970s, when "the influx of inner-city populations" or, as another author puts it, the "'encroaching' blacks or other nonwhites" were perceived as a direct threat to their privileged status as suburban homeowners (Traber 35; Parker 11). The graffiti and destruction in "Possessed" thus help the "invading" skate punks to place themselves within this discourse of urban decay, while gang insignia such as bandanas and the Suicidal Tendencies logo further strengthen the impression of the racially connoted threat of inner-city criminality.[8] The skate punks' disruption of middle-class normality is enmeshed in a pattern of intersectional signification as it signals a rejection of this privileged environment through the evocation of cultural markers of marginality. Basically staging the "encroachment" or "influx" of exactly those populations that the skate punks' parents "fought [in] battles over taxes, property values, and neighborhood boundaries" (Traber 35), the protagonists in "Possessed" exemplify how the intersectional categories of space, race, and class can be deployed to critique the normativity of white middle-class suburbia. They do not only move within Californian suburbia on their skateboards, but also and simultaneously within "discursively mediated sensescapes" that are demarcated by vectors of race and class differentiation which ultimately "signify social taste and distinction, ideology and meaning" (Urry 48). The fact that these interconnections are necessarily bound to the category of gender becomes evident through an analysis of how women are represented in the video's narrative.

8 Cf. Blush, who describes Suicidal Tendencies as a "loose-knit gang with *cholo*-style bandanas" (97).

The only female character directly involved in the video's plot is the mother. Together with the father she is part of the narrative frame, but whereas the father represents the authoritarian head of the family, the mother worries about leaving her son alone at home, tells him to eat the sandwiches she prepared for him, and advises him about possible emergencies. This almost oedipal scene is cut short by the father declaring that his son is a "big boy." He then leads the mother to the passenger seat of the van (needless to say that *he* is driving) and reinstalls patriarchal order by reducing the mother to his supplement as a passenger. The mother is represented as passively obeying the traditional hierarchies of suburban family life. Mary Woronov, who plays the mother, had already appeared in several films in which she represented a similar image of conservative femininity, most notably in the 1979 movie *Rock 'n' Roll High School*, in which she plays an authoritarian school principle who confiscates the protagonist's ticket for a Ramones concert. To cast her as a conservative Californian suburbanite in "Possessed" thus consciously evokes the stock character of a white middle-class woman. The video reveals the patriarchal organization of suburbia while articulating an ironic comment on the sexist heteronormativity of the American middle class in the 1980s. However, the narrative depends on—and thus reinforces—this image of femininity; it thus seems as if "Possessed" cannot offer an alternative to patriarchal gender hierarchies. The only other female characters in the video are two girls in bikinis who do not participate in the skateboarding at the swimming pool but are only cheering and admiring spectators. In this overly clichéd short sequence, it becomes evident that while the physical movement of the skate punks constitutes a challenge to suburban space and the middle-class values it represents, the video's reinforcement of a stereotypical and sexualized femininity compromises its subversion of white middle-class gender politics. Whereas the lyrics of the song "Possessed to Skate" suggest that it is possible to become an "outcast of society" through skateboarding, the video's depiction of female characters reveals to what extent the skate punks unintentionally adhere to a masculinist gender ideology.

The skaters' treatment of architecture turns it into something that literally is mobile.

Grinding on the Most Tenuous Borders of Discourse

Resistance not only needs to engage categories of intersectional differences, but must also be "semiotically sophisticated in its counter-practices" (Lowe 176). The analysis of "Possessed" has shown that the video does not meet this requirement as its representation of skate punk unwittingly relies on the discourse of patriarchal middle-class suburbia. The protagonists cannot escape the discursive restrictions of their ideological surroundings or, more precisely, the capitalist conformity of Californian suburbia. But I concur with Traber, who "[does] not accuse them of a 'failed rebellion' because they cannot get outside that system"

(50). Rather, I intend to avoid a too pessimistic conclusion by insisting that a critical contestation of capitalism is possible and necessary. "There is only one culture: capitalist culture," Félix Guattari states. "It is a culture that is always ethnocentric and intellectocentric (or logocentric), because it separates semiotic universes from subjective production" (*Molecular* 33). This explains why Lowe's conception of successful resistance is always already undermined by the capitalist exploitation of semiotic representation. Following Guattari's interventionist approach, it appears useful to shift the focus to the micropolitics of skate punk culture and its deployment of mobility. With Guattari's conception of change on what he calls the "molecular level," skate punk can be read as an "apparatus [that is] changing the life of the neighborhood" (Guattari, *Chaosmosis* 21). It is within the neighborhood of suburban California that skate punk operates and fosters "processes of singularization." Guattari defines these processes as "simply being able to live or to survive in a particular place, at a particular time, and to be ourselves," which applies to the skate punks' reappropriation of their environment: skateboarding and hardcore punk music constitute their ways of being themselves (*Molecular* 94). Guattari adds that this

> has nothing to do with identity (things such as: my name is Félix Guattari, and I am here). It has to do with the way in which, in principle, all the elements that constitute the ego function and are articulated; in other words, with how we feel, how we breathe, how we want to speak or don't want to, being here or going away. (*Molecular* 94–95)

Guattari avoids any kind of identity politics and thus indicates a momentum that challenges the categories of race, class, gender, and space differentiations. He shifts the focus to feeling and breathing, to aspects of agency in speech and, ultimately—via the notion of "being here or going away"—to mobility. Guattari's inquiries into the micropolitical processes allow for an analysis of skate punk as a "Molecular Revolution" (cf. Guattari, *Molecular*). Despite the inflationary usage of the term "revolution" by youth cultures (which often just cater to mainstream conceptions of marginality in order to present themselves as credible "outcasts") I regard Guattari's "Molecular Revolution" as a useful metaphor for the potentiality of skate punk, as it implies change or differentiation on a micro level. Additionally, the term "revolution" references the movement of spinning or rolling, which makes it even more adequate in connection to the movement of a skateboard (i.e. the literal revolution of the wheel).

Micropolitics, or "[t]he attempt to assemble things in such a way that the processes of singularization are not mutually neutralized, not co-opted in the reconstitution of molar pseudoentities" (Guattari, *Molecular* 110) not only disrupt the essentializing fixity of a normative and masculinist white middle-class suburbia, but also open up "the existence of an entire world of unconscious micropercepts, unconscious affects, fine segmentations that grasp or experience different things" (Deleuze and Guattari 235). "There is a micropolitics of perception, affection, conversation, and so forth" which can be located in the tiny moments of skate punk articulation that loosen its discursive ties to suburban normativity (235). Butler notes that "there is an 'outside' to what is constructed by discourse" (8); thus, skate punk can enter that "outside" in order to escape American middle-class normativity. However, she explains that

> this is not an absolute "outside," an ontological thereness that exceeds or counters the boundaries of discourse; as a constitutive "outside," it is that which can only be thought—when it can—in relation to that discourse, at and as its most tenuous borders. (8)

Applying this conception of the discursive and the "extra-discursive" to the physical movement and mobility in skate punk helps to locate its potential between discursive restriction and material contingency (cf. Butler 11). The skate punks skating in the swimming pool and moving their hands over the fretboard of their guitars in "Possessed" produce actions that literally *grind* on the "most tenuous borders" of discourse and thus create micro or molecular moments of possible disruption (8).[9] Despite being entangled in the restrictive discourse of Californian suburbia and thus in the contradictory effects that are produced by the categories of race, class, gender, and space, skate punk

9 "Grinding" in skateboarding refers to the maneuver of sliding over edges with the board's trucks (axles). Additionally, "grinding" is used to describe fast and aggressive guitar playing.

upsets its boundaries. The potentiality of skate punk culture is characterized by the moment when gravity is challenged in a skateboard maneuver and by the contingency of the maneuver's outcome. Will the skater land the trick? Will the skater fail? The trick or the maneuver will never be the same. At least on a micro level it develops infinitely different forms and outcomes. The same holds true for the fraction of a second between two guitar chords in a punk song. The movement, the grinding momentum between the fixed frets of the guitar constitutes the micropolitical and molecular condition which provides for the possible expression of rebellion. Similar to gravity which pulls back a skater to the concrete surface of a swimming pool, the discursive grip of suburban normativity will constantly affect skate punk's disruptive potential. Discourse thus restricts skate punk rebellion to an infinitely short moment of disruptive relevance. However, as Rudolph Lablan notes, "[m]ovement can say more, for all its shortness, than pages of verbal description," which indicates that the shortness of skate punk's transgressive moments at the boundaries of discourse can be interpreted as its most important feature (quoted in Adey 142). These moments cannot be coopted; they can hardly be represented or linguistically grasped, and they do not dissolve into the normativity of "molar pseudoentities" (Guattari, *Molecular* 110).

Skateboarding and hardcore punk have the potential to disrupt normative discourses.

The representation of skate punk in "Possessed" fails to evade normative discourses of race, class, gender, and space, but this does not prevent me from believing that skateboarding and hardcore punk have the potential to disrupt normative discourses and to provide an alternative to middle-class values. Ole B. Jensen, in the foreword to a recent anthology on *The Cultures of Alternative Mobilities*, mentions skateboarding as a counter-practice and reemphasizes the importance of movement for its success by reminding us that "we construct identities, constitute places, and make sense of our environment as we move" (cf. xv, xviii). By implication, this points toward the opportunity for skate punk culture to also question, alter, and challenge these constructions through movement. However, the fact that it mainly attracts young white men emphasizes the importance of Guattari's demand that, in order to really generate effective change, "[i]ndividuals must become both more united and increasingly different" (Guattari, *Three Ecologies* 69). The example of skate punk shows that, even while drifting in the delimited space of a suburban backyard, it is possible to strive for this ideal as long as we *move*.

References

Adey, Peter. *Mobilities*. London: Routledge, 2010. Print.

Baldassare, Mark. *Trouble in Paradise: The Suburban Transformation in America*. New York: Columbia UP, 1986. Print.

Black Flag. *Nervous Breakdown*. SST, 1978. Vinyl record.

Blush, Steven. *American Hardcore*. Los Angeles: Feral House, 2001. Print.

Borden, Iain. "Speaking the City: Skateboarding Subculture and Recompositions of the Urban Realm." *Research in Urban Sociology* 5 (2000): 135–54. Print.

Brah, Avtar, and Ann Phoenix. "Ain't I A Woman? Revisiting Intersectionality." *Journal of International Women's Studies* 5.3 (2004): 75–86. Print.

Brooke, Michael. *The Concrete Wave: The History of Skateboarding*. Toronto: Warwick Publishing Inc., 2005. Print.

Butler, Judith. *Bodies That Matter*. New York: Routledge, 1993. Print.

Collins, Patricia Hill. *Black Feminist Thought*. New York: Routledge, 2000. Print.

Crenshaw, Kimberlé. "Demarginalizing the Intersection of Race and Sex: A Black Feminist Critique of Antidiscrimination Doctrine." *University of Chicago Legal Forum* (1989): 139–67. Print.

The Decline of Western Civilization. Dir. Penelope Spheeris. Atlantic Television, 1980.

Deleuze, Gilles, and Félix Guattari. *A Thousand Plateaus*. New York: Continuum, 2004. Print.

Descartes, René. "Second Meditation: Of the Nature of the Human Mind; and That It Is Easier to Know than the Body." *The Body*. Ed. Tiffany Atkinson. New York: Palgrave Macmillan, 2005. 27–33. Print.

Fishman, Robert. *Bourgeois Utopias: The Rise and Fall of Suburbia*. New York: Basic Books, 1987. Print.

Foucault, Michel. *Discipline and Punish: The Birth of the Prison*. New York: Vintage, 1995. Print.

Foucault, Michel. *Power/Knowledge: Selected Interviews and Other Writings 1972–1977*. Eds. Colin Gordon et al. Brighton: Pantheon, 1980. Print.

Guattari, Félix. *Chaosmosis*. Bloomington: Indiana University Press, 1995. Print.

Guattari, Félix. *Molecular Revolution in Brazil*. Cambridge, MA: Semiotext(e), 2008. Print.

Guattari, Félix. *The Three Ecologies*. London: Continuum, 2000. Print.

Greenblatt, Stephen, et al. *Cultural Mobility: A Manifesto*. Cambridge: Cambridge University Press, 2010. Print.

Halberstam, Judith. "Notes on Failure." *The Power and Politics of the Aesthetic in American Culture*. Eds. Klaus Benesch and Ulla Haselstein. Heidelberg: Winter, 2007. 69–90. Print.

Jensen, Ole B. "Foreword: Mobilities as Culture." *The Cultures of Alternative Mobilities: Routes Less Travelled*. Ed. Phillip Vannini. Burlington, VT: Ashgate Publishing Company, 2009. Print.

Lewis, Jon. "Punks in LA: It's Kiss or Kill." *Journal of Popular Culture* 22.2 (1988): 87–97. Print.

Lock, Margaret, and Judith Farquhar. "Introduction." *Beyond the Body Proper*. Eds. Margaret Lock and Judith Farquhar. Durham: Duke UP, 2007. 1–16. Print.

Lowe, Donald M. *The Body in Late Capitalist USA*. Durham: Duke UP, 1995. Print.

MacLeod, Dewar. "'Social Distortion' – The Rise of Suburban Punk Rock in Los Angeles." *America Under Construction: Boundaries and Identities in Popular Culture*. Eds. Kristi S. Long and Matthew Nadelhaft. New York: Garland Publishing, 1997. 123–48. Print.

Middle Class. *Out of Vogue*. Joke Records, 1978. Vinyl record.

Moore, Ryan. *Sells Like Teen Spirit: Music, Youth Culture, and Social Crisis*. New York: New York UP, 2010. Print.

Mullen, Brendan, and Marc Spitz. *We Got the Neutron Bomb: The Untold Story of L.A. Punk*. New York: Three Rivers, 2001. Print.

Parker, Richard. *The Myth of the Middle Class*. New York: Liveright, 1972. Print.

Possessed to Skate. Dir. Bill Fishman, 1986. Film.

Sobin, Dennis P. *The Future of the American Suburbs*. Port Washington, NY: Kennikat, 1971. Print.

Suicidal Tendencies. "Possessed to Skate." *Join the Army*. Caroline Records, 1987. Vinyl record.

Traber, Daniel S. "LA's 'White Minority' Punk and the Contradictions of Self-Marginalization." *Cultural Critique* 48.1 (2001): 30–64. Print

Urry, John. "The Mobilities Paradigm." *Mobilities*. Ed. John Urry. Cambridge: Polity, 2007. 44–60. Print.

Weyland, Jocko. *The Answer Is Never: A Skateboarder's History of the World*. London: Century, 2002. Print.

Yochim, Emily Chivers. "'This Is How I Think': Skate Life, Corresponding Cultures and Alternative White Masculinities." Dissertation, University of Michigan, 2007. Print.

Francisco Vivoni

City of Social Control *Skateboarding and the Regulation of Public Space*

Social control through built forms is a key dynamic within processes of contemporary urban development. The proliferation of new forms of control and exclusion in cities takes shape through urban beautification programs, the enforcement of public codes of conduct, and the privatization of public spaces. These programs set out to improve the "quality of life" of urban cores through new forms of controlled inclusion intent on "cleansing" downtowns for the proper circulation of capital. The most recent wave of urban revitalization efforts produces downtown public spaces that cater to the leisurely pursuits of affluent newcomers while pricing out tenured working poor and indigent people from their neighborhoods and single occupancy residences (cf. Smith). Contemporary public space users increasingly experience surveillance technologies that control public conduct and limit access to public life. Social control measures include the pervasive use of Closed Circuit Television (CCTV) cameras, high-intensity street lighting, wrought-iron spiked gates, and enforced rules, regulations, and curfews (cf. Davis). Recent arrangements between state, market, and civil society actors shape the emergence of privately owned public spaces such as corporate plazas, atriums, and walkways as well as the enclosure of urban parks and other open spaces within the city (cf. Kayden).

This essay examines the production and contestation of new public spaces through a discussion of skateboarding as a meaningful social practice. Public space within the city of social control is a site of struggle, negotiation, contestation, and cooperation (cf. Mitchell). The essay focuses on street skateboarding as an ephemeral spatial tactic, an everyday practice, and an aesthetic playful intervention that undermines the intended uses of built forms and the moral panics inherent to the "cleansing" project concerned with regulation, privatization, and urban beautification. Through ethnographic research experiences in Emerica's Wild in the Streets, Red Bull's Manny Mania, and the DC King Of Chicago skateboarding events; the essay chronicles recent processes of corporate branding as a key dynamic in the making of Chicago as a city of exclusion and leisure. Street skateboarders participate in the production of a city of social control while challenging prescribed notions of public exchange and forwarding the potential for alternative visions of the city.

Public space is a battleground.

Order and Disorder in the City

In contemporary cities, multiple public spheres unravel through competing visions of order and disorder that guide the production of public spaces (cf. Mitchell). Visions of order involve the top-down regulation of public behavior in which prescribed users participate in sanctioned uses of public space. A homogeneous public is enforced in order to assure the complementary imperatives of leisure and consumption. Conversely, visions of disorder are founded on the tolerance of difference and dissent. Multiple and plural spheres of publics are envisioned through this take on disorder (cf. Fraser). From this vantage point, public space is a battleground subject to heterogeneous usurpations for the fulfillment of political claims to the city.

Competing visions of order and disorder in the city center on new forms of social control and the contestation of a uniform public sphere. Public order takes place through the outright militarization of urban space by way of social policies and building practices intent on transforming cities into fortresses (cf. Davis). Everyday surveillance spreads thick across public squares through add-on technologies such as CCTV cameras or built-in features such as hostile seating (cf. Staples; Coleman). Defensible space tenets underline a hardening of urban landscapes through measures founded on the rational choice belief that the built environment determines social behavior (cf. Newman). These tenets justify the enforcement of crime prevention through urban design. Defensible space translates into the building of paranoia evident in a series of interdictory spaces characterized as stealthy, slippery, crusty, prickly, and jittery (cf. Flusty, "Building paranoia"). Walls and gates most forcefully trigger the eradication of public space by repelling potential users of fortress cities spanning from pervasive policing throughout central business districts to gated communities across suburban fringes (cf. Caldeira; Low, *On the Plaza*).

The city of social control also takes shape through the reproduction of commercial images across the built environment. This aesthetic strategy complements the social exclusion policies of hard spaces. The branding of public space signals a shift toward privatization/colonization of social landscapes through corporate image saturation (cf. Klein). It effectively contracts out the construction and maintenance of public spaces in exchange for advertisement space. Through public-private partnerships and corporate sponsorships, these urban redevelopment projects produce public spaces in which the "trappings of private ownership and commerce are woven into the fabric of the place" (Staeheli and Mitchell xviii). The corporate brand disseminates throughout the urban landscape and in the process transforms cities into marketing ventures.

The arrangements between market and state forces that increasingly privatize public space often take shape through nostalgia as a key force for the collusion of historic preservation and economic development across downtowns (cf. Isenberg; Herzog). The turn toward nostalgia in urban design results in the proliferation of festive marketplaces, waterfront destinations, and shopping malls that resemble theme parks and forward the Disneyfication of cities (cf. Sorkin). Pay-to-play rules and regulations along with simulated environments override the possibility of public dissent and unscripted encounters in these theme park spaces.

Know Skateboarding

As skateboarders drift through the city, traces remain as evidence of an alternative use of the built environment. Similar to the dirt shortcuts created by pedestrians that venture off sidewalks (cf. de Certeau; BondGraham), skateboard scuff arises from an unspoken collective effort. Traces of filth adorn concrete surfaces as both markers of previous use and harbingers of unscripted encounters in public space. Candle wax and board art coalesce on concrete ledges as skateboarders glide across varied surfaces. Skateboard scuff markings are works-in-progress, smudge palimpsests, and friction-regulating technologies. If left unused, spots tend to dry up. Pieces of candle wax are often left behind as gestures of solidarity. The upkeep of a skate spot is a communal practice that entails discretion and fine-tuning.

An integral dynamic in the production of skate spots consists of crafting direct action measures to elude anti-skateboarding regulations. Skateboarders' exclusion from public space is most often justified through appeals to public safety and property maintenance. Noise pollution, loitering, property defacement, and trespassing figure among the offenses incurred while skateboarding on unsanctioned grounds. Private security guards, state police officers, and vigilante property owners work toward ridding city streets of skateboarders. Among the strategies employed, NO SKATEBOARDING signs are posted in places where this improper use of space is discouraged. Skateboarders have taken on the challenge of subverting these signs with the same ingenuity employed to redefine downtown workplaces as spaces of play (cf. Flusty, "Thrashing downtown").

The theft or alteration of NO SKATEBOARDING signs constitutes a symbolic act of skate spot liberation. Ferrell claims that

> for skaters, such acts exist as skirmishes in an ongoing battle, a battle to liberate public space from legal regulation, and to reencode the meaning of public space within the experience of skating. Toward this end, skaters who don't bother removing "No Skateboarding" signs from strip

> malls and parks still counter them with a touch of subcultural signage, pasting them over with "Know Skateboarding" stickers that have become almost as common as the signs themselves. (72)

Knowing skateboarding entails the recognition of skateboarders as legitimate public space participants and the symbolic victory over anti-skateboarding spatial regulation. A similar culture jamming tactic was devised by the Emerica skateboard shoe company through the purchase-free distribution of "de-sign" kits that consisted of a 14 × 21.5cm sheet of different sized letter "G" stickers. Proctor states "the idea was to place the 'G' sticker over the letter 'N' of a 'No skateboarding' sign, reversing the meaning to [...] 'Go skateboarding'!!" (Ferrell 72). The defacement of posted rules of conduct is a second-order subversion of dominant meanings inscribed in the built environment that harbors the potential for imagining alternative social horizons.

NO SKATEBOARDING signs are just one component of an intricate system of public space regulation that includes police-issued fines for trespassing, loitering, and defacement of public and private property, skateboarding deterrents designed into the built environment, and purpose-built skateboarding terrains such as skate parks and skate plazas. Skateproofing devices, much like NO SKATEBOARDING signs, dot the urban landscape. Metal brackets are fastened to concrete ledges, knobs are welded to handrails, and ornamental features are strategically placed in hopes of deterring scuff. An advertisement slogan for a company in the business of skateproofing reads: BECAUSE SIGNS ALONE ARE NOT ENOUGH!

Skateproofing conforms to recent practices of urban spatial regulation informed by the ideological tenets of defensible space (cf. Newman) and broken windows[1] (cf. Wilson and Kelling). Crime prevention through environmental design forwards a holistic approach to community policing founded on a strong correlation between rising crime rates and the deterioration of built environments (cf. Schneider). From this social policy perspective, unlawful activities in public space are addressed through built forms. Critics contend that defensible space and

1 Policing informed by broken windows theory is overwhelmingly concerned with street activity. Artists, musicians, acrobats, and vendors making a living on sidewalks and streets become targets for increased law enforcement. In New York City, the broken windows theory informs zero-tolerance policies and stop-and-frisk practices. These policing procedures result in a deeply racialized and class-based "cleansing" of the public realm.

broken windows constitute instrumentalist policing ideologies founded on environmental determinism that effectively only relocate lawlessness rather than addressing longstanding social inequalities (cf. Rentschler; Shaftoe). Among the new spatial relations that emerge from the practice of these ideologies, hard plazas result in defensible spaces lacking trees, shrubbery, and ornamental vegetation in order to increase visibility set on deterring crime and reducing public spending on maintenance (cf. Low, *Behind the Gates*). Unexpectedly, these hard places built from smooth concrete, granite, and marble slab, and intentioned on securing public safety, also comprise desirable skateboard destinations. Skateproofing most often takes place only after scuff has settled across the new surfaces.

Anti-skateboarding landscapes form part of a series of surveillance technologies including graffiti-proof walls, CCTV cameras, automated sprinkler systems, pigeon-proof ledges and bum-proof benches (cf. Davis). These material expressions of power (cf. Hodder) forge social relations through geographies of exclusion (cf. Sibley). Under these social conditions of exclusion, dirt, filth, and scuff are construed as evidence for the reproduction of dominant truth claims and social inequalities. From the standpoint of public safety, scuff-producing skateboarding bodies must be deterred in order to uphold the symbolic purchase of private property and state authority.

Set against a stage of systematic social exclusion, skate spots constitute material expressions of resistance (cf. Hodder) that proliferate under the wire (cf. Mitchell). The Skatespot Liberation Front promises the steadfast eradication of anti-skateboarding devices inscribed into the built environment. Rather than a hierarchal organization, this clandestine collective is composed of anyone willing to trespass, deface, and loiter on public/private property for the purpose of reclaiming space for skateboarding. Along with inverting the message of anti-skateboarding signage, hacking metal brackets fastened to low-set ledges, sawing knobs welded onto handrails, and smoothing ground surface cracks with automotive body dent fillers all figure among skate spot liberation tactics (cf. Panhead). Construction materials such as QuikCrete and Portland Cement are applied to sidewalk cracks to allow for smooth entries and landings in and out of spots and used to produce ad hoc transitioned surfaces allowing for vertical prowess. Also, angle iron is fastened to ledges in tandem with the application of wax to assure greater speed. These pro-skateboarding devices adapt the city and constitute built counter-narratives to skateboard deterrents and the privatization of public space.

Leisure and Exclusion

Chicago lakefront development is driven by an amalgam of social forces with diverse motives such as commercial profit, historical preservation, public safety, and citizen participation. The recent proliferation of leisure practices along the lakefront corresponds to a paradigmatic shift in urban governance from securing ideal conditions for industrial manufacturing to more often allocating local government resources toward the everyday spaces of entertainment and consumption. Built environments, security, and citizenship become further entwined within a context of increased interdependence between leisure spaces and economic development. As a result, public resources are unevenly distributed toward the social reproduction of tourists and local elites who can afford leisure, while poor racialized populations are systematically excluded from the city. Urban development projects such as high-rise condo buildings, multilevel parking garages, wrought-iron gated parks, and fine-dining restaurants cater to affluent city dwellers. The development of these amenities tends to price out poor populations and contribute to efforts that seek to make poverty invisible.[2] Municipal governments increasingly envision public safety and citizenship participation in urban spaces as an exclusive domain of affluent populations.

The punitive regulation of public life is on the rise. Defensive design measures contribute to a high surveillance scenario that spreads thick across varied urban centers. With the dramatic rise in global wealth disparities and disinvestment in social welfare programs, governing differences among popu-

2 Both Berman and Harvey discuss Baudelaire in order to tease out key linkages between social inequality and built environments. In "The Eyes of the Poor," Baudelaire describes an exchange between wealthy cafe-goers and a poor family lurking outside. The eyes of the father say: "All the gold of the poor world must have found its way onto those walls" while a patron begs: "Those people are insufferable with their great saucer eyes. Can't you tell the proprietor to send them away?" (53). As part of Haussmann's military plan for Paris, the spectacle of the new cafe is contingent on keeping poverty out of sight.

3 Spielman reports that even as it endures its current economic crisis, the state of Illinois will spend $16 million to promote tourism. The mayor of Chicago justified the spending by stating that "We're competing against Atlanta. We're competing against Las Vegas and Orlando. You have to put packages together to get the conventions here. At the same time, you have to publicize. You have to do marketing worldwide and throughout the United States" (9)

lations becomes increasingly challenging. In Chicago, the linkages between lakefront leisure and urban unrest contribute to longstanding race, class, and gender inequalities. In uncertain times, new immigrants join the ranks of the descendants of the Great Migration as scapegoats for the source of endemic social problems that include economic decline, street crimes, and dwindling social welfare programs. New arrangements of urban space on the defensive arise from the multiplication of plural publics in the contemporary city.

The widespread embrace of urban tourism is a key component of postindustrial urban development. The marketing of cities as centers of culture and entertainment is common ground among local government officials seeking growth beyond industrial production.[3] Instead of a stage for jobs, the city and its amenities are increasingly promoted as the main attraction. Publicity campaigns abound advertising local destinations such as convention centers, shopping malls, museums, theaters, and restaurants through a plethora of media that include television and print ads. Furthermore, both virtual spaces such as web pages and social networking sites and built forms that follow current trends within elite architecture promote cities as tourist destinations.

Skate spots constitute material expressions of resistance.

In contemporary Chicago, tourist city dynamics mostly align with the "converted city" model in which infrastructure is built to produce tourist spaces that Fainstein and Judd describe as "insulated from the larger urban milieu within a process of uneven development" (262). Vast social disparities characterize the urban landscape segregated along racial, ethnic, and class fault lines. Chicago remains a divided city in which government officials in partnership with finance speculators and private developers seek to hide poverty behind a veneer of tourist attractions. These attractions consist of large-scale infrastructure projects that include sports stadiums, convention centers, museums, theaters, parks, gardens, and public art. Tourist city dynamics in Chicago funnel public resources and symbolic purchase toward projects that will attract visitors and away from citizens' claims such as affordable housing and public education.

Amenities such as entertainment zones, theater districts, and museum campuses not only serve to lure in tourists, but also attract a new affluent class of urban dwellers engaged in so-called creative work (cf. Florida). The shift “from urban renewal to the city of leisure” (Spirou and Bennett), urban beautification projects (Spirou), and the “amenities drive urban growth” thesis (Clark) all contribute to visions of a contemporary Chicago that has shaken off its industrial rust, embraced a turn toward culture as motor of development, and transformed itself into a city that plays.

The band shell designed by Frank Gehry in Millennium Park helps construe an image of Chicago intended on luring tourists, investors, and affluent urbanites to the city. The urban redevelopment dynamics that take place in Millennium Park create diverging experiences founded on an increased control of potential users. Although access to the park is free of charge, its financing scheme and the policing of its grounds conform to a growing trend within the production of new public spaces. Like most sports stadiums, Millennium Park is a corporate-sponsored destination turned into an advertisement landscape. The selling off of naming rights is a key public-private partnership scheme that raises issues of access and ownership. Corporations such as McDonald’s, Chase, and BP advertise their brands across the park’s grounds. Furthermore, sections of the park are often off-limits to the public and rented for private events, while an enforced curfew dissuades homeless sleeping. Corporate sponsorship and highly controlled access make for unforeseen arrangements within public space. Staeheli and Mitchell describe the park as follows:

> With its heavy corporate sponsorship and curfew, Millennium Park seems like some confusing hybrid space. It *is* publicly-owned, but the trappings of private ownership and commerce are woven into the fabric of the place. (xviii)

Millennium Park combines trends within official sporting venues that showcase corporate brands with the work of star architects in order to advertise the city on a global stage.

Chicago Skate Parks and Skate Spots

The construction of poured-in-place skate parks along the lakefront contributes to the broad urban development schemes that seek to transform Chicago into a city of leisure. Burnham Skate Park, Wilson Skate Park, and Grant Park Skate Plaza represent a municipal embrace of skateboarding while increasing the regulation of public spaces. These projects work as a political concession that justifies the controlled exclusion of skateboarders from downtown (cf. Németh). Recent legislation prohibits skateboarding in the Central Business District. An unsettling scenario emerges as skaters are subject to stiff fines if caught skating beyond the fence. A purpose-built conundrum unfolds. Designated skateboard sites such as the poured-in-place lakefront skate parks stimulate the growth and popularity of skateboarding while justifying its further criminalization on city streets.

Although the enclosure of skateboarders within skate parks along the lakefront is in full swing, skate spots continue to flourish throughout Chicago's built environment. The *Accessories to an Event (Plaza)* installation at the Museum of Contemporary Art and the McCormick Place Gap are two noteworthy examples. The first was the inspiration for the development of the Grant Park Skate Plaza, while the second was the setting of an impromptu "best trick" contest during the 2009 GO Skateboarding Day events. Another Chicago skate spot example is the Shedd Aquarium seawall. As a notorious skateboarding destination, it figures among a list of "10 Spots You Gotta Skate Before You Die" (Salo) and consists of a ten-foot-high curved barrier along the aquarium perimeter intended to protect the building from breaking waves. Skateboarders frequent the wall and perform exhilarating maneuvers. They collectively redefine the seawall through its creative, spontaneous, and ephemeral appropriation. The predictability of the skate park and its prescribed uses contrasts with the risks of confronting security guards or witnessing your board sink into Lake Michigan. The differences between found and planned skateboarding terrains hinge on the potential for the flourishing of practices founded on alternative uses of public space. Street skateboarding thrives on the creative exploration of the built environment rather than on ready-made, regulated, and enclosed parks.

Getting Wild on Michigan Avenue

Wild in the Streets was a hybrid skate spot and skate park corporate-sponsored event that galvanized Chicago skateboarders' struggles for use and access to urban space within the city. During the early afternoon of June 21, 2006 thousands of skateboarders fleetingly occupied a stretch of Michigan Avenue in downtown Chicago. With the harsh winter behind them, they pushed forward by taking to the streets. The deafening roar of skateboard wheels felt like a communal cry for change. Their political goals were to disrupt business as usual, gain recognition as legitimate users of the city, and lobby for the second phase of the Grant Park Skate Plaza.

The six-mile journey from Buckingham Fountain in Grant Park to Wilson Skatepark on Lake Shore Drive was part of a global movement sponsored by the International Association of Skateboard Companies. GO Skateboarding Day encourages skateboarders to take to the streets in unison across the world. Skateboarders' access to and use of urban space are at the center of the claims made through this one-day event. Sponsored by the Emerica skateboard shoe company, the event played a key role in the massive participation in the 2006 GO Skateboarding Day event through the draw of its professional skateboarders. Much like the purchase-free distribution of "de-sign" kits of "G" stickers for jamming NO SKATEBOARDING signs (cf. Proctor), the Emerica-sponsored Wild in the Streets event and advertisement campaign seek to bridge the global reach of skateboarding and localized struggles for public space.

Once skateboarders took to the streets, congratulatory posing gave way to defiant performance. The most skilled skaters pushed ahead of the pack. The rest weaved through traffic trying not to fall. The sound of roaring wheels left the city at a momentary standstill. Even though a Xeroxed hand-drawn map of the sanctioned route had been distributed previous to the departure, skateboarders managed to trace their own unforeseen lines across the city. By veering off of the intended path, they challenged the prescribed expectations of the event organizers. The Wild in the Streets event proved fertile ground for furthering spatial appropriation and creative play within a highly orchestrated corporate-sponsored event.

While traces of skate spots remain in the form of scuffed ledges and jammed NO SKATEBOARDING signs, the space produced through the collective push through the city was ephemeral and fleeting. This social product constitutes a sonorous space characterized by the roaring thunder of thousands of skateboard wheels rolling on the street and echoing off of downtown skyscrapers. Beyond the one-day protest event, skateboarders produce sonorous spaces through everyday practices. The "clack-clack" sound made by quickly skating over sidewalk groves is a form of sonorous space that communicates the presence of a skater on the move. The "skaters'-eye-view" (Flusty, "Thrashing downtown") of the city also requires a sharp ear for skateboard sounds. Both street and sidewalk skating produce distinctive roaring and "clack-clack" noises that contribute to the making of urban space. Sonorous skate spaces are examples of representational space that is "directly lived" by users and experienced as dominated spaces which "the imagination seeks to change and appropriate" (Lefebvre 39). The loud takeover of city streets by skateboarders unearths the potential redefinition of urban space for pleasure and protest.

Street skateboarding thrives on the creative exploration of the built environment.

The unchartered collective push culminated in Wilson Skate Park. After momentarily usurping the streets, Chicago skateboarders claimed the skate park for an Emerica-sponsored barbeque, product giveaway, and skate demo. Unlike other skate park demos, a sense of shared accomplishment seemed to linger as skateboarders rejoiced in having collectively survived street traffic and the long journey under the glaring sun. The Wild in the Streets event spearheads a trend toward the staging of promotional skateboarding venues beyond purpose-built settings. The demo proves to be a popular medium through which to cultivate brand awareness and loyalty. Emerica buys multiple two-page ads in skate magazines to promote Wild in the Streets that build name recognition and a corporate image in tune with street skateboarding.

Daley Plaza, Clemente Skate Spot, and the Staging of Street Skateboarding

The Red Bull Manny Mania Am Series and DC King Of Series competitive events showcased skateboarding through the temporary appropriation of Chicago skate spots. These corporate-sponsored events were staged in the streets rather than within the sanctioned confines of a skate park. The built environments redefined by street skateboarders as skate spots were made official for the staging of contests that sought to display skateboarding within an authentic urban setting. Corporate branding is at the center of these street contests. However, the events also take up the skateboarders' claims to public space. While Emerica's Wild in the Streets event enabled skaters to take to the city in a fleeting motion accentuated by the roaring thunder of thousands of skateboard wheels, these competitive events set up camp and temporarily occupied a corner of the city. Furthermore, they constitute sanctioned skateboarding spectacles that promote Chicago as a leisure city in tune with youth, street cultures, and alternative sport. The street contest enables the temporary decriminalization of street skateboarding while providing cities with tourism, consumption, and media coverage.

On July 18, 2009, the Chicago stop of the Red Bull Manny Mania Am Series took place at the western entrance of Soldier Field after a last-minute change of location. Initially, the event was scheduled to take place at Daley Plaza in downtown Chicago. Promotional materials for the event included copies of folders in which local skateboarders were encouraged to submit designs for the contest obstacle: "Manny Pads designed by and built for Chicago Skaters!" A manny pad, or manual pad, consists of a low-set stage with a variety of inclined planes and ledges. Skateboarders perform manuals through an assortment of technical maneuvers that most often include balancing on two skateboard wheels across an elevated surface. The manny contest is most similar to the almost defunct freestyle competition. During the months leading up to the Red Bull event, the promotional folders surfaced in the Uprise Skate Shop that advertised an "under the Picasso" setting and a participatory planning process.

Daley Plaza is a hard space at the base of a 648-foot-tall skyscraper at 50 W. Washington Street. Completed in 1965, the towering Daley Center was erected during a boom of high-rise construction due to the relaxing of height regulations and the adoption of floor-area-ratio limits and density bonuses (cf. Schwieterman and Caspall). Its exterior surface consists of self-weathering steel that has enabled the building to mutate over time into a rusty veneer. The centerpiece of Daley Plaza is a fifty-foot-tall steel sculpture made by Pablo Picasso to match the building's exterior. While the plaza was conceived as a barren defensible space, it is regularly retrofitted to accommodate lunchtime performances, ethnic festivals, holiday celebrations, and a weekly farmers' market. Furthermore, Daley Plaza often hosts political demonstrations, Critical Mass cyclists, and skateboarders seeking thrills on the inclined surfaces of the Picasso sculpture.

The Red Bull Manny Mania event was set to claim Daley Plaza for skateboarding. Instead, the venue was unexpectedly moved outside of Soldier Field. The lakefront sport stadium is a marginal space in which participants and spectators enjoyed views of the city skyline rather than the experience of skateboarding among skyscrapers. The event consisted of a day-long elimination process as local skateboarders showed off their skills to each other, the public, and the judges. Red Bull banners, tarps, coolers, and a DJ vehicle adorned the event while massive quantities of the energy drink were given away. A fence separated skateboarders with wristbands proving they had registered for the contest from other skateboarders and spectators. While the main event played out on the Red Bull-branded manny pad within the fence, a series of impromptu skate sessions unfolded throughout the perimeter of Soldier Field. Some found refuge from the corporate-branded caffeinated frenzy by waxing a couple of ledges and making lines across a side entrance of the stadium.

A different set of social dynamics shaped the DC King Of Series in Chicago. In previous years, the event was hosted in skate spots across Dublin and Vancouver. Unlike the Red Bull Manny Mania series in which a stage designed through a participatory process is built for the competition, the King Of contest takes place on a found space originally conceived for uses other than skateboarding. On October 10–11, 2009 the event was staged on a plaza at Roberto Clemente High School in the Humboldt Park neighborhood. Although by no means a skyscraper, the built infrastructure of the school consists of a single steel-framed building anchored by a hard plaza. Much like Little Village, Humboldt Park remains a densely populated working-class neighborhood. Its Puerto Rican population struggles against gentrifying forces set to price out longstanding residents. However, the King Of event was lacking a political agenda other than to promote a corporate brand and forward struggles toward skateboarders' right to the city. A comment made by an out-of-town event announcer disheartened with the metal detectors placed at the school entrance hinted at the persistent social inequalities shaping the Puerto Rican experience in Chicago and the Humboldt Park neighborhood.

The two-day spectacle was staged across four distinct groupings of built features within the Clemente High School plaza. The first day featured tech zones consisting of a two-stair and ledge followed by a bank to ledge and long stair. Six heats of five skateboarders each competed on the spots for ten minutes at a time. The second day followed the same format across a different section of the plaza named the gnar zone. It featured a long flat rail and ledge followed by a party deck wall short and long gap. Much like the Chicago stop of the Red Bull Manny Mania Am Series, corporate branding saturated the King Of venue through the copious numbers of DC banners, tarps, flyers, and stickers. Furthermore, a product giveaway left lucky spectators sporting DC hats and T-shirts. Overall, the organizers of the event managed to appropriate a variety of architectural features throughout the plaza in order to showcase a wide set of street skateboarding skills.

The success of the DC King Of Series highlights both the gender inequalities that shape skateboarding and the political potential of skateboarding as a tactic of public space appropriation. As a male-dominated spatial practice, skateboarding perpetuates the exclusion of girls and women from public life. The title of the DC competitive series makes no qualms about the masculinist overtones inherent to skateboarding as sport. Skateboarding as crime most often takes place far from the immediate grasp of corporate branding and sport spectacle. Street contests stage male-dominated spectacles through the merging of skateboarding's criminal and sporting dimensions. The collusion between crime and sport is further complicated by the emergence of skateboarding as art. Similar to gallery curators, the DC event organizers retrofit space for the proper display of works of art. They filled gaps across the concrete ground surface and capped ledges with metal veneers to allow for greater speed. These modifications to found space constitute a form of corporate-sponsored skate spot liberation. The corporate branding spotlight shines over the tactical public space appropriations achieved through the social practice of skateboarding.

City of Play

Whether on planned or found spaces, street skateboarding more closely embodies a politics of resistance and social inclusion. Practitioners of this style skate over distinctions between human-made and natural surfaces through spatial tactics of appropriation that transform the city into playground (cf. Woolley and Johns). Street skateboarding as a critical spatial tactic undermines the enclosure of skateboarders within skate parks and contributes to a vision of the city that fosters collective uses and creative experimentations with built environments. Unintended pleasurable engagements with architectural forms challenge prescribed uses by welcoming unexpected encounters. Furthermore, street skateboarding fosters communal land use practices that undermine the primacy of market-rate private property (cf. Blomley). While purpose-built skateboarding spaces may work as training facilities to further this quest, the appropriation of found urban spaces through street skateboarding contests the given meanings of cities as theme parks (cf. Sorkin). Street skateboarders scout, usurp, and maintain spots of spatial desire by practicing an ethic of care for the built environment that transforms ordinary urban spaces into temporary autonomous play zones (Bey). The spaces crafted through the ethic of care outlined above are both subject to an urban politics of disciplined accommodation and figure as a groundwork toward resistance to punitive spatial regulation.

References

Baudelaire, Charles. "The Eyes of the Poor." *Paris Spleen*. New York: New Directions, 1947. 52–53. Print.

Berman, Marshall. *All That is Solid Melts into Air: The Experience of Modernity*. New York: Simon and Schuster, 1982. Print.

Bey, Hakim. *T.A.Z.: Temporary Autonomous Zone, Ontological Anarchy, Poetic Terrorism*. New York: Autonomedia, 1991. Print.

BondGraham, Darwin. "Anarchitecture: A Manifesto for Rebuilding Place and Community." *Z Magazine* 19.9 (2006): 49–52. Print.

Blomley, Nicholas. *Unsettling the City: Urban Land and the Politics of Property*. New York: Routledge, 2004. Print.

Caldeira, Teresa. *City of Walls: Crime, Segregation and Citizenship in Sao Paulo*. Berkeley: University of California Press, 1999. Print.

Certeau, Michel de. *The Practice of Everyday Life*. Berkeley: University of California, 1984. Print.

Clark, Terry Nichols. "Amenities Drive Urban Growth." *Journal of Urban Affairs* 24.5 (2002): 493–515. Print.

Coleman, Roy. *Reclaiming the Streets: Surveillance, Social Control and the City*. Portland, OR: Willan, 2004. Print.

Davis, Mike. *City of Quartz: Excavating the Future in Los Angeles*. London: Verso, 1990. Print.

Fainstein, Susan, and Dennis Judd. "Cities as Places to Play." *The Tourist City*. Eds. Dennis Judd and Susan Fainstein. New Haven, CT: Yale University Press, 1999. 261–72. Print.

Ferrell, Jeff. *Tearing Down the Streets: Adventures in Urban Anarchy*. New York: Palgrave, 2001. Print.

Florida, Richard. *The Rise of the Creative Class: And How It's Transforming Work, Leisure, Community, and Everyday Life*. New York: Basic Books, 2002. Print.

Flusty, Steven (2000). "Thrashing Downtown: Play as Resistance to the Spatial and Representational Regulation of Los Angeles." *Cities* 17.2 (2000): 149–58. Print.

Flusty, Steven. "Building Paranoia." *Architecture of Fear*. Ed. Nan Ellin. New York: Princeton Architectural Press, 1997. 47–60. Print.

Fraser, Nancy. "Rethinking the Public Sphere: A Contribution to the Critique of Actually Existing Democracy." *Social Text* 25.26 (1990): 56–80. Print.

Harvey, David. "The Political Economy of Public Space." *The Politics of Public Space*. Eds. Setha Low and Neil Smith. New York: Routledge. 2006. 17–34. Print.

Herzog, Lawrence. *Return to the Center: Culture, Public Space, and City Building in a Global Era*. Austin: University of Texas Press, 2006. Print.

Hodder, Ian. "The Interpretation of Documents and Material Culture." *Handbook of Qualitative Research*. 2nd edition. Eds. Norman K. Denzin and Yvonna S. Lincoln. Thousand Oaks, CA: Sage, 2000. 703–15. Print.

Isenberg, Alison. *Downtown America: A History of the Place and the People Who Made It*. Chicago, IL: University of Chicago Press, 2004. Print.

Kayden, Jerold. *Privately-Owned Public Space: The New York City Experience*. New York: Municipal Art Society of New York, 2000. Print.

Klein, Naomi. *No Logo*. New York: Picador, 2000. Print.

Lefebvre, Henri. *The Production of Space*. Oxford: Blackwell, 1991. Print.

Low, Setha. *Behind the Gates: Life, Security and the Pursuit of Happiness in Fortress America*. New York: Routledge, 2003. Print.

Low, Setha. *On the Plaza: The Politics of Public Space and Culture*. Austin: University of Texas Press, 2000. Print.

Mitchell, Don. *The Right to the City: Social Justice and the Fight for Public Space*. New York: The Guilford Press, 2003. Print.

Németh, Jeremy. "Conflict, Exclusion, Relocation: Skateboarding and Public Space." *Journal of Urban Design* 11.3 (2006): 297–318. Print.

Newman, Oscar. *Defensible Space: Crime Prevention Through Urban Design*. New York: Macmillan, 1972. Print.

Panhead. "Taking Back the Streets." *Transworld SKATEboarding* 23.4 (2005): 175–84. Print.

Proctor, Yogi. "Go Skateboarding!" *Skateboard Stickers*. Eds. Steve Cardwell and Mark Munson. New York: Laurence King, 2004. 72–73. Print.

Rentschler, Carrie. "Designing Fear: How Environmental Security Protects Property at the Expense of People." *Foucault, Cultural Studies, and Governmentality*. Eds. Jack Z. Bratich, Jeremy Packer, and Cameron McCarthy. Albany: State University of New York Press, 2003. 243–72. Print.

Salo, Adam. "10 Spots You Gotta Skate Before You Die." *Skateboarder* 15.7 (2006): 32. Print.

Schneider, Richard. "Introduction: Crime Prevention Through Environmental Design (CPTED): Themes, Theories, Practice, and Conflict." *Journal of Architectural and Planning Research* 22.4 (2005): 271–83. Print.

Schwieterman, Josef P., and Dana M. Caspall. *The Politics of Place: A History of Zoning in Chicago*. Chicago, IL: Lake Claremont Press, 2006. Print.

Shaftoe, Henry. "Behaving Badly in Public Places." *Urban Design* 97 (2006): 19–21. Print.

Sibley, David. *Geographies of Exclusion: Society and Difference in the West*. New York: Routledge, 1995. Print.

Smith, Neil. *The New Urban Frontier: Gentrification and the Revanchist City*. New York: Routledge, 1996. Print.

Sorkin, Michael, ed. *Variations on a Theme Park: The New American City and the End of Public Space*. New York: Hill and Wang, 1992. Print.

Spielman, Fran. "Daley: Tourism Money Worth It." *Chicago Sun-Times*, September 23, 2009: 9. Print.

Spirou, Costas, and Larry Bennett. *It's Hardly Sportin': Stadiums, Neighborhoods, and the New Chicago*. DeKalb: Northern Illinois University Press, 2003. Print.

Spirou, Costas. "Urban Beautification: The Construction of a New Identity in Chicago." *The New Chicago: A Social and Cultural Analysis*. Eds. John Koval et al. Philadelphia, PA: Temple University Press, 2006. 295–304.

Staeheli, Lynn. A., and Don Mitchell. *The People's Property?: Power, Politics, and the Public*. New York: Routledge, 2008. Print.

Staples, William. *Everyday Surveillance: Vigilance and Visibility in Postmodern Life*. Lanham, MD: Rowman and Littlefield, 2000. Print.

Wilson, James Q., and George L. Kelling. "Broken Windows." *The Atlantic Monthly* 3 (1982): 29–38. Print.

Woolley, Helen, and Ralph Johns. "Skateboarding: The City as a Playground." *Journal of Urban Design* 6.2 (2001): 211–30. Print.

Kai Reinhart

"Concrete Carving on the Berlin Wall" *Skateboarding in East Germany*

Translated by Konstantin Butz

"Ready for labor and defense!" was the motto of the GDR sports badge (cf. Bernett 77). Leisure and recreational sports were supposed to systematically educate people in terms of responsibility, discipline, collective unity, and first and foremost ideological firmness and strict commitment to the party (cf. Schwidtmann and Budzisch 361). "Skate and Create" or "Skate and Destroy" were the slogans of skateboarding (cf. Peralta, "Future Primitive"; Howell 83; Brooke 95). When skate parks were closed in the US during the 1980s and the American scene shrank to a small group, a hardcore group, skateboarding became "synonymous with a special way of life. A myth was born" (Doren and Pramann 21).[1]

1 All quotations that do not stem from English publications have been translated by Konstantin Butz.

Skateboarding and socialism were as far removed from each other during the 1970s and 1980s as were the US and the Soviet Union. Still, skateboarding found its way into the socialist world from the end of the 1970s onwards and even reached the USSR (cf. "Moskauer Staatszirkus!" 13; Bauer 50f.; Borden 183).

When a few American skateboard companies received letters by skaters from Czechoslovakia and Poland they were really surprised: "Feature it: people are building ramps behind the Iron Curtain, they're freestyling in the Arctic, they're concrete carving on the Berlin Wall" (Peralta, "Interview" 20). However, the evolution of skateboarding in the East lagged decades behind developments in the West (cf. Ludewig 77). East Berlin—the capital of the GDR that was located right within the small state but had an inner-city border to the Western world and the liberal "island" of West Berlin—became the skateboard center of the GDR.

Berlin, Alexanderplatz

It is hard to say who the first skateboarder in the GDR was, but during the mid to late 1970s there was certainly already a small group of about five skaters in East Berlin. They were approximately fifteen to twenty years old and were riding together with a few roller-skaters. Some of them owned skateboards from the West. About ten years later, when new kids joined the scene, these early pioneers slowly retreated and lost contact with the younger skaters. Apart from the memories of some contemporary witnesses, the photographs that Harald Schmitt shot at Alexanderplatz and which were partly published in the Western magazine *Stern* constitute the only evidence of the existence of these first GDR skateboarders (cf. "Kein Bock Auf Honecker" 20f.).

Before German reunification, East Berlin displayed none of the hectic bustle of a Western capital city and Alexanderplatz was one of the few lively urban squares. It had a traffic junction, a diner, benches, flower boxes and—in contrast to the mostly rough and holey streets—a very smooth surface. Unsurprisingly, the "Platz," as the skateboarders called it, quickly became their meeting point and the place where they spent much of their free time (cf. Haak; Thomasius; Geisler). When the surface was replaced by small wave-shaped cobblestones for the 750th anniversary of Berlin in 1987, the scene moved to the neighboring passage of the town hall which still had a smooth surface and was also roofed over, making it skateable in rain and in the winter (cf. Mofo 68). During the first half of the 1980s younger kids joined the older skateboarders. Among the first to become influential characters of GDR skateboarding were John Haak (son of the well-known GDR musician Detlef Haak, Haak had a Finnish mother, meaning that he enjoyed extensive freedom of travel because of his Finnish passport) and René-Falk Thomasius.

In addition to Alexanderplatz, this "second generation" of skaters used a new prestigious GDR landmark for skateboarding. Between 1977 and 1981 a sports and recreation center (*Sport- und Erholungszentrum*, abbreviated to SEZ) was built near the *Volkspark* (people's park) in Berlin-Friedrichshain, providing much space for leisure activities. Compared to the circumstances in East Germany at the time, these pleasure grounds constituted a "colorful place," housing a wave pool, sauna, gymnasium, workout studio, billiard tables, and an ice- or roller-skating rink all under one roof (cf. Kluge 186). This place became an additional breeding ground for the skateboard scene of East Berlin where "at first everybody rode roller skates [...] but eventually switched to the skateboard" (Thomasius). While roller skaters went in circles, the skateboarders stood in the center of the rink and presented an improvised show to everyone standing in line at the entrance (cf. Geisler). Their self-confident and unconventional demeanor in combination with the astonishing maneuvers and tricks attracted even more kids. Since there was no formal organization it is difficult to estimate the scene in numbers. According to Marco Sladek there were twelve skaters at Alexanderplatz at the time (cf. Groth 69). Overall, however, the skateboard scene of East Berlin was probably slightly bigger and comprised perhaps twenty to thirty, exclusively male, skateboarders (cf. Weinreich, "Zirzensisches auf den rollenden Brettern"). Once further new skaters had joined in, a "third generation" emerged, including even younger kids. All in all, however, East Berlin's skateboard scene remained rather homogenous and small.

"Bo(a)rderline"

A unique characteristic of the scene in the divided city was its connections to the skaters of West Berlin. In 1982, a few of the Western skaters took notice of the skaters beyond the wall, having seen them in *Stern* magazine (cf. "Kein Bock Auf Honecker"). Real contacts, however, were first established a few years later by Easterners who had left the country, by East Berliners such as John Haak or Holger Will who had Western passports, by contests in the CSSR that were attended by skaters from the East and the West, and also by chance meetings in East Berlin. Intrigued by stories from the "Wild East," West Berliners became curious and reached out across the border. During visits to "the other side" they learned about life in the GDR and traveled to the unknown part of the divided city, including its skate spots. Andreas "Elle" Gillmeister remembers that the Western skaters felt like "stars" during these visits; just like the American skate pros who came to West Berlin.

In order to enter the GDR, the Westerners needed a one-day visa, which was not always granted. In Article 18, paragraph one of the constitution from April 6, 1968 the GDR committed to fighting against the "imperialist *Unkultur* [anti-culture] serving psychological warfare and the vilification of human beings" (Verfassung Art. 18, 219). In paragraph three of the same Article, body culture and sports were emphasized as "elements of socialist culture" serving the corporeal and mental evolution of the people. Skateboarding, however, was obviously not regarded as an element of "socialist culture" but rather as part of the "imperialist *Unkultur*." Skaters appeared suspicious to the border officials and were always rigorously inspected: address books were photographed; stickers had to be removed from skateboards; and if they were unlucky skaters could be interrogated and questioned for hours. "It was like taking a round-the-world trip although it was basically just next door. You never knew if you would make it, particularly if you carried the wrong stuff with you" (Graetsch). Bigger groups of skaters appeared extremely suspicious at the border, as Karl Johann "Kalle" Richter experienced in 1988 when he wanted to travel to East Berlin with about ten to fifteen friends: "They were like: 'Where do you want to go with these devices?' and we were like: 'Well, we want to go skate there and meet a few guys.' Of course, they became very wary and immediately questioned every one of us individually with two officers" (Richter).

Body culture and sports were emphasized as "elements of socialist culture."

Attempts at Socialist Integration

Since their activities not only included remarkable maneuvers, but also created loud and unknown sounds, the Eastern skaters—just like their friends in the West—were quickly regarded as a public nuisance and provocation. As a self-organized youth group, they did not fit into the system of the GDR, where leisure time was also defined in accordance with socialist ideology; sociologist Dieter Voigt comments that "'Leisure time'—mostly determined heteronomously in the GDR—thus constitutes an element in maintaining the system; first and foremost it serves to increase labor productivity and combat readiness as well as the assimilation to the norms of the state party" (Voigt 153; quoted in Stündel 21). Consequently, in all cities with bigger skateboard scenes, attempts were made to remove skaters from the streets in order to integrate them into established structures.

At the end of 1986, a representative of the DRSV, the Deutscher Rollsport Verband (German Cycling and Roller Skating Association) approached the skaters at Alexanderplatz (cf. Sladek; Thomasius). As they were currently looking for construction material with which both to build a new ramp and a spot to skate on during the winter, the skaters appreciated the contact with the association and became members of the cycling section of a company sports group: the *Betriebssportgemeinschaft Empor HO Berlin*, BSG for short (cf. Weinreich, "Zirzensisches auf den rollenden Brettern"). Their coach, Jürgen Grosche, was only about ten years older than the skaters and did not really care about formalities. He simply handled the official administration and did not intervene otherwise, with the result that some participants from that time valued the official *Rollsport* activities very highly (cf. Mamach; Haak). Marco Sladek himself became an official coach, even earning some money through this job (cf. Groth 70). Other skaters from that time, however, have no recollection of membership cards or membership fees and were probably not official members of the BSG. There was also some skepticism concerning the understanding of skateboarding within the association: "They tried to push us into a certain frame but did not really know how to do it" (Haak). The BSG granted the skaters a time frame within their gymnasium but removed them after the first scratches appeared on the surface of the hall floor. They were relocated to a paved space that was located next to the Friedrich Ludwig Jahn Sports Park, close to where record-holding soccer champions BFC Dynamo played their home matches. This space at the sports park—nicknamed Cantianstadion because of the neighboring Cantianstraße—was a great advancement for the skaters as it gave them somewhere to place their homemade ramps.

The BSG also booked the skaters for public performances. Marco Sladek and Dirk Maretzki of the "first generation" participated in this kind of show, skating in a professional capacity. They regularly appeared at events presented by the famous TV host Gerhard "Addi" Adolph (cf. Sladek). Nevertheless, Berlin's sports administration could not expect too much support for the BSG from the skaters. For the most part, they clearly distanced themselves from the association and refused to participate in "stupid club activities" (Rotenhagen). The skaters were hardly content to integrate or subordinate themselves and thus remained outsiders. "They did not manage to organize us. Our individuality could not be controlled" (Haak). It therefore seems that the BSG did not play a decisive role in the evolution of the Berlin skateboard scene, and the main meeting point remained at Alexanderplatz.

Material

For kids in the East, it was impossible to buy a skateboard from the West. A board of Western quality would have cost about four thousand (Eastern) marks. Given that the older skaters had a monthly income of about eight hundred marks, this was clearly unaffordable (cf. Sladek 41). The sense of frustration over this situation is expressed in a letter by René-Falk Thomasius: "Too bad that nobody wants our Eastern cash. That sucks. I'm starting to really feel desperate here!" (Thomasius, second letter from January 18, 1989).[2] Relatives living in the West might have offered a solution but approximately three hundred (Western) marks for a quality board was also a lot of money over there. The relatively cheap department-store skateboards that some Eastern skaters obtained from the West were insufficient for the improving skaters (cf. Mamach). They enviously dreamed about the West where skaters enjoyed comparatively paradisiacal conditions.

Those who were in touch with the scene in the West at least tried to get hold of secondhand material. But for the GDR skaters, writing the necessary "begging letters" was highly uncomfortable: "Do you know what? It really sucks big-time to write these letters. It makes me feel so cheap," wrote René-Falk

2 Meike Jung provided her correspondence with René-Falk Thomasius for this text. Sections that were too personal have been edited.

Thomasius (letter from December 6, 1988) to his skating friend Meike "Häksa" Jung from Münster who worked for the Titus skate shop and thus was located right at the source. International contests in Czechoslovakia offered a concrete chance to get hold of relatively affordable material as Western skaters sold their used equipment there (cf. Richter; Sladek; Geisler). Additionally, Czechoslovakian skaters offered boards that they had made themselves (cf. Thomasius; Sladek; Bogner).

In 1986, to the great surprise of the skaters, a skateboard manufactured in the GDR entered the shops: the Germania Speeder. State officials had recognized the trend and tried to equip the respective sections that were to be established in sports clubs with a special state skateboard (cf. Götze, "Rollenstudium auf dem Brett"). At the Berlin sports and recreation center (SEZ), one could even borrow a *Rollbrett* ("rolling board"), as it was called by the officials (cf. Mamach; Wagenknecht). Peculiarly, the *VEB Schokoladen-Verarbeitungsmaschinen* (a factory for the construction of chocolate production machines) in Wernigerode produced the board. VEB is short for *Volkseigener Betrieb*, translating more or less to "people's enterprise." Alongside the enterprise's name, the board read NAGEMA, an acronym for *Nahrungsmittel, Genussmittel, Maschinenbau*, meaning: food, luxury food, mechanical engineering. The Germania Speeder cost 135 (Eastern) marks, which was still a lot of money in the GDR, and the boards were difficult to acquire. Even in Berlin it was not easy to get hold of a Germania Speeder, as René-Falk Thomasius had to realize. He had planned to send one of the boards to the Titus skate shop in the hope of getting a quality board from the West in exchange (cf. Thomasius, letter from January 11, 1989). The "chocolate-board," as the skaters disparagingly called it in view of its producer, was of better quality than the department store boards from the West but apart from the ball bearings skateboarders were not impressed: "They should have asked us how to build a skateboard. Probably, that would have turned out much better than the shit they threw on the market" (Sladek). The board was completely straight with no griptape, a break block at the tail, slippery wheels, axles which were too narrow, and an unstable kingpin (cf. Sladek 41).

Some East Berlin skaters even tried to build a real concrete pool.

As a result of the poor supply of useful skateboards, many skaters depended on homemade boards. Similar to what had been done in the US a few decades earlier, roller skates were taken apart and screwed on to wooden boards. The Germania Speeder was also exploited as a useful "materials store" for these endeavors. Any available template, either in the form of a board from the West or in the form of pictures from skate magazines, was evaluated, copied, and redrawn. The kids encouraged and motivated each other so that the quality of the constructions constantly improved. Since most of the boards did not last too long anyway, there was a continuous need to keep on building new ones. When the magazine *practice* released a manual in 1987 and even the TV show *Wie wär's?* explained the construction of a skateboard (cf. "Skateboard-Fahren" and Ulbricht, "Wie wär's?"), the active skaters already knew much about how to go about it with very limited material and equipment.

It was, however, not just the functionality of the board that was important, but its appearance, too. At first, the design was rather plain, but it slowly evolved to emulate its American role models, enhanced with colorful drawings and stickers. Even though the boards would break after a very short time, particularly during jumps, the skaters paid great attention to their design, right down to the smallest details. On the one hand, having to build their own boards was a nuisance for the skaters, but on the other, they took great pride in their craftsmanship: "Did you ever build your own board?" Thomasius asks Jung in a letter (February 1, 1989), "A board which even has a tail and an inflected nose and that really lasts! I tell you, that's an incredible feeling!"

From around 1986, skaters began to not only build skateboards themselves but also their own moveable ramps. Once again, a lack of material forced them to find creative solutions, as Eric Dressen and Wiley Weenie, two American skateboard professionals, realized during a visit to East Berlin: "Due to lack of materials, i.e. plywood, the ramp is made out of sheet metal, and various scraps of two by fours" (Mofo 69). Skaters were constantly looking for useful construction materials and quite obviously they were successful: There were jump-ramps, ramps for wall-rides, quarter-pipes, rails for slides, and some East Berlin skaters even tried to build a real concrete pool, which, however, remained only half-finished upon German reunification (cf.

Thomasius, letters from January 18, 1989, January 24, 1989 and September 20, 1989; Geisler).

Berlin Solidarity

The proximity to the West made it easier for people in the capital city to get hold of Western material. Skaters from the "first generation" already owned quality boards from the West and during the 1980s the West-East transfer increased. Westerners brought used material and B-stock to the "Platz" so that East Berliners could slowly begin to equip themselves with Western material. The border regime of the GDR, however, remained unpredictable. Sometimes skaters from the West were turned away because of their boards; sometimes they were admitted. "Nobody knew what was legal and what was illegal. After a while that wasn't even the question any more. What counted was: Will you get through or not?" (Graetsch). East Berlin skater John Haak established the route that allowed for the most material from the West to be brought over to the East. This was only possible thanks to his Finnish citizenship. He made contact with Andreas Gillmeister in West Berlin who worked in one of Berlin's first skate shops, California Sports. Gillmeister pitied the East Berliners as they had great talent and potential but could hardly evolve due to their "prehistoric material." He used his position in the shop and his contacts in the West Berlin scene to organize help for the Easterners.

> We were right at the source and the boards were still kind of affordable. Everyone had an old but still okay board somewhere in the basement or in the attic that was not used any longer as new boards had been bought [...] We collected these for John and he took them with him. (Gillmeister)

René-Falk Thomasius, even almost twenty years after the fall of the Berlin Wall, was still thankful for this support, as the East Berliners would have had almost no opportunity to improve their skating skills without it (cf. Bogner 53). "The funny thing was that, at Checkpoint Charlie, I always had to remove all the stickers from the boards. That was a little annoyance for them, you know. After all, this could have been some kind of Western propaganda" (Haak).

The material was highly cherished within the East Berlin scene. When, during the Münster Monster Mastership (MMM), Meike Jung was able to convince professional skateboarder Tony Hawk to donate his board to the Easterners, they almost "tattered" it (cf. Jung). Those who did not have personal contacts sometimes had to pay five hundred marks or more for a heavily used skateboard. "You gave everything to be able to be part of this thing" (Wagenknecht).

Many things were swapped and exchanged: "Since my wheels were so run down, I had to give away my pink-colored hoodie, but instead I now have brand-new OJ Teamrider wheels" (Thomasius, letter from October 19, 1988). Sometimes three to four different skaters shared just one skateboard until it literally fell apart (cf. Rötschke; Geisler). It was hard to prevent splinters and breaks while practicing difficult tricks. In such a case "you immediately ran home, took some special glue and tried to get the board back to its original state" (Thomasius).

After the Wall fell in 1989, California Sports became a meeting point for East Berlin skaters in the Western part of the city (Geisler; Wagenknecht). Gillmeister had distributed his business card during an earlier visit to East Berlin and "the guys then showed up in the shop. That was amazing" (Gillmeister). Many of them invested their *Begrüßungsgeld* (welcome money GDR citizens received from the West German government) in skate equipment and thus ended the era of homemade boards and collected materials.

Skate Style

The art of riding a skateboard in the GDR evolved similarly to the way it had developed in the US. The skating style of the "first generation" more or less imitated the Sidewalk Surfing in 1950s and 1960s America (cf. Sladek 41). The first GDR skateboarders, however, were already capable of some spectacular maneuvers and were characterized by a distinct willingness to take risks:

> Patrick rode down these slopes at Alexanderplatz, these spikes. He ran up there, jumped on his board and then went downhill at full speed over this little tip with a little hole next to it. You have to carefully raise your board to cross this ledge; otherwise you will hit the floor at like 70 to 80

> kilometers per hour. And that guy went down there without protection, without anything. And then he switched into a handstand when he arrived down there. (Graetsch)

Special protective gear was not available in the GDR and you could only use protectors that were meant for playing volleyball.

When, in 1986, the skaters of Alexanderplatz were approached by top skater Luděk Váša from the CSSR—who had come to Berlin as a tourist and only saw them skating by chance—they received fresh impetus for their practice. Freestyle techniques improved and vert skating started to play a more important role, while the Czechoslovakian skateboard scene still wielded strong influence over the GDR skaters (cf. Sladek 41; Thomasius). Many of them frequently went to Prague in order to buy material and attend contests, sometimes even as active participants. "It's still sick to think of the many new tricks I saw in Czechoslovakia," writes Thomasius in a letter (September 9, 1988) about the Euroskate 1988 in Prague. Visits by West Berlin skaters were also highlights, as they provided one of only very few firsthand opportunities to learn about skateboarding in the West. "They [the East Berlin skaters] really listened to anything you said [...] they really absorbed it as it was something new. For us it was daily routine to talk about pool skating or something like that. And they were like: 'Pool? What do you mean? A swimming pool?'" (Richter). Furthermore, skate magazines that made it into the GDR through West Berlin were used as inspiration and the lucky few who already owned VCRs, such as John Haak, were also able to enjoy skate videos (cf. Rötschke; Bogner 54).

Particularly in view of the difficult conditions, the West Berlin skaters had tremendous respect for the achievements of the East Berliners. "I don't know how they did it but they really knew everything [about skateboarding] a hundred percent" (Richter). The East Berliners appeared as "gnarly dudes" that reminded the Westerners of the pioneering days of skateboarding (cf. Gillmeister; Richter). John Haak, who was able to travel to West Berlin because of his Finnish passport, even became honorary member of the First Berlin Skateboard Club in 1988.

The skills and performance capability of the GDR skaters improved year after year. During the 1980s, top riders such as

Marco Sladek and René-Falk Thomasius were definitely able to compete on an international level and some of them dreamed of a professional career (cf. Thomasius, letter from October 19, 1988). Sladek could do a one-armed handstand kickflip, an extremely difficult trick that only very few international skaters managed to do successfully. In 1988, *Thrasher Skateboard Magazine* published a photograph of Sladek and in 1989 he was interviewed for the West German *Monster Skateboard Magazin*, which also published further photographs of him shortly after (cf. Mofo 62; Sladek 41). After German reunification, he became the *Vorzeige-Ossi* (Geisler) or token Easterner capable of competing on a national level, as he demonstrated by coming fourth in the Northern German Mastership in 1990.

Skateboarding and Socialist Sport

The GDR was known as the country of world record holders and Olympic champions but the skateboarders had other priorities: "You can present the craziest tricks but if you don't have style it's only half as good" (Wagenknecht; cf. Rotenhagen). In contrast to traditional sports and despite its athletic ambition, skateboarding was characterized by its freedom and its unruliness. One example might be the fact that there were no real coaches: "You are your own coach. You don't have a training schedule that asks you to practice ollies for four hours a day" (Rötschke). As a consequence of this independence and autonomy many skaters experienced their achievements as particularly satisfying (cf. Rotenhagen). Accordingly, skaters were hardly ever interested in practicing conventional and efficiency-oriented sports. During an official talent selection (*Einheitliche Sichtung und Auswahl*, or ESA) John Haak was chosen to become a weightlifter:

> That is almost like in the Third Reich, I have to say. They muster everyone. You have to stand in a row and they measure your body. So, if you are small and chunky, you become a weightlifter. But I couldn't be bothered as I was already skating. (Haak)

Tobias Voigt practiced track-and-field five times a week in a training camp of the GDR program for competitive sports. "The coach constitutes the unquestionable authority and he demands effort and if you are unable to cut it, it's: bye-bye!" (Voigt).

Matthias "Mike" Ernst and Lu Hartmann emphasize the openness and dynamics of skateboarding: they explain that "We are creative and we keep on advancing our sport," and add that "a new idea does not have to be officially announced in order to check if it is allowed or not." Skaters ostentatiously distanced themselves from "normal citizens": "I think that was just it: being different" (Wagenknecht). This included punk music as "the musical equivalent of the way we lived" (Wagenknecht). It was not easy to get hold of the desired bands and songs, particularly those from the West, but there were also East German groups that produced punk music with critical lyrics that were popular among skaters: e.g. Feeling B or Die Art.

GDR and Berlin Championships

In 1987, the East Berlin skaters organized the first "GDR evaluation" with some financial support from the BSG Empor HO Berlin. All in all, however, the funding remained very restricted: "We mounted the mastership on our own without any officials" (Sladek 41). Consequently, the skaters were not allowed to use the official sounding title "mastership" for their event. Instead, they called it "unofficial GDR qualifier" or merely "skateboard contest" (*Skateboard-Wettkampf*), as was printed on the certificates of the Deutscher Rollsport Verband (cf. Püschel 30; Groth 70). The contest was held at the space the BSG assigned to the skaters near Cantianstadion and in addition to the East Berliners, some skaters from the CSSR who were in touch with Marco Sladek joined the event (cf. Sladek; Graetsch). Sladek took first place in freestyle and thus became the first unofficial GDR champion in skateboarding (cf. Püschel 30f; Groth 70).

Skaters ostentatiously distanced themselves from "normal citizens."

In the spring of 1988 the contest was held again and this time it was much bigger. There was a freestyle and a streetstyle competition and the riders could win minor prizes such as records. During various workshops and performances, the Berlin skaters had established contacts within the whole GDR and also with West Berlin, with the result that the invitation was spread by word-of-mouth within the local scenes. The main sensation of the contest was the participation of the Westerners, among them the First Berlin Skateboard Club. There had been some problems in passing the border due to a T-shirt featuring a giant skull logo, but most of the skaters were eventually able to enter East Berlin (cf. Bogner 54). The hosts picked them up at the Rotes Rathaus (Red Town Hall) and then everybody went to Cantianstadion together enjoying a sort of "biker-gang feeling" (cf. Thomasius). The total number of skateboarders in the contest included fifteen to twenty-five Westerners and twenty to thirty Easterners, according to the estimations of the participants (cf. Haak; Richter; Gillmeister). As the Berliners from both sides of the city dominated the contest both in terms of numbers and performance, those participants that had not been involved in the organization of the event rather experienced it as a Berlin and not a GDR contest: "Actually, this was already a unified Berlin; a Berlin where, as a consequence of skateboarding, the Wall no longer existed" (Graetsch; cf. Gillmeister; Voigt).

At first, the atmosphere was friendly and relaxed. The emphasis was on enjoyment rather than competition. There was music and Michael "Scheune" Thummerer, guitarist of West Berlin skate punk band Disaster Area, handed out records. In addition to the riders themselves there were a few spectators and even parents of the skaters watched their children perform their tricks. However, there were also obviously a few observers from the Stasi (the State Security Service of the GDR) among the audience who did not approve of the way the event was shaping up. Given that not even the organizers themselves had known which and how many Westerners to expect in advance, the Ministry of State Security had been unable to prepare adequately (cf. Thomasius). Karl J. Richter recognized that some people who were not part of the scene observed them constantly, while the Westerners lacked this experienced eye and were only informed about the observation by the Easterners (cf. Gillmeister). After a while, the Ministry observers ordered the skateboarders to disband their *Zusammenrottung* (riotous assembly). They checked the passports of the Westerners and confiscated a few cassettes of Western music (cf. Richter; Graetsch). One of the persons in charge who belonged to the official host, the BSG Empor HO Berlin, was officially interrogated: "We were not allowed to participate in this interrogation but we definitely knew that the shit had hit the fan," John Haak remembers.

The BSG representative had no other choice but to try to dissuade the East German skaters from going through with the contest. In an article in *Junge Welt* (a left-wing German newspaper), Steffen Kaden from Dresden recalls a "suit": "He informed us that we could not start a mutual contest with the class enemy. This would damage German-German sports relations" (Weinreich, "Skateboard-Roll on" 1). When some skaters started to directly argue with the "suits," the situation almost escalated. "There was huge turmoil and it came really close to a cancellation of the whole event" (Hartmann). Eventually, an agreement was made: the Westerners were not allowed to participate in the contest but they could stay and judge (cf. Thomasius). After the official contest had ended, the skaters did not go home but skated through the city together. For many of them this became the defining experience of the day:

> I just remember a crazy pack. The way we sped through the city after the contest; that was an awesome feeling. There had never been anything like that before. Such a mass of people speeding through the streets together [...] That was the primal day for everyone. We had such a blast. Legendary! (Mamach)

In 1989, another contest was held in East Berlin. Both Easterners and Westerners participated. However, the total number of about thirty riders was lower than the previous year (cf. Jung).[3] This time the contest winner received a pro model skateboard by Ralf Middendorf (West German skateboard professional), which Meike Jung—who also participated as a judge—had brought from the Titus skate shop. Apart from the top skaters, the level matched the local scenes in the West, according to Jung. The event was officially registered and this time there was no disruption by the Stasi (cf. Wagenknecht; Haak).

3 Groth (71)—probably referring to a conversation with Marco Sladek—mentions a total number of fifty riders.

GDR Authorities

The presence of skaters in public space in East Berlin—just as in many Western cities—caused conflicts and disputes time and again. The underside of the Germania Speeder read: "Do not use in public traffic" and the do-it-yourself magazine *practice* explicitly stated that "it is forbidden to use the skateboard on public streets and sidewalks" ("Skateboard-Fahren" 109). However, skateboarders ignored such warnings. In congruence with the slogans "Skate and Destroy" or "Skate and Create," the riders developed a new approach to the city and society. They used their skating to question architecture and the systems hidden behind its facades (cf. Borden 192).

At Alexanderplatz, the skaters quickly caused a sensation as their demeanor and tricks led to frequent confrontations (cf. Groth 69f.). Skating on the spike-like constructions of the TV tower could even lead to an official report on the charge of "disruption of socialist coexistence," as John Haak had to learn. During a nightly downhill session René-Falk Thomasius was stopped by the police and held in custody until the next morning. Sometimes it seemed as if one or the other side was actually attempting to provoke a confrontation. Police officers stepped in the way of skateboarders and skateboarders did not deliberately avoid collisions (cf. Thomasius, letter from February 5, 1989).

When Meike Jung became familiar with the East Berlin skaters she recognized "that they always conceived [the confrontations and conflicts] as symptomatic of the regime. 'It has to do with the fact that we practice such a Western sport.' I just thought: It's totally normal" (Jung). Jung was surprised by the Eastern skaters' glorification of the West and she tried to correct and put into perspective their image of the West. However, in reverencing the West, the GDR skaters did not so much aspire to the capitalist system as imagine an alternative to the dreariness of socialism and a way to escape it:

> Skateboarding, and now I refer to the GDR, required that one distanced oneself from the East during that time. Skating, coming from America, was obviously a little bit outlawed. (Wagenknecht)

Within the dreariness of the daily routine of East Germany, skateboarding opened the door to a fascinating, different world: "For me, skateboarding at that time had a total glamour and gleam to it" (Geisler). When popular West Berlin skater Christian Wasdaris brought the two US professionals Eric Dressen und Wiley Weenie to East Berlin for the first time in 1988, the GDR skaters were very excited (cf. Mofo): "I can tell you, you are standing there at the border and you get weak at the knees" (Sladek). The occasion constituted a unique experience for the Americans as well: "Everyone is excited by this first-time meeting of skate cultures and Weenie almost cries with excitement" (Mofo 69). Because of Berlin's interesting location as an "island" and the involvement of several skate shops, further American pro skaters visited West Berlin, among them Stephanie Person and Mark Gonzales. "And, of course, they also went over there to East Berlin to check the known spots. That was something new [...] That was a culture clash" (Gillmeister; cf. Haak; Sladek).

For many protagonists of the time, skateboarding as well as punk was connected to a leftist political attitude. Thus, right-wing skinheads, as well as the system of "the East," embodied an additional enemy. John Haak, along with friends, even founded the Red Front Pankow to spray-paint anti-Nazi slogans onto walls. The skinheads took up the challenge and, particularly in Berlin, skaters needed to be on their guard to avoid being beaten up. During BFC Dynamo soccer matches, events that attracted many hooligans, the skaters did not use the space near Cantianstadion (cf. Thomasius; Rötschke; Rotenhagen; Voigt). Being "leftist," however, was little more than a tendency among the skaters, and it was definitely not a political attitude that could be associated with the GDR. "The GDR, the state, was not leftist. That was a dictatorship and that was the East" (Wagenknecht).

The majority of skaters did not reflect upon politics. Fun was definitely at the heart of skateboarding and the younger kids in particular lacked a political consciousness (cf. Voigt; Rötschke). Nevertheless, for many participants skateboarding went much deeper than mere enjoyment, in a way that was felt rather than understood: "Back then we always had revolutionary thoughts, too—not thoughts but a feeling; a feeling of being something special. We were able to kind of break out of the system" (Mamach). With regard to Western society, Becky Beal analyzed the "grassroots practice of skateboarding resistance" (258). Within a socialist dictatorship this resistance was much more distinct. "You did not have to say that you did not care for the East. You just took your skateboard and rode on Alex-

[anderplatz]. That totally symbolized it" (Wagenknecht). These activities were acknowledged by the West Berlin skaters: "That was courageous. These guys sometimes risked everything" (Graetsch; cf. Richter).

For the GDR skaters, education and career prospects were particularly at stake, with many favoring skateboarding over career advancement. Their disinterest in social status and progression made them immune to the smaller pressures of the regime and the smaller everyday compromises everyone had to make. "We did not care, as this whole hierarchy and this whole setup was not for us" (Thomasius). In the chaos of the first years after reunification, many skaters enjoyed the anarchic conditions, scratched along with odd jobs, and conquered the city on their skateboards (cf. Deckwerth, "Mit Skateboard durch den Palast der Republik"; Deckwerth, "Auf Rollen brettern sie ziellos durch die Stadt"; Haak).

In view of their individualistic demeanor, René-Falk Thomasius conceives of skateboarders in the GDR as the "forerunners of decline." The GDR magazine *Freie Welt* also regarded skateboarders as an obvious sign of change and created a minor scoop in the media. In February 1988, when Mikhail Gorbachev's politics of *glasnost* and *perestroika* had already started to take effect, the magazine printed a double-page spread of photographs of the "artists on wheels" (cf. Püschel 30f.). In addition, the magazine cover showed Marco Sladek on his skateboard with "Bones" and "Titus" prints on his clothing. Ambiguously, the story starts as follows: "Whether in Leipzig, Karl-Marx-Stadt, Erfurt, or Berlin—there is a lot of movement in the streets and squares. Partly [i.e. not only] on boards" (Püschel 30).

Even if the GDR was already dead to many teenagers by the late 1980s, the protagonists of the time considered skateboarders to be very distinct from their contemporaries. "Normal" teens were still raised within socialist structures despite all sorts of criticism, and after reunification many of them had difficulties adapting to the new circumstances. But given their comparatively Western way of living, skaters did not face such problems: "We were already in the West with one foot. We just followed suit with the other one" (Haak). Pierre Geisler agrees: "I had the feeling that skateboarding made it very easy to find an entry to the West" (Geisler; cf. Rötschke). And the Westerners needed to make no effort to understand the East Berlin skaters: "There was no wall. The wall might have been between skateboarding and not skateboarding. It was as if you had already known each other for ages" (Graetsch; cf. Sladek).

After reunification, skaters rode all over the unified city in any wind and weather (cf. Rötschke). In particular, the squares in front of the Gedächtniskirche (Memorial Church)—nicknamed "Schnalle"—and the National Gallery became meeting points for East and West Berlin skaters, with gatherings comprising up to one hundred riders at a time. Alexanderplatz became a permanent construction site and it became almost impossible to skate there. The East emptied out rapidly but around one year later attractive skate spots such as the Spittelkolonnaden on Leipziger Straße and the Palast der Republik (Palace of the Republic) were rediscovered by both Easterners and Westerners alike. "That was [...] a very fast accomplishment of German reunification on skateboards" (Rötschke).

References

Bauer, Mathias. "Bei uns zu Gast: Der Moskauer Staatszirkus." *Monster Skateboard Magazin* 8.38 (1989): 50–51. Print.

Beal, Becky. "Disqualifying the Official: An Exploration of Social Resistance Through the Subculture of Skateboarding." *Sociology of Sport Journal* 12 (1995): 252–67. Print.

Bernett, Hajo, ed. *Körperkultur und Sport in der DDR: Dokumentation eines Geschlossenen Systems.* Schorndorf: Hofmann, 1994. Print.

Bogner, Manuel. "Skateboarding in Berlin Vor Und Nach Der Wende." *Monster Skateboard Magazine* 28.12 (2009): 53–55. Print.

Borden, Iain. *Skateboarding, Space and the City: Architecture and the Body.* Oxford: Berg, 2006. Print.

Brooke, Michael. *The Concrete Wave: The History of Skateboarding.* Toronto, Los Angeles: Warwick, 2003. Print.

Deckwerth, Sabine. "Auf Rollen brettern sie ziellos durch die Stadt." *Berliner Zeitung*, January 27, 1997: 22. Print.

Deckwerth, Sabine. "Mit Skateboard durch den Palast der Republik." *Berliner Zeitung*, January 20, 1997: 18.

Doren, Martin von, and Ulrich Pramann. *Faszination Skateboarding. Ein Lehrbuch Für Theorie Und Praxis.* Munich: Heyne, 1991. Print.

Götze, A. "Rollenstudium Auf Dem Brett." *Junge Welt*, August 26, 1986: 201B. Print.

Groth, Katrin. "Skatin' GDR." *Unser Berlin* 2.2 (2015): 66–71. Print.

Howell, Russ. "Gymnastics Meets Freestyle." *The Concrete Wave: The History of Skateboarding.* Ed. M. Brooke. Toronto, Los Angeles: Warwick Publishing, 2003. 83. Print.

"Kein Bock Auf Honecker." *stern* 35.17 (1982): 20–32. Print.

Kluge, Volker. *Das Sportbuch DDR.* Berlin: Eulenspiegel-Verlag, 2004. Print.

Ludewig, Jörg. "Das Waren Die Achtziger." *Monster Skateboard Magazine* 9.4 (1990): 74–77. Print.

Mofo [Möritzen Föche]. "From Here to There. Pain and Rain on Cobblestone Terrain, or, Where's My Wallet." *Thrasher* 8.12 (1988): 62–69. Print.

"Moskauer Staatszirkus!" *Monster Skateboard Magazin* 7.36 (1989): 13. Print.

Peralta, Stacy. dir. *Future Primitive. Bones Brigade Video II.* 1985. Film.

Peralta, Stacy. "Interview." *Thrasher* 2.5 (1982): 17–21. Print.

Püschel, Andreas. "Brett-Bezüge: Artisten Auf Rollen." *Freie Welt* 35.2 (1988): 30–31. Print.

Schnabel, Jens. "Berlin City Report." *Monster Skateboard Magazine* 11. 70 (1992): 22–29. Print.

Schwidtmann, Heinz, and Margot Budzisch. "Körperkultur und Sport der jungen Generation unter dem Aspekt der Anforderungen der wissenschaftlich-technischen Revolution in der entwickelten sozialistischen Gesellschaft. Gedanken und Probleme, Feststellungen und Vorschläge als Beitrag zur weiteren Auswertung des X. Parteitags der SED." *Theorie und Praxis der Körperkultur* 31 (1982): 361–60. Print.

"Skateboard-Fahren." *practic* 21.3 (1987): 106–09. Print.

Sladek, Marco. "Ten Questions..." *Monster Skateboard Magazin* 7.36 (1989): 41. Print.

Stündl, Herbert. *Freizeit- und Erholungssport in der DDR. Marxistische Grundlagen, Ziele und Organisationen 1946–1976*. Schorndorf: Hofmann, 1977. Print.

Ulbricht, Venadis. dir. *Wie wär's?* DDR-F-1. 1987. Film.

Voigt, Dieter. *Sportsoziologie in Der DDR.* Überblick, *Entwicklung, Ergebnisse, Kritik.* Postdoctoral thesis. Justus-Liebig-Universität, Gießen, 1973. Print [unpublished].

"Verfassung der Deutschen Demokratischen Republik Vom 6. April 1968." *Die Verfassung Der DDR. Entstehung, Analysen, Vergleich, Text*. Ed. Herwig Roggemann. Opladen: Leske, 1970. 211–39. Print.

Weinreich, Jens. "Skateboard-Roll on! DDR-Brettartisten Ermittelten Erstmals Ihren Besten."
Junge Welt 44.123 (1990): 1. Print.

Weinreich, Jens. "Zirzensisches Auf Den Rollenden Brettern." *Junge Welt* 41 (1987). Print.

Interviews

Ernst, Matthias "Mike," b. 1964, grew up in West Berlin, skater since the mid-1970s, slalom world champion 1987, owns a skate shop. Interview. November 19, 2004.

Geisler, Pierre, b. 1974, grew up in East Berlin, skater since 1987. Interview. November 21, 2004.

Gillmeister, Andreas "Elle," b. 1962, grew up in West Berlin, skater since 1976. Interview. January 26, 2005.

Graetsch, Volker, b. 1971, grew up in West Berlin, skater since 1985. Interview. February 20, 2006.

Haak, John, b. 1971 (Helsinki), grew up in East Berlin, skater since 1985. Interview. January 25, 2005.

Hartmann, Lu, b. 1973, grew up in Halle, skater since 1982. Interview. November 19, 2004.

Jung, Meike "Häksä," b. 1970, grew up in Münster. Interview. February 21, 2006.

Mamach, Andreas, b. 1973, grew up in East Berlin, skater since 1986. Interview. January 25, 2005.

Richter, Karl Johann, b. 1964, grew up in West Berlin, skater since 1977. Interview. January 27, 2005.

Rötschke, David, b. 1976, grew up in Dresden and East Berlin, skater since 1981. Interview. January 24, 2005.

Rotenhagen, Christian, b. 1972, grew up in East Berlin. Interview. November 21, 2004.

Sladek, Marco, b. 1970, grew up in East Berlin, skater since 1984. Interview. July 2, 2006.

Thomasius, René-Falk, b. 1969, grew up in East Berlin, skater since ca. 1984. Interview. January 28, 2005.

Vick, Thomas, b. 1972, grew up in Dresden, skater since 1985. Interview. October 26, 2004.

Voigt, Tobias, b. 1975, grew up in East Berlin, skater since 1989. Interview. January 24, 2005.

Wagenknecht, Hans, b. 1972, grew up in East Berlin, skater since 1987. Interview. November 21, 2004.

Ocean Howell

The "Creative Class" and the Gentrifying City *Skateboarding in Philadelphia's Love Park*[1]

Introduction

This is about consumer culture, class politics, and urban space. Specifically, it is a story about skateboarding in John F. Kennedy Plaza—better known as Love Park—in city-center Philadelphia. The plaza was completed in 1965—at the height of the Great Society, in an era of public works and social welfare programs—as part of the Penn Center redevelopments. It was created in a modernist mode of development, which is to say that it was centrally planned, publicly funded, state-led, and aesthetically intended to represent a broadly conceived public or citizenry. In the first two decades, the plaza was a favorite lunch spot for local office workers, but also attracted users of all classes with protests and spontaneous street games. Under the strain of "re-forms" to public welfare programs set into motion by the Reagan administration, however, the plaza became a makeshift home for the homeless by the late 1980s.

Around this same time skateboarders—almost all teenage males from the surrounding working-class neighborhoods and suburbs—began using the plaza. At first the skaters were treated much like the homeless by the police and by the local press. But by the late 1990s, the skateboarders were widely praised by city elites like planners, local architecture critics, the editorial boards of major newspapers, and over half of the city council members. In the public eye, the skateboarders were tempering the activities of the homeless population, injecting skateboard industry capital into the plaza, and generating a hip image for the city. Even so, Mayor John Street's administration had the plaza redesigned at public expense in order to deter the skateboarders. At the time of writing there is a high-profile debate in the city of Philadelphia about whether the skateboarders should be allowed back into the plaza. I will argue that what is at stake in this debate is not only access to Love Park, but the city of Philadelphia's transition to a new mode of urban economic development.

1 This essay was first published in the *Journal of Architectural Education* 59.2 (2005): 32–42. It documents a particular moment in the story of Philadelphia's Love Park. Together with Ocean Howell we decided to include the text in its original form and without any adjustments concerning the developments and changes that have occurred in and around Love Park since. The essay still provides a nuanced insight into a site- and time-specific situation and thus—even thirteen years after its first publication—constitutes an exemplary approach within the realm of skateboard studies. [The editors]

In order to trace the contours of this transition, I will review some recent policy documents from the Philadelphia city government, alongside the influential writings of Richard Florida, a professor at Carnegie Mellon University who has weighed in on the side of the skateboarders. In Florida's framework, the best strategy to stimulate urban growth is to appeal not to employers, but to gay, bohemian, and foreign-born populations. Whether they have money or not, these members of the "creative class" will attract the employers—largely in technology-based industries—by generating an "organic" street culture.

I will argue that what is obscured in the novel particularities of the Love Park case is a familiar story of urban class conflict. As with so-called bohemian populations from San Francisco's SOMA district to New York City's SoHo district, the skateboarders have here served as both the subject and object of class displacement. The next wave of renewal in Love Park is being carried out according to the logic of gentrification.

As Neil Smith shows, gentrification is something of a "chaotic concept"—sometimes it is state-initiated, sometimes it is led by corporate-scale capital, sometimes it is instigated by loose consortiums of individual investors with or without direct subsidies from city governments, and often it is effected by some combination thereof. Though the term is at times understood to refer only to the "upscaling" of working-class residential neighborhoods, I use this term to refer to any reclaiming of urban space by people of a higher socioeconomic position than the current users.

Writing in 1996, Neil Smith said that he no longer felt that it was useful to make a strict distinction between the fine-grained gentrification of the 1990s and the large-scale urban renewal of the postwar decades: both modes of development were geared toward a class remake of central cities, after all, so both must be understood in terms of a more inclusive rubric of gentrification (39). I agree with Smith that urban renewal and gentrification both remake cities in the image of the upper classes. However, I will maintain this strict distinction, referring to urban renewal projects as *modernization*, and to piecemeal "reinvestment-" and "reclamation"-based development as *gentrification*. I do so for several reasons. The first is that the spatial programs of the respective modes of development are completely different: while urban renewal tended to level and then replace existing urban fabric, gentrification tends to rehabilitate existing urban fabric; urban renewal was almost always carried out with state monies, gentrification may or may not be. The second reason is to respect the discursive contexts in which these modes of development have taken place: few people were talking about the Penn Center redevelopment in terms of "gentrification" in 1960s Philadelphia, and few people are talking about the modernization of Love Park today. The third reason, closely related to the second, is that I wish to analyze the discourses that underwrite these modes of development.

I will also draw insights from recent work on the geographies of youth culture, particularly the work of Iain Borden. Borden's groundbreaking work—*Skateboarding, Space, and the City: Architecture and the Body*—demonstrates how skateboarding reasserts "*use* values as opposed to exchange values" in the "left-over spaces of modernist planning" (237; 188). "Architecture," he writes, "is intended for the production of things—either products as commodities in factories, knowledge in universities and museums, labor power in housing, information and decisions in offices, and so on [...] Skateboarding however offers no such contribution, consuming the building while not engaging with its productive activity" (231). I argue that Borden is correct that skateboarding "performs a critique" of modernist space, but that when viewed from the framework of the gentrifying city, skateboarding can be reconfigured as productive—it produces marketable "street culture" imagery, and it reclaims space. I seek to build on Borden's work by showing that, while skateboarding does perform a critique of the modernist mode of development, in Love Park it has been reconfigured as an instrument of development.

As shock troops of gentrification, young skateboarders—with no personal memory of the postwar contract between labor and capital—must be understood as a kind of individualized labor, producing surplus value by leading the reclamation of this space. Finally, I will argue that the story of Love Park is also a story about the continuing privatization of citizenship. In the Love Park debates, the populace has been splintered into interest groups who must fund their own use of the space in order to gain legitimate access.

The History of Love Park

The modernization of Philadelphia began with the arrival of the City Beautiful in 1906, when Paul Cret, Horace Trumbauer, and Charles C. Zantzinger designed the Benjamin Franklin Parkway. This Hausmann-esque boulevard cut through Penn's grid from a site on the Schuylkill River—which would later house the new Museum of Art—in the northeast, to city hall at its southeast terminus. In 1917 the Parkway would be converted "from an urban boulevard to a green wedge of park" by the landscape architect Jacques Greber (Brownlee 31). But no architect had yet addressed the problem at the southeast terminus of the Parkway: an unceremonious six-way intersection at the foot of city hall.

Edmund Bacon's 1932 master's thesis at Cornell—a Burnham-inspired Civic Center for Philadelphia—removed City Hall and relieved the traffic jam with a half roundabout, surrounding a plaza. When Bacon took over as director of the Planning Commission in 1949, he had given up on the civic center, but started advocating for the plaza. It appeared first in the West Plaza-Hahnemann redevelopment area, which was later broken into two smaller redevelopment projects (cf. Philadelphia Redevelopment Authority 1963; 1964). The plaza ended up part of the Penn Center developments, receiving both federal and local funding. Designed by Vincent Kling, the park opened in 1965, and was dedicated as John F. Kennedy Plaza in 1967.

Judging from a survey of reportage on the plaza in the *Philadelphia Inquirer*, the park appears to have hosted a vibrant public life. There are descriptions of a crowded lunch hour, a lively "chess scene," regular double Dutch competitions, and an annual ritual dating from at least 1974 in which the local Catholic high school girls jumped into the fountain on the last day of school (cf. Deleon; Pothier; and Keating). The space seems to have been well-used, well-liked, and well-integrated in terms of class:

> Even with the fountain shut off, the lunchtime crowd gathered around the empty basin at JFK Plaza. Executives from Bell Telephone across the street sunned themselves, a woman shooed a bumblebee away from her ginger ale, [...] a young man made kissing noises at pretty women who passed, and when the breeze was right, the inevitable odor of marijuana wafted by. (Deleon)

Located across the street from City Hall, the space was a favorite for staging protests. Given that Philadelphia suffered deep cuts to both public housing and programs for the mentally ill, the "Rally to stop Reaganomics," staged in the plaza in 1982, appears now to have had an ominous prescience (cf. "Hud's Sins Phila"; Cooke). Later in the decade the bill came due, as the *Inquirer* began reporting in 1989 that Philadelphians were "watching JFK Plaza turn into an open-air dormitory," and an ""open-air mental-health clinic" (cf. "Hud's Sins"; "The Mental-Health"). From there reportage on the plaza was dominated by accounts of "urine stains and patches of vomit," panhandling, and drug abuse, all conveyed with metaphors of darkness and death (cf. "Hud's Sins"; Rosenberg, "Mayor Unveils"; and Ferrick Jr. and Odom). By 1991 the paper was publishing articles with titles like "Who Eats at JFK Plaza? Brown-Baggers, Homeless – and Rats" (Wiegand).

Skateboarders had discovered that Love Park was "skateboard heaven."

Around this time, the paper also started reporting on the increasing presence of what they would later call the "the skate rats" (Rubin). Skateboarders had discovered that Love Park—with its open plan, stairs, handrails, marble benches, and granite planters—was "skateboard heaven" (cf. *Love Story*).[2] As an industry, skateboarding was financially "in the depths of despair," during this period, but it did continue to produce magazines and videos, and to distribute them internationally (K. Heller). Following the model of San Francisco's Justin Herman Plaza, Love Park became a darling of the skateboard media, appearing countless times in both editorial content and in advertisements for skateboards, wheels, bearings, clothing, shoes, and retail shops.

2 In 1987 the *Philadelphia Inquirer* suggested that it was the homeless who gave JFK Plaza the name "Love Park" during this period (cf. Loeb).

The primary users of the park during the early 1990s were homeless and skateboarders, and both were occasionally painted with the same brush in popular discourse. When a police officer described entering Love Park as follows: "It's like when you've got a room full of roaches and turn on the light," he was talking about skateboarders, though homeless, like skaters, were compared to rats often enough (Goodman). The *Inquirer* registered an ambivalent position on this new group. "A park for skateboarders? For those dudes in backward baseball caps who dart between cars, plow into pedestrians, and gouge the granite in public plazas? It's an idea whose time has not quite come. The dominant trend continues to be punitive, with more and more communities restricting or banning skateboarding as dangerous, destructive, even anti-social" (McCullough). In 1995 a Common Pleas Court Judge, Richard B. Klein, complained that the "average person has been taken off the plaza. This is a total waste of city money and frankly, gross stupidity" (Rubin).

By the millennium, the problem intensified, as the skateboard industry grew to about $1.5 billion. There were not only four retail skateboard shops in the center of Philadelphia, there were also at least a dozen professional skateboarders, skate photographers, and skate videographers who were based in the city. Love Park was everywhere—simulations of the plaza even appeared in video games that reached a market much broader than only skateboarders—making the space "a world famous icon" for youth culture (*Love Story*). The plaza was overflowing with skateboarders.

In 2000, the council passed a citywide ban on skateboarding that specifically called out Love Park (cf. Pennsylvania). The ban was enforced with sweeps and often violent police tactics, which are well documented in skateboard videos (cf. *Love Story;* and *Sight Unseen*). But public support for the skateboarders was mounting. On August 11, 2001, Inga Saffron, the *Inquirer* architecture critic, wrote an opinion piece titled "Don't trash thrashers": "Are skateboarders bad for JFK Plaza? No. They're the good users. Banning them won't make the poorly designed park inviting to others." "Frankly," she wrote, "I really miss the dudes."

The plaza had enough notoriety in the skateboard world to attract ESPN's X Games in 2001 and 2002. ESPN wanted to hold the event in the plaza itself, but the mayor's office offered Dilworth Plaza on the west side of City Hall across the street instead, which was where the Games were ultimately held (*Love Story*). The Games generated an estimated $80 million in revenue for the city of Philadelphia, but shortly before ESPN arrived in the summer of 2002, the city fenced off Love Park to prepare for a redesign of the space (*Love Story*). ESPN did not renew its contract with the city for a third year.

Mayor Street promised to find another site where the city would build a "world-class facility" for skateboarders, but in the meantime, the city had hired architects Synterra & Buell Kratzer Powell to renovate Love Park, for a price tag of $800,000. The architects installed a new drainage system and introduced planters, teak benches, and patches of grass. Saffron's review in the *Inquirer* called the work "slapdash" and "badly executed." "To block the skateboarders' path, they installed an array of sickly pink concrete planters and trash cans." The problem with this "Pepto-Bismol-tinted makeover," Saffron wrote, was "the city's priorities. Its main goal was to get rid of skateboarders; it wasn't to make LOVE Park a good urban space" ("Disappointing developments"). Saffron's review was only the first salvo in a barrage of negative press.

In September 2002 "an assortment of the city's leading business and policy organizations" flew in Richard Florida— the holder of a Columbia Urban Planning Ph.D. and a bestselling author—to speak to an audience of 350 on the subject of urban economic development. Commenting on the remake of Love Park, Florida said "Skate parks are very important to young people, an intrinsic part of their creative culture, part of their identity. We should be expanding skate parks [...] To take the park away is to tell them that they are not valid. Big mistake" ("I Can Fix Your City"). In October, Edmund Bacon showed up in the new Love Park with television crews and a skateboard. After skateboarding across the space, the 92-year-old Bacon announced that "by this act of civil disobedience, I am showing my displeasure with the mayor's actions." Vincent Kling was also in attendance to protest the ban and the redesign (Altman).

By 2003, skateboarding had become an issue in the mayoral election. As part of his ultimately unsuccessful campaign, Republican candidate Sam Katz skateboarded across Love Park, declaring that if he were elected, the skateboarders would be returned. It was later revealed that Street's campaign finance manager repeatedly asked him to reconsider the ban—"It will do wonders for the re-election"—calling Street's position "wrong, both operationally and politically" (Gelbart).

Skateboarders created a nonprofit lobbying group.

In response to the Street administration's policies the skateboarders created a nonprofit lobbying group called the Skateboard Advocacy Network (SAN), led by a skater named Scott Kip who worked in the woodshop at a local arts college. Enlisting the help of local activists, editors, lawyers, architects, and planners who were sympathetic, SAN began negotiating with the city for a compromise, producing what it called a "balanced solution" proposal. If some of the obstructing planters were removed, the skateboarders would agree to use only certain areas of the park, only after 3 p.m., to avoid conflict with the lunch crowd. The city told SAN that it would have to consider how much money it would cost to maintain the park, given the skaters' high-impact use. SAN then found a 1999 report from the city controller's office stating that "In fiscal year 1998, the City spent approximately $3100 to repair damage to the park's granite pavers that was caused by skateboarders [...] In addition, according to Fairmont Park officials, the City may have to spend approximately $50,000 in the near future to repair granite capping in the park damaged by skateboarders" (Saidel et al. 138). When SAN said that it could easily raise this amount, the city's managing director, Phillip Goldsmith, replied that the findings of that report were out of date and that the city would have to conduct another study. Goldsmith returned with a report estimating that if skateboarding were permitted, maintenance of the park would cost $100,000 a year.

When, at the beginning of 2004, SAN came back with a pledge for $1 million over the next ten years—if the skateboarders were allowed to return to Love Park—the Street administration was taken aback. The money came from a $100 million, California-based skateboard shoe manufacturer called DC, who sponsored several Philadelphia-based professional skateboarders. Barbara Grant, the mayor's spokeswoman, "said the skateboard advocates overstepped their bounds by negotiating the million-dollar pledge, despite the fact that Street said he'd consider their compromise plan" (Anderson). "We just don't see skateboarding in LOVE Park," Grant said. In a city that was planning to "close dozens of recreation centers [and] fire stations" because of ever-tightening budgets, the decision to reject the money generated even more unfavorable press ("For LOVE, Money"). John Dougherty, the city's Democratic Party treasurer and a union leader stated that "This kind of investment in public resources represents the type of creative thinking and public-private partnership that will push our city forward [...] In the end, this means more jobs for our members, more commerce on our streets, and more vitality for our city" (Anderson). The *Inquirer* wrote that rejecting the money was "a stunningly backward move" ("For LOVE, Money").

At the time of writing, the city has selected a parcel of land near the Museum of Art, at the opposite end of the Parkway, as the site for a future skateboard park. The skateboarders will be expected to raise $4 million in private funding if it is to be built (Saffron, "Changing Skylines"). But the debate over whether the skateboarders will be returned to Love Park is ongoing. They have the public support of the editorial boards of the *Inquirer* and the *Daily News*, Vincent Kling, Edmund Bacon, local professors, over half of the city council members (eleven out of seventeen), the Executive Director of the Pennsylvania Economy League, and the Independence Hall Association (a preservation group), among many other influential figures in Philadelphia. On June 6, 2004, the *Inquirer's* Chris Satullo published an editorial titled “LOVE Park remains a test case of Philadelphia’s will to thrive.” Invoking the work of Richard Florida, he wrote that

> the editorial page I lead has crusaded to restore skateboarding to LOVE Park, a.k.a. JFK Plaza, the awkward little square with the Robert Indiana sculpture near City Hall. This has convinced many serious sorts that the Editorial Board has lost its mind: “What is it with you guys and these obnoxious skaters? They’re scruffy, rude, chip the concrete and annoy the lunchers. Why not worry about something important?” This is important. LOVE Park is a test case of whether this city can do the things that cities must do to thrive. Smart cities don’t spit on serendipity. They open themselves to spirit, creativity, happy accident, and innovation—with all the messiness they entail. They don’t just tuck in the coverlet and try to keep things peaceful while they die.

What has changed in theories of urban economics that so many opinion makers in Philadelphia see “scruffy skaters” as not only an opportunity for development, but as an indicator of whether or not the city can survive?

Skateboarding on the “Boho Index,” Skateboarders as a “Creative Class”

To understand the terms of this debate, I turn now to the writings of Richard Florida, a consultant who has worked with cities all over the US and Canada. Florida’s 2002 book *The Rise of the Creative Class: And How It’s Transforming Work, Leisure, Community and Everyday Life* is becoming standard reading on syllabi in graduate urban planning, public policy, and economic development programs. A basic premise underlying his argument is that

> [t]he economic need for creativity has registered itself in the rise of a new class, which I call the creative class. Some *38 million* Americans, 30 percent of all employed people, belong to this class. I define the core of the creative class to include people in science and engineering, architecture and design, education, arts, music and entertainment,

whose economic function is to create new ideas, new technology and/or new creative content. Around the core, the creative class also includes a broader group of *creative professionals* in business and finance, law, health care, and related fields. (8)

In an increasingly consumer-based economy, Florida sees an inversion of the socioeconomic hierarchy between the professionals and the artists. The creative class is the "norm-setting class," the new "dominant class in America" (317, xi).

What does Florida believe these new circumstances mean for urban planning and policy? For starters, it means that cities should no longer be catering to the traditional professions, trying to bring in jobs by bringing in companies by creating infrastructure and offering tax breaks. Rather, cities should be bringing in members of the "creative class" with lifestyle amenities. So, the city is no longer industrial engine, or even "growth machine," but rather an "entertainment machine" (Molotch).

This phrase was coined by Terry Nichols Clark, Professor of Sociology at the University of Chicago and the Coordinator of the Fiscal Austerity and Urban Innovation Project (FAUI). Florida's ideas influenced Clark to take amenities seriously, and ultimately to devote an entire volume, *The City as an Entertainment Machine*, to the subject. In Clark's chapter, "Amenities Drive Urban Growth: A New Paradigm and Policy Linkages," he cites his research from the FAUI: "We completed a national survey in 1984 and 1996 of mayors in all U.S. cities over 25,000 population. Results suggest the national importance of a pattern of leadership that we have termed the New Political Culture, which is distinctly responsive to consumption rather than just production" (Clark et al. 302). The New Political Culture is one in which cities respond to the reality that "Contemporary consumption practice extends to the consumption of space. The lifestyle concerns of social participants are increasingly important in defining the overall rationale for, and in turn driving, other urban social processes. Quality of life is not a mere byproduct of production; it defines and drives much of the new processes of production" (299).

The city is no longer industrial engine but rather an "entertainment machine."

The 1968 *Annual Report of the Philadelphia Redevelopment Authority* opens with a paean to the modernizing, and modernist city: "Center City, riding the momentum created by the [urban renewal] program, was a forest of cranes and booms as new buildings popped up like spring flowers, glistening with promise of more tax returns to the city" (Philadelphia Redevelopment Authority 4). At the beginning of the new millennium, the modernist growth machine was sputtering. Writing in 2001, Florida quoted then CEO of Hewlett Packard, Carly Fiorina, addressing "a conference of governors recently: 'Keep your tax incentives and highway interchanges, [she stated,] we will go where the highly skilled people are'" (Florida and Gates 2). The glimmer that 1960s urban leaders saw in office towers, 2000s leaders see in renovated art galleries, cafes, and plazas.

There is, in Florida's phrase, a new "Hegemony of the Street" (Florida, *Rise* 182). One conclusion to be drawn from this observation is that cities should no longer put so many resources into what Florida refers to as ""SOB'—the high-art triumvirate of a symphony orchestra, an opera company, and a ballet company" (182). Stadia are also off the agenda, since the "creative class" favors individual sports, where they "set their own pace and create their own rules" (175). As the *Inquirer* opined "Think skateboarding, that is, before baseball stadiums" (Satullo). "[T]he creative class is drawn to organic and indigenous street-level culture [...] Much of it is native and of-the-moment, rather than art imported from another century for audiences imported from the suburbs" (Florida, *Rise* 182). "To prosper in the creative Age," Florida writes, "regions have to offer a people climate that satisfies this group's social interests and lifestyle needs" (295). Seattle and San Francisco started as bohemian and gay meccas: "New York had Christopher Street and SoHo long before Silicon Alley erupted," Florida writes, "All of these places were open, diverse and culturally creative first. *Then* they became technologically creative and subsequently gave rise to new high-tech firms and industries" (206).

In his 2001 piece "Technology and Tolerance: The Importance of Diversity to High-Technology Growth," published by the Brookings Institute, Florida set out to quantify this observation. He developed a Gay Index, a Bohemian (or "Boho") Index, a Foreign-Born Index, and a Composite Diversity Index, which is the sum of the rankings of the other three. "We compare our diversity measures to a measure of high-technology industry concentration and growth developed by the Milken Institute" (3). Florida finds striking correlations: "The leading indicator of a metropolitan area's high-technology success is a large gay population [...] A high concentration of artists or 'bohemians' follows gays," and a high concentration of foreign-born residents also helps to predict high-tech success (1).

When Florida weighed in on the side of the skaters during his trip to Philadelphia in 2002, presumably he understood them under the rubric of the "Bohemian Index." While the "scruffy," "rude" skateboarders may have been viewed as marginal in the early 1990s, by the 2000s they were beginning to be represented as the new model citizens and new model workers. "In culture as in business," Florida believes, "Everything Interesting Happens at the Margins" (Florida, *Rise* 184).

While Philadelphia has begun to cater to specialized lifestyles—with a gay-oriented tourist marketing campaign and negotiations with SAN for a new skate park—I will argue in the following section that the city has not adopted Florida's more inclusive conception of class.

New Century Neighborhoods, Exclusivity Avenues, and the Question of Class

Under Mayor Street the city has launched programs called the Neighborhood Transformation Initiative and New Century Neighborhoods. The programs set out to "advance the quality of life in neighborhoods with a coordinated and targeted code enforcement program to abate public nuisances." And: "Use limited public resources to leverage private investment dollars to provide higher levels of maintenance, service, and amenity. Encourage rehabilitation and new development to appeal primarily to middle and upper income households, but also to maintain fair housing opportunities for low-moderate income households" (Florida, *Rise* 20). The $1 million offer from DC seems in line with the strategy of leveraging "private investment dollars to provide higher levels of maintenance, service, and amenity"—the conflict is about whom the amenities are for. While the Inquirer's Satullo, or Florida, might view the skateboarders as a bohemian or creative class, the Street administration views the skateboarders as a "public nuisance"—or as Goldsmith put it "a pimple on an elephant's hide"—perhaps one that doesn't "appeal" to "middle and upper-income households" (Satullo).

The City Controller's Report offers another possible insight into the city's policy toward skateboarders. In a section titled "Potential Future City Marketing Avenues," the controller writes that:

> Selling exclusivity is a way that the City can further capitalize on marketing efforts. By offering companies the right to be the exclusive providers of a product in Philadelphia, the City can multiply the value of its concessionaire-type contracts. Companies have demonstrated their desire to pay private and public entities a premium for arrangements that create official sponsors, vendors, or suppliers. (Philadelphia City Controller 145)

Love Park is listed as one of the six "Potential Future City Exclusivity Avenues" (146). Perhaps a private company may want to open a restaurant in the now vacant visitor center, the report suggests; and in exchange for exclusivity, the company would "provide maintenance services" in the park, which "suffers from neglect" (146). Even though they are not restaurateurs, again DC's offer seems to fit the bill; indeed, the controller himself, Jonathon Saidel, urged the city to accept the offer (Anderson).

Of the many who supported the plan (including the *Inquirer*) and the few who opposed the plan (including *The Sentinel*), the only voice that objected to the very principle of "corporate sponsorship or support of municipal functions or properties" was the cantankerous lefty weekly, *The Daily News* (cf. "Skateboard grant"; "Skate Off"). While acknowledging the city's fiscal problems, the paper opined that "The line between selling our citizenry and pimping them is a thin one" ("Skate Off"). Given the negative press, the city was largely quiet about its reasons for rejecting the offer, yet—in light of its policy reports which recommend that the city actively seek out corporate "sponsorship"—it is clear that protecting the citizenry against the corporatization of municipal property was not among them. With no other prospects for private "sponsorship"—at least none that have been made public—why give up such an offer?

Debates about this kind of public/private "partnering" seem to always employ a specific vocabulary (like "consumer" or "client" instead of "citizen") and I want to suggest that the language itself offers a clue. For example, consider one of the other Potential Future Marketing Avenues identified by the controller: "a boutique to sell used City property, including old street signs, parking meters, demo voting machines, and memorabilia from the City's defunct Civic Center" (Saidel 144). Is Love Park one of the items being sold, or could it even be the boutique itself?

Many American cities are facing fiscal problems that have led them to begin treating their public space as intellectual property. Philadelphia is no exception. The controller suggests that "The city can explore legally trademarking and copyrighting images and representations of much reproduced icons, or it could issue licenses to vendors to sell 'official City of Philadelphia' Liberty Bell and Independence Hall souvenirs" (Saidel 145). Richard Indiana's LOVE sculpture would be a natural candidate for such an exploration. Would LOVE's further association with skateboarding dilute or preclude a future exclusivity deal?

Whatever the case, the administration's policy reports make clear that the city is proceeding from a belief that people of whatever class location "oppose the introduction" of people "perceived to have lower socio-economic characteristics than those that already exist in the community" (Philadelphia City Planning 6). Furthermore, given that the reports also state the city needs to appeal to people of "upper-income" brackets, it is clear that the city is trying to nurture upper-class community in Love Park (20). And as the *Inquirer* has observed: "Serious skateboarding largely attracts working-class kids" (K. Heller).

Gentrification as Equalizer

Florida's book is a call to class consciousness: "The members of the creative class today need to see that their economic function makes them the natural—indeed the only possible—leaders of twenty-first-century society. But being newly emergent, the creative class does not yet have the awareness of itself, *as a class*, that is needed" (Florida, *Rise* 315). Without this class consciousness, the creative class will be unable to realize its historical calling—to "pursue a collective vision of a better and more prosperous future for all" (xii). But if class is understood in terms of economic status and the type of labor that one performs, then there is something counterintuitive about Florida's creative class, where a high school teacher and a neighborhood artist are of the same class as a biotech researcher and a hedge fund manager. On what basis would these people identify with one another? Is the answer really something so amorphous as "creativity"?

In Florida's account, what holds all of these people together is that they drive urban growth. "Bohemian presence," Florida writes, "predicts [...] high-tech industry concentration" (Florida, *Cities* 42). But Florida has no predictions about what happens to the bohemians once the high-tech capital has been concentrated. What holds "bohemians" and "creative professionals" together is not class at all, but their participation in the process of gentrification. However, they each play different roles, at different stages, and they each benefit unequally.

If the city is an entertainment machine, then Adorno and Horkheimer's "culture industry" no longer serves as just ideological legitimation for the economy, but as the urban economy's main motor. And with the creative class, we see not only "culture" that elides and naturalizes class inequalities, but also a *class politics* that elides and naturalizes class inequalities. Such inequalities were not entirely lost on the skateboarders in Love Park.

"We Made This Place Alive": Skateboarders as the Shock Troops of Gentrification

I spoke with a Philadelphia planner who observed that Ed Bacon's "understanding what skaters were doing in Love Park was like his understanding that Society Hill needed to be preserved" (G. Heller). In the 1950s, when his counterparts in other US cities were clearcutting struggling neighborhoods with Title 1 money, Bacon used this money to rehabilitate a distinguished but distressed housing stock in Philadelphia's Society Hill (Smith). In this early and influential model of gentrification, Bacon showed that renewal could happen on a more fine-grained scale. There are many obvious differences between the Society Hill and Love Park stories—for one thing, the former project was carried out by old money elites, with federal subsidies, while the skaters in Love Park were banned—but both are stories of "reclamation."

In an interview recorded on video in 2002 in front of the fenced-off Love Park, a frustrated skateboarder named Ricky Oyola said:

> We should be able to do whatever we want here. We made this place. We made this place alive. Honestly we made this place worth anything. It was just fuckin' drug dealers, dudes chillin' up there, fightin' each other all the time, every day, you know what I mean. Like that's all it was. We came here and we gave it life. We gave it to where people could walk by and not feel scared because you got these little scrawny kids on skateboards here next to these fuckin' big time drug dealers: if these little kids aren't scared, why should I be scared? I'm a thirty-year-old man coming from work. (*Love Story*)

Oyola's predicament is familiar to artists and bohemians from San Francisco's SOMA district to Manhattan's SoHo district. As the unwitting shock troops of gentrification—injecting a small capital flow into a distressed area—they eventually suffer from the same process that they precipitate (Smith 20). The first wave of elites in 1950s Society Hill, of course, benefited enormously from their reclamation—what stories of gentrification have in common is not who the winners are, or even necessarily who the losers are, but the fact that the losers are typically erased from the story. Just as Oyola erased the homeless population in his statements, he is now being erased by the anti-skate redesigns of the plaza. While many of the skateboarders point out that they had befriended and built community with the homeless, it is certain that one of the reasons local opinion makers sided with the skateboarders was their belief that they deterred the homeless (*Love Story*). Challenging the skateboard ban, Saffron asked: "why chase out the park's main constituency, leaving it to the sort of people who use the space for long naps and personal grooming?" (Saffron, "Don't Trash the Thrashers").

The *Inquirer* editor Satullo opined that "Ed Bacon celebrates how skaters' discovery of LOVE breathed *life* into his design [emphasis added]" (Satullo). As in Oyola's assertion that skateboarders made this place *alive*, it follows that Love was only death before the skaters arrived. This is another expression of the narrative that equates homeless populations with darkness or, worse yet, nothingness. Saffron, for example, referred to Love Park as "an urban black hole" ("City planner's legacy"). When a square full of people is described as "empty," those people are typically homeless. Before receiving federal funding, Society Hill needed to be officially diagnosed with "blight" (a plant biology term used to describe a spreading disease), and as with Love Park, Society Hill was described using terms like "barren" or "dead space." What Society Hill and Love Park have in common is a mode of describing social problems in terms of *natural* decay, when in fact those problems are better understood through an analysis of policy: redlining and federally subsidized suburbanization in the 1950s, and the evisceration of public housing and mental health programs in the 1980s.

Skateboarders were compared to rats and cockroaches.

In the early 1990s skateboarders were, like homeless, compared to rats and cockroaches. But as skateboarding grew to a $1.5 billion industry in the early 2000s, bringing in millions to the city coffers, the activity rose out of the category of "quality of life crime" in local elite opinion (Saidel 201). A survey of the *Inquirer* from January to December of 2004 shows that not only did the reportage on skateboarding increase as the stories on homelessness decreased, but the skaters began to serve as a syntagmatic substitution for homeless populations in political discourse. In fact, many local politicians—like councilwoman Jannie Blackwell—who had fought for the homeless on the grounds that everyone was entitled to access to public goods, now fight for skateboarders, invoking the same modernist ideal of universal access (cf. Rosenberg, "New Strategy"). As the homeless are phased out of the debates about access, the bottom rung on the social ladder is now occupied by the skateboarders, a group who everyone understands can pay the price of admission. Homelessness, then, is emptied of its political subjectivity, and is reconceived as an unfortunate fact of nature, and the homeless themselves as an "element" that ebbs and flows like the tides.

Conclusion

In the shift from the city of the Great Society to the gentrifying city comes a shift in outlook. Florida presents a sanguine view of this transition: "People have come to accept that they are on their own—that the traditional sources of security and entitlement no longer exist, or even matter. This is a sea change" (*Rise* 115). This sea change has been acted out in the space of Love Park. While it is not the case that all people have accepted the condition Florida describes, the statement does seem to accurately represent most of the skateboarders. Indeed, they have no personal memory of there ever having been "traditional sources of security and entitlement," having been born in the 1970s and 1980s, and having come to adult consciousness in the 1990s and 2000s.

Borden's *Skateboarding, Space and the City* makes the case that the activity is a "critical exterior to architecture" (1). Skateboarding, he argues, interrogates and challenges the meanings of "the left-over spaces of modernist planning, or the spaces of decision-making (typically the urban plaza) which symbolize not through overt iconography but through the expansivity of space" (188). The book provides a history of skateboarding beginning in the 1970s, yet since the book's publication in 2001, the relationship between skateboarding and the city has been reconfigured in ways that force a reevaluation of Borden's argument. From the 1970s to the 1990s modernist plazas like Love Park were largely abandoned by municipal governments; and at this same time, skateboarding was a marginal industry. Observing this period, it makes sense to argue, as Borden does, that skateboarding "involves great effort, but produces no commodity ready for exchange" (1). But in recent years, skateboarders have delivered Love Park to the city of Philadelphia in a new, more marketable form. In the 2000s, as the skateboard industry has grown to over a billion dollars, and as cities have begun to reinvest in their leftover modernist spaces, many opinion makers have begun to perceive some "synergies." Skateboarding may have been a wrench in the modernist "growth machine," but in Philadelphia it has been retooled as a cog in the entertainment machine.

The modernization of Philadelphia began when the Parkway was cut through Penn's grid in 1906. Love Park was constructed at the Parkway's terminus in front of City Hall in 1965. Even through the fiscal crisis of the 1970s, the park was well used by Philadelphia citizens of all classes. With the "reforms" of the welfare state in the 1980s came a different sort of inhabitation of the park—if there were no housing or mental health services, at least there was public space. In recent years the youthful defiance of skateboarders has serendipitously reclaimed Love Park—generating revenue through media exposure and producing a marketable image for the city—all while deterring the presence of homeless. Now the skateboarders, in turn, are being phased out to make way for the next reclamation. Love Park was an expression of the modernist city, both architecturally and socially. On the same site is now emerging the gentrifying city, where you are on your own.

Acknowledgments:
In the Architecture and Geography departments at U.C. Berkeley, I would like to thank Kathleen James-Chakraborty, Allan Pred, and Paul Groth who offered insightful comments on various versions of this essay. Special thanks go to Greig Crysler who has commented on all of those versions. I also thank the *JAE*'s anonymous reviewers for their excellent critiques of this piece. Finally, this essay could not have been written without information provided by Scott Kip. For all of the assistance that I received, any errors of fact or interpretation remain my own.

References

Altman, Howard. "LOVE Burns Bacon." *Philadelphia City Paper*, October 31–November 6, 2002. Print.

Anderson, Carla. "Cover Story: City to Boarders and Shoe $$: Keep Walking." *Philadelphia Daily News*, June 2, 2004. Print.

Borden, Iain. *Skateboarding, Space, and the City: Architecture and the Body.* New York: Berg, 2001. Print.

Brownlee, David B. *Building the City Beautiful: The Benjamin Franklin Parkway and the Philadelphia Museum of Art*. Philadelphia, PA: Philadelphia Museum of Art, 1989. Print.

Clark, Terry Nichols, Richard Lloyd, Kenneth K. Wong, and Pushpam Jain. "Amenities Drive Urban Growth: A New Paradigm and Policy Linkages." *City as Entertainment Machine.* Ed. Terry Nichols Clark. Oxford: Elsevier, 2004. Print.

Cooke, Russell. "Reagan Budget Cuts Prompt Phila. Rally Next Month," *Philadelphia Inquirer*, April 7, 1982. Print.

Deleon, Clark. "The Scene in Philadelphia and Its Suburbs." *Philadelphia Inquirer*, February 19, 1981. Print.

Ferrick Jr., Thomas, and Maida Odom. "Living on the Streets of Center City Ranks of the Homeless Soar." *Philadelphia Inquirer* November 26, 1989. Print.

Florida, Richard. *Cities and the Creative Class*. New York: Routledge, 2005. Print.

Florida, Richard. *The Rise of the Creative Class: And How It's Transforming Work, Leisure, Community and Everyday Life*. New York: Basic Books, 2002. Print.

Florida, Richard, and Gary Gates. "Technology and Tolerance: The Importance of Diversity to High-Technology Growth." *The Brookings Institution, Survey Series*. Washington, DC: The Brookings Institution, 2001. Print.

"For LOVE, Money." Editorial. *Philadelphia Inquirer*, June 2, 2004. Print.

Gelbart, Marcia. "Street's Musings, Worries, in E-Mails." *Philadelphia Inquirer*, March 27, 2005. Print.

Goodman, Howard. "The City's Love Park – A Gateway for Visitors – Is Home to the Homeless and Lures Skateboarders." *Philadelphia Inquirer*, August 15, 1996. Print.

Heller, Greg. Personal interview. November 5, 2004.

Heller, Karen. "Chairman of the Board." *Philadelphia Inquirer*, August 2, 2000. Print.

"Hud's Sins." Editorial. *Philadelphia Inquirer*, September 17, 1989. Print.

"Hud's Sins. Phila. Could Have Used Some Of That $2 Billion." Editorial. *Philadelphia Inquirer* July 14, 1989. Print.

"I Can Fix Your City." *Philadelphia City Paper*, September 12–18, 2002. Print.

Keating, Douglas. "TV/Radio Talk: Original Writers, Crew Rehired To Revive 'Saturday Night Live.'" *Philadelphia Inquirer*, July 28, 1981. Print.

Love Story. 411 Productions, 2004. DVD.

McCullough, Marie. "Skateboarders Slowly Gain Right-of-Way – And a Few Parks / The Sport Long Has Been Restricted or Banned as Dangerous. Some Communities, However, Are Building Places Just For It." *Philadelphia Inquirer*, April 30, 1995. Print.

Molotch, Harvey. "The City as a Growth Machine." *American Journal of Sociology* 82.2 (1976): 309–32. Print.

Pennsylvania. City of Philadelphia. Committee on Public Property and Public Works. *An Ordinance Amending Title 10 of The Philadelphia Code relating to "Regulation of Individual Conduct and Activity," by amending Section 10-610 entitled "Skateboarding on Public Property," by prohibiting skateboarding on all public property unless otherwise authorized, and by creating additional penalties, all under certain terms and conditions*. By Nutter, Reynolds-Brown, Goode, Cohen, Ortic, Kenney, DiCicco, Krajewski, Miller, Verna, Marino, Clarke, Longstreth, Ricco, and Tasco. Title 10, Chapter 10-600, Section 10-610 of the Philadelphia Code. Philadelphia, PA: City Council, 2000. Print.

Philadelphia Redevelopment Authority. *Annual Report of the Philadelphia Redevelopment Authority*. 1963. Print.

Philadelphia Redevelopment Authority. *Annual Report of the Philadelphia Redevelopment Authority*. 1964. Print.

Philadelphia, City of. City Planning Commission. *New Century Neighborhoods. Philadelphia, City of Office of the Controller*. Philadelphia, PA: A New Urban Direction. Print.

Philadelphia, City of. Philadelphia Redevelopment Authority. *Annual Report of the Philadelphia Redevelopment Authority*. Philadelphia, PA: Redevelopment Authority, 1968. Print.

Pothier, Dick. "Chess Fans Find Friendly Challenge at JFK Plaza." *Philadelphia Inquirer*, August 19, 1986. Print.

Rosenberg, Amy. "Mayor Unveils New Strategy for the Homeless. Panhandling Will Be Discouraged. So Will On-Street Feeding. Instead, Long-Term Solutions Will Be the Focus." *Philadelphia Inquirer*, October 1, 1993. Print.

Rosenberg, Amy. "New Strategy for the Homeless Panhandling." *Philadelphia Inquirer*, May 14, 1993 and *On Video* (2004).

Rubin, Daniel. "No 'Love' for Skateboarders. Instead, A South Philadelphia Home." *Philadelphia Inquirer*, March 3, 1995. Print.

Saffron, Inga. "Changing Skylines." *Philadelphia Inquirer*, May 6, 2005. Print.

Saffron, Inga. "City Planner's Legacy Not the Sweet Deal WHYY Sells." *Philadelphia Inquirer*, September 23, 2004. Print.

Saffron, Inga. "Disappointing Developments on 15th St." *Philadelphia Inquirer*, August 23, 2002. Print.

Saffron, Inga. "Don't Trash Thrashers." *Philadelphia Inquirer*, August 11, 2001. Print.

Saidel, Jonathan A., Brett H. Mandel, Kevin J. Babyak, and David A. Volpe. *Philadelphia: A New Urban Direction*. Philadelphia: Saint Joseph's University Press, 1999. Print.

Satullo, Chris. "LOVE Park Remains a Test Case of Philadelphia's Will to Thrive." Editorial. *Philadelphia Inquirer*, June 6, 2004. Print.

Sight Unseen. Dirs. Jon Holland and Greg Hunt. Transworld Skateboarding, 2001. Video cassette.

"Skateboard Grant Hides an Agenda." Editorial. *The Sentinel*, June 3, 2004. Print.

"Skate Off." Editorial. *Philadelphia Daily News*, June 3, 2004. Print.

Smith, Neil. *The New Urban Frontier: Gentrification and the Revanchist City*. London: Routledge, 1996. Print.

"The Mental-Health Puzzle Some May Think They've Come Up With an Easy Answer, But They're Wrong." Editorial. *Philadelphia Inquirer*, September 17, 1989. Print.

Wiegand, Ginny. "Who Eats at JFK Plaza? Brown-Baggers, Homeless - and Rats." *Philadelphia Inquirer*, November 5, 1991. Print.

DOWN A HATCH (
EINE HECKE ENTLANG (
( ) UP A TREE
UP A TREE ( )
( ) EINEN BAUM HINAUF
EINEN BAUM HINAUF ( )
( ) AROUND A TOWN
AROUND A TOWN ( )
( ) UM EINE STADT HERUM
UM EINE STADT HERUM ( )

Emily Chivers Yochim

"Freedom on Four Wheels" *Neoliberal Masculinities in Skate Life*

Introduction

Brian, a twenty-nine-year-old skater with a history degree and a tattoo on his neck, started skateboarding at age nine at the urging of his "hippie dad." When Brian was ten, his father divorced Brian's mother, an alcoholic, and Brian described spending much of his childhood playing freely outside to avoid conflicts at home. At the time of our interview in 2004, he had recently moved to Michigan from California in order to be closer to his young children. Passionate about skateboarding, Brian had plans to open a skate park in order to give his own and others' kids "a safe place to go": a place where young people would feel welcome, build lasting friendships, and stay away from video games. He explained to me his love for skateboarding:

> Skating, you come up to the same obstacle, and if you can't tackle it right away, you get another chance. You just keep going at it [...] Skateboarding is always something I was able to do on my own terms [...] It's me against me. I'm

> my own obstacle. Getting past those stationary obstacles is just my mental challenge, really. It's on my own terms; I tackle it head-on, and if I don't feel like tackling it anymore that day, it's still always going to be on my mind, but it's my own terms [...] There's so many things I need to overcome as far as what I want to do skating-wise, so that's just a constant push. But it's a freedom! I feel free when I'm skateboarding and I can forget about everything that's bothering me for that hour or two of the day. It's liberating, it's kind of like therapy.

When I asked Brian to define skateboarding, he summed things up this way: "Skateboarding is freedom on four wheels." Like so many of the skateboarders I interviewed in Ann Arbor, Michigan between 2002 and 2004, Brian saw skateboarding as an opportunity to express his own desires, to enhance his own abilities, and to escape from the grind of daily life. I met Brian in a small Michigan skateboard shop tucked below the street, where I spent much of my time in the summers of 2002, 2004, and 2006. There, amidst a jumble of skateboard gear, skater boys gathered regularly to meet up with one another between skateboarding sessions and to watch skateboarding videos. More a clubhouse than a place of business, the skate shop was home to a few worn out lounge chairs, a 13" television/VCR, and a metal rail sitting approximately eight inches off the ground, upon which skateboarders could practice their tricks. A multitude of worn-out skateboard decks were woven into the shop's exposed metal rafters, and all four walls were covered in handmade pictures and professional posters, with racks of skateboarding shoes and new skate decks layered over them. Skate magazines and videos peppered the counters and the floors around the TV. Here, amid the detritus of skate life, Ann Arbor's skate culture was consolidated; skaters (almost all adolescent boys and young men) debriefed skate sessions, debated the merits of various skate videos, paged through magazines together, and proposed ideas for making their own amateur videos. The skate shop, in other words, was a place where the skate community developed and articulated its norms and its primary values.

The skateboarders who populated this shop loved skateboarding, imagined it as central to their lives and identities, and considered it an everyday part of their lives. As twenty-four-year-old Kiran told me, "It's like addictive too, you know. If I don't skateboard for three or four days, I start going crazy. I'm just like, 'Oh man, I need to skate!'" Indeed, without fail, skateboarders spoke passionately and lovingly of their practice, making it clear that skateboarding was deeply important to their lives—some even suggested that it had changed their lives. Their descriptions of the community and its practices were delivered with a sense of reverence that contrasted profoundly with the irreverent images of young men we see in most media. Though mainstream culture has managed to paint skateboarders as an aggressive, highly competitive group of adrenaline junkies or as slacker-stoners, these skaters were far more passionate about the value their culture placed on freedom, individuality, and self-expression. They imagined skate culture as a location of difference, an alternative to dominant demands that adolescent boys, as exemplified by "jocks," should overvalue competition, physical dominance, and emotional repression. For them, skate culture's esteem for freedom and individuality seemed to be an alternative to mainstream adolescent culture and an opportunity for various expressions of masculinity.

What to make of a group of mostly white, mostly middle-class boys and young men who sought to distance themselves from dominant culture, and more importantly, dominant forms of masculinity? How to think about boys who spent so much time roughhousing in homosocial groups and attempting aggressively physical stunts, but who also described their practice, as I detail below, as noncompetitive, artistic, therapeutic, even spiritual? In my 2010 book *Skate Life: Re-Imagining Masculinity*, I argued that skaters were articulating a nascent critique of dominant masculinities while preserving skaters' patriarchal, white, and heteronormative cultural power. This not-anti-patriarchal critique of dominant masculinities was important, I argued, for it revealed the ways in which young men could express dissatisfaction with status quo gendered norms while also holding fast to larger structures of power that maintained their own dominance. What's more, as I noted, skaters' discussions of their identity as skateboarders and their devotion to skateboarding culture revealed that masculinity posed a problem for them. In reverent descriptions of the experience of skateboarding, the adolescent boys I interviewed disclosed a yearning for the opportunity to express themselves and a space in which to feel a sense of freedom or transcendence. Though, in important ways, white middle-class boyhood is entirely focused on freedom and self-expression, in the minds of the skateboarders, male adolescence and adulthood are both framed by institutions that serve to stifle such individualized joy. Work, school, family, and most importantly, organized team sports, all operate as personifications or institutions of patriarchy that place limitations on the type of transcendent, inspirational, and boundless sensation imparted by skateboarding.

In this essay, I want to move beyond showing how skateboarders' subcultural critique is quintessentially American and toward examining how skateboarders occupy an idealized neoliberal masculine subjectivity. Indeed, skaters' not-fully-formed gender critique reimagines white masculinity, but it does so through gendered discourses and a subcultural sensibility that highlight skaters as idealized gender subjects in neoliberal times.

When Brian exclaimed that "skateboarding is freedom on four wheels," he was articulating a decidedly neoliberal idea of freedom: the freedom to strive for one's own, self-defined goals, the freedom to tackle obstacles independently, the freedom to express one's individually defined identity, and the freedom to escape from the demands of the day (work, family) through inwardly focused pastimes. Of course, what is absent here is a larger sense of the collective good, a broad structural critique, or simply a sense that the world could be different. The freedoms skaters celebrate are centered on self-determination, a powerful sensibility that they can do whatever they like—so long as they forge their own way, accept others' similar desires to act as wholly independent subjects, and continually enhance their own value as neoliberal subjects.

In what follows, I trace how skaters' burgeoning critique of masculinity was leveled in large part through the norms of neoliberal subjectivities. Skaters' more expansive views of masculinity in the skateboarding world—as an expressive, spiritually fulfilled, inclusive, and passionate experience—map neatly onto neoliberal subjecthood. In this way, though neoliberalism opens a door toward reimagining white masculinities, it simultaneously shuts down the reimagination of political horizons.

"You're on Your Own Team": The Enterprising Subject

Like Brian, many of the skateboarders pinned skateboarding's appeal on its location outside of mainstream sporting culture. Thirteen-year-old Eric told me:

> Like a team sport, you have like, coaches yelling at you, and people depending on you. You have a time limit. But um, with skateboarding, you're on your own, you're like on your own team, you just push each other. It's not, it's not, you don't compete against each other. Like, you see the X Games, it's not skateboarding, like it's not about competing. It's just skating together.

Jim, aged fifteen, said, "It's just awesome, to ride and do it wherever you can do it. There's not a court, it's not like basketball or something that, where you have certain limitations. There's like no limitations at all. And, you can do it wherever you want, and do whatever you want or anything." For each of these skateboarders, the trappings of team sports, including sanctioned spaces for participation, established rules, and coaches, all signify patriarchal control, and for skateboarders, their practice offers an escape from such control.

But what signals as freedom from patriarchal control for the skaters also operates as capitulation to the norms of the neoliberal entrepreneurial self. As David Harvey writes, "Neoliberalism is in the first instance a theory of political economic practices that proposes that human well-being can best be advanced by liberating individual entrepreneurial freedoms and skills within an institutional framework characterized by strong private property rights, free markets, and free trade" (2). The state's role becomes not the protection and provision of citizens' lives, but instead the endowment of private enterprise and economic growth (cf. Brown 26).

Not simply a theory, though, neoliberalism is a logic that, as Wendy Brown says, "governs as a sophisticated common sense, a reality principle remaking institutions and humans everywhere it settles, nestles, and gains affirmation" (35). Indeed, more than orienting the state toward the well-being of the global marketplace, neoliberal rationality privileges the suffusion of privatized, market logics through most all of social and political life. As Harvey explains, "The market is presumed to work as an appropriate guide—an ethic—for all human action" (165). Accordingly, this "reality principle" comes to shape contemporary subjects as first, foremost, and always *homo oeconomicus* (Brown 31), with "the model of the market" governing our decisions about relationships, schooling, work, and leisure. Human beings become human capital, leveraging the self through entrepreneurialism for profit.

According to Pierre Dardot and Christian Laval, enterprising subjects orient themselves as if they were working for themselves—not for an employer. They write: "The individual must work as his own efficiency, at intensifying his own effort, as if this self-conduct [...] was commanded from within by the imperious order of his own desire" (260). Entrepreneurial conduct is constantly represented as a vehicle for "individual flourishing, as the instance where individuals' desire for self-realization, their material well-being, the commercial and financial success of the work 'community,' and their contribution to the general prosperity of the population can finally be combined" (261).

Indeed, in their impassioned descriptions of skateboarding's virtue as an unorganized practice, skaters demonstrated their neat adherence to the creative, flexible, and self-improving entrepreneurial self. Timmy, a twenty-year-old skateboarder who worked at a local diner, explained, "There's no teams [...] It's completely up to you, how much better you get, and what you want to work at, and it's like self-propelled." Matthew, a twenty-one-year-old college graduate, claimed:

> It's just like disassociated from the rest of the normal world, almost [...] With snowboarding [...] you're in the mountains, in a place where they allow you to be, where you pay to go there, and you ride a chair lift and go down the mountain and everything's fixed, they have little slopes built for you, but skateboarding is not like that, you know. You are in places that you are not meant to be for skateboarding, and [...] you have to look at things like, "How can

I use this for skateboarding, even though it's not meant for it," you know. And, I don't know, it makes you think a little different, right?

Sixteen-year-old Jack, a student simultaneously earning his high school degree and associate's degree at a local community college, made this point most adamantly:

> It's just that you don't skate to be better than anyone; there's not a coach who's saying, "I want you to do a 360 first, and then a kickflip, by the end of the week!" you know? You don't have to wake up at 5:30 in the morning to go skate. That's what sports are all about. It's like tournaments. They're not worth it! You better be good, and that's not how I see skating.

Jack concluded, "The possibilities are endless in skating, and there's no restrictions, there's no, like, codes, there's no rules; it's just like, open, you know. Just get on your board and ride."

Skaters claim their practice as a unique opportunity to step outside of the boundaries of traditional masculine culture. Nineteen-year-old Joe perhaps put this best in his disavowal of the tradition of passing masculine norms from father to son: "[Football players are] told their whole life that that's what they should do 'cause their dad probably was a football player for [the university] or something, and sometimes their dads won't even let 'em skateboard. I've seen it happen." For Joe and the other skateboarders, participation in football represents submission to inherited masculinities and compliance with the stifling rules of the older generation. While skateboarding rejects these norms, it also celebrates the self-propelled and creative entrepreneurial self.

"It's Just You and Your Board": Self-Expression, Creativity, and Self-Branding

In dreamy and passionate descriptions, many of the skaters waxed lyrical about the expressive and individualistic nature of skateboarding. Responding to the question "Why do you skate?" with descriptions of their love for the practice, skateboarders usually shifted tone, staring off into space, grappling for words that would describe the joy of the experience. Far from the overly aggressive, in-your-face skateboarders on mainstream television, these boys spoke quietly and ardently of their devotion to skating. Jeremiah, aged twenty-two, said, "It's just you and your board [...] It's like an art form in a sense. The only limitations you have in skateboarding [are] your own. And the idea that you can just take a thought, a pure idea, a thought in your head and go attempt to do it, it's kind of like art." Mike, twenty-nine, echoed Jeremiah: "And it's not a choreographed thing, so it's not like you go out and have a play, you know. It's like, the play is in your head, you make it up. Um, that's part of the art of it too, it all just comes from your soul and your heart [...] And I think that's part of the joy that builds up in style."

The only limitations you have in skateboarding are your own.

The skaters' devotion to artistic self-expression certainly undercuts emotionally reticent masculinities, and in their thoughtful accounts we can read some movement toward expanding the possibilities for male emotional, spiritual, and bodily expression. But their descriptions also, in some ways, echo the requirements of the entrepreneurial self, which must not only be self-propelled, but also willing and ready to adapt to the changing needs of the marketplace. The enterprising subject manages this requirement through ongoing self-work. As Dardot and Laval put it, "It is the efficient, competitive individual who seeks to maximize his human capital in all areas, who not only seeks to project himself into the future and calculate his gains and losses [...] but above all seeks to *work on himself* so as to constantly transform himself, improve himself, and make himself ever more efficient" (265). This self-work is designed to improve not only efficiency but also flexibility. Understood through these logics, skaters' creative self-expression might be read less as a kind of "pure" emotion and more as the development of entrepreneurial habits of self. Taking "a pure idea" and trying it out; "making up the play" on your own: these are the hallmarks of a "good" entrepreneur, who will allegedly fare better in a neoliberal economy by leveraging new ideas and adapting old ways to maximize their capital in a rapidly changing environment.

More than an opportunity for creative flexibility, the pleasures of skateboarding also figure for skaters as the expression of personal style, an expression that can easily adopt the logics of self-branding that feature as a strategy for investing in the self. As Wendy Brown argues, *homo oeconomicus* is not only entrepreneurial, but also financialized: increasing its value with self-investment in the form of schooling, training, self-branding, and the like. In her discussion of girls' and young women's self-branding work online, Sarah Banet-Weiser writes, "self-branding is positioned by marketers and brand managers as the proper way—perhaps even the necessary way—to 'take care of oneself' in contemporary advanced capitalist economy" (54). My interviews with the skateboarders took place at the cusp of the emergence of Web 2.0, but, as I describe in *Skate Life*, skaters spent much of their time constructing "sponsor-me tapes" designed to highlight individual skaters' skills *and* style, sometimes in an effort to get sponsored by a skateboarding company. They were no strangers to the logics of self-branding, and their poetic descriptions of artistic self-expression slipped easily into these logics.

Sixteen-year-old Jack, for example, told me, "It's an art. That's the only way you can define it [...] So with skating, like I take who I am as an individual and bring it to my skating [...] Watching a skateboard video, you'll see people with [...] dreds and stuff, they'll have the whole rude style, and the hesh rats, and like, I don't know, it just seems that you take the exact individual that you are and put it in your skateboarding." Twenty-nine-year-old Mike explained how one expresses style via skating:

> Once you learn a trick, you start to appropriate your own style, like squeak out a trick, like slide it out, the way you use your foot [...] You just teach yourself, like different ways, like you would do it the way you're more comfortable. And when you teach yourself that, you know, you completely make it your own at that point, because not only have you learned to do the trick, and maybe do it quite well, but you're able to put your piece on something that's already been done many times, and you do it in a way that no one does it.

So many of the deep feelings that skaters revealed about their practice suggested that skaters were "baring their souls," or tapping into some deep sense of self, through their highly individualized styles. The practice of putting these selves on display—either during skate sessions or in sponsor-me tapes—tended to register as a moment free of constraints, including gender constraints. The self-on-display, for the skaters, was not a performance laden with identity norms, but instead felt like an expression of the "authentic self." Indeed, as Banet-Weiser shows, contemporary ideals of the self as self-determined and principles of self-improvement fold easily into brand culture—and self-branding comes to be understood in the context of these discourses about the self. Far from simply being "just you and your board," self-expression in skate culture, when inflected with the neoliberal logics of self-branding, is taken up as a mode of increasing one's human capital; that is, investing in the self.

Claiming the Outside: Multiculturalism as Brand

Beyond acclaiming skateboarding as a mode of individualized self-expression, the Michigan skaters celebrated it as a practice and culture populated by outcasts and accepting of racial and cultural difference. As twenty-one-year-old Jeremiah, an employee of a chain skate shop, put it, "I wasn't really attracted to skateboarding by the actual sport. I was more attracted to the fact that nobody did it and I was like 'wow, this is cool, I'm going to try this.' And that's pretty much how I got into it. A desire to be different, I guess, at a young age." Many of the skateboarders voiced similar desires, and together the community claimed outsider status with recourse to both their youth and various—and acutely contradictory—gender and racial discourses. It is critical to see that skateboarders don't simply accept and manage outsider status; rather they claim it proudly, in fact wielding it as a distinctive feature of their culture: we can understand skaters' outsider status as a key axis of their brand.

Many skaters distinguished themselves from their nonskateboarding peers by defining themselves as outsiders who both reject dominant norms of masculinity and must negotiate generalized suspicion from adults. In part, these claims helped to express the fraught relationship many of them had to their nonskateboarding peers, and they also gestured to the ways in which skaters are policed and surveilled by parents, teachers, security guards, and sometimes, municipal police. Jeremiah, aged eighteen, said, "It's a subculture [...] because we get sort of a raw taste of life. We have to argue with people on a regular basis about getting out of the area." Fifteen-year-old Jim said, "I think, skaters are, they're more open, not as uptight. Like we're stupid little kids that got made fun of, like some jock or something would be like, 'Dude, that's stupid!'" Joe described how skateboarding made space for his "scrawny" body: "You'll always be accepted into skateboarding, and unlike football or something, kids'll make fun of you if you're small or something like that."

The skateboarders' descriptions of being teased about skateboarding or body type and their references to arguments with authorities about the practice of skateboarding make it clear that they feel as if they have been somewhat forcibly excluded from dominant groups—such as the jocks in high school. Skate media and culture does tend to suggest a lanky body type as an ideal—one need only look at Tony Hawk to see this—and I suspect that bulkier men who would be valorized as football players or wrestlers may feel excluded from skateboarding culture. It is important to note, however, that the dominance of this body type in skate culture may play a role in skaters' attraction to it. The boys' assertions of difference serve as a strategy by which they establish a sense of agency; if one chooses not to participate in a particular group, then he cannot be excluded from it by others. More germane to my argument, however, is that the skateboarders' solution to the exclusion is highly individualized and lacks an articulation of larger structural issues, such as the idea that a "real man" would be big—and physically dominant—not "scrawny" like Joe. Skateboarding in this sense becomes a type of enclave (cf. Bellah et al.), a location in which skateboarders can feel comfortable with themselves and escape from the demands of dominant norms. Skaters' inability or unwillingness to live up to established markers of masculinity does not necessarily effect an articulate critique of those norms, nor does it inspire a conscious effort to change them. Instead, it results in withdrawal from—or repudiation of—dominant elements of the culture. This renunciation consequently becomes a distinguishing feature of the culture; part of its brand.

While gendered discourses and skaters' youth established distinct defining lines around their culture, skaters also drew on racialized discourses to cement their own worth in profoundly paradoxical ways. On the one hand, some skaters claimed minority status, a discursive move that not only disavowed race as a structuring element of society but also conceived self-worth in terms of competition between various identity groups. On the other hand, skaters affirmed the exceptionality of their culture and the value of their experiences as outsiders by both celebrating the multicultural branding of skate companies and suggesting that skateboarding was a practice that transcended race.

Skaters clearly felt like outsiders to mainstream culture.

Many skaters clearly felt like outsiders to mainstream culture and experienced everyday life as a series of gender hurts and conflict with adults. But one skater, through highly racialized and coded language, redefined these daily frustrations as oppression. Brian told me:

> And we gotta band together. It's the only way we're gonna be able to fight oppression. We're still being oppressed. Wanna talk about a real minority. Skateboarders, is a true minority. 'Cause you know, cops hate us, uh, everybody hates us. Middle-class people, oh we're so dangerous, yet somebody can barrel down the street on a mountain bike, they never say nothing about that. You know what I mean? [...] They profile us, big time, skaters. Just have a skateboard, even if you're walking with one, the cops'll watch ya. It's terrible [...] I've never been ticketed for skateboarding. I'm proud to say that. Never been ticketed for skateboarding.

This skater's claim that he is continually surveilled—and even targeted—but has never received a ticket is curious and suggests a feeble attempt to claim special status via an unrealized oppression. Studies of whiteness and masculinity have both described such behavior, and surely a proclamation of oppression is one manifestation of what George Lipsitz calls "the possessive investment in whiteness." After all, it takes only a small step to move from claiming to be "a real minority" to suggesting that other minorities are inflating claims of oppression or asking for "special treatment" when it is not needed. But Brian's discussion also highlights identity politics as a kind of zero-sum game, wherein one's difficulties in public life translate into claims to be a "real minority" (with the unstated flip side being that others claiming minority status, and the supposed benefits that status entails, are not "real" minorities).

While Brian doubles down on racialized *competition* for minority status, many other skateboarders frequently translate their outsider status into assertions of cultural *acceptance*. Referencing such stylistic markers as music and clothing, skateboarders deemed their community "multicultural" or "diverse," and indicated that their acceptance of multiple peoples stemmed from their own experiences of exclusion or oppression. Using code words such as "rasta," "punk," and "hip hop," skaters implied that their culture is racially diverse, but these words seemed to weigh equally with generic terms associated with high school cliques—"geeks," "nerds," and so on. The skateboarders' explanations of difference served to elide race, making it seem as if any and all racial differences were easily subsumed by a common devotion to skateboarding. Even when explicitly discussing race and class, skateboarders slid easily into references to lifestyle or music, as evidenced in Kiran's explanation:

> One of the things I've always liked about skateboarders is that it's diverse [...] Like culturally diverse, it's socioeconomically diverse. It's not about rich people that skateboard, poor people that skateboard, middle-class people, there's like, all sorts of different races. It's awesome. There's pro skaters that are half Indian like me [...] In India there's not really a skateboarding scene, but in most other countries, like in Africa and stuff like that, there's skateboarders, South America. It's so cool. That's one of the things that makes skateboarding, in my opinion, a superior culture to any other kind of youth culture, or like, thing that other people would consider cool. That's one of the reasons that it's cooler than snowboarding. Like who snowboards? Rich white kids. For the most part [...] I think that's what keeps the majority of people out of it... they can't afford to buy a five-hundred-dollar board and lift ticket [...] Skate-

> boarding's low cost keeps it diverse and that rules. There's so many different things you can be into and still be a skateboarder. Punk rocker kids, hip hop kids, metal, whatever. There's dudes that listen to Britney Spears and they all skateboard. 'Cause that's their common bond. There's diversity.

Kiran slips, without pause or transition, from a fairly sophisticated discussion of the race and class politics of extreme sports to describing skateboarding's diversity through popular culture. This kind of racial elision is not surprising in a community of youth who have come of age in a culture celebrating tolerance, diversity, and multiculturalism while rarely explicitly discussing the continued effects of racism and racial differences. Indeed, as Lisa Duggan explains, "the rhetoric of 'official' neoliberal politics shifted during the 1990s from 'culture wars' alliances, to a superficial 'multiculturalism' compatible with the global aspirations of U.S. business interests" (44). This "nonredistributive form of equality" (xii) put multiculturalism up for sale.

Indeed, as I have argued with Matt Atencio and Becky Beal, the lifestyle and action sports marketers use racialized bodies in their campaigns to signal their brands' supposedly nonconformist, oppositional, and inclusive values. Skaters echo the marketing. Brian said, "I think the type of people it attracts [...] very multicultural, multi-diversity crowd [...] 'Cause when you're skating, it doesn't matter if you're a geek, a moron, a nerd, any of that stuff. It kind of transcends all that kind of behavior." Joe agreed, "Skateboarding's for everybody. Like everyone can skateboard, and like, skateboarding's full of so many—it's so diverse, like there's so many different kinds of pros [...] [T]here's like rasta dudes, there's like hip hop soldier whatever, there's little like punk rock kids." Matthew also swapped style for race: "[Skateboarding is] a mesh of cultures [...] You know, people who listen to punk rock music, and then there's your rocker, there's your hip hop heads, and then there's everything in between [...] [L]ike style of clothing, right, you know, like there's people who look like rockers, people who look like hip hop heads [...] There's people who dress real nice like [pro skater] Andrew Reynolds, you know, he wears a sports coat."

In many ways, skaters' claims to outsider status, to oppression, and to inclusivity all function as branding strategies that highlight skaters' individual senses of self. Put another way, they suggest that skaters are individuals disembedded from the social, possessive of unique attributes that could be mobilized in order to garner self-value.

"It's like spiritual fulfillment": Self-Actualization and Disembedding

Though (and in part because) skateboarding requires a high level of concentration, it offered a sense of transcendence, escape, meditation, or fulfillment seemingly unavailable in the boys' other domains. School, work, families, and relationships all produced stress in the skaters' lives; the practice of skating mitigated that stress. Matthew, aged twenty-one, explained, "When I'm skateboarding, there's nothing else on my mind but skateboarding. So, in that aspect, it's freeing. If I have exams or stress from anything else [...] like, I could have a midterm tomorrow and I go skateboarding, I, for that time [...] I'm thinking about nothing but skateboarding. And just, like totally immersed in how much fun I'm having." Kiran, twenty-four, and an employee at the skate shop, echoed him: "This is gonna sound cheesy but it's like spiritual fulfillment. In a way, where it's just, if there's any problems any time, you go skating and you don't really think about it and it feels good." Timmy explained, "When you're skating, there is sort of an escape involved. Like, when you're really concentrating on just skating, I mean, it's that sense of focus that you don't really, I don't get it from anything else. It's almost like meditation in a way [...] It even helps me think about things [...] It just makes you feel good about yourself." And fifteen-year-old Marc said, "It's just so fun, it's like, you're just in your own world when you skate. Like it's really fun [...] You're focused just on skateboarding, and [...] you can like get away and stuff, you know."

Despite the fact that skateboarding is, to some degree, inherently risky (and thus, conventionally masculine), skateboarders' reflective and passionate tones contradict dominant images of surly white male teens as well as notions that men are not and cannot be expressive, emotive, or introspective. Furthermore, their discussions of stress and problems belie suggestions that young men are unable to reflect on or talk about what's troubling them. Both the practice of skateboarding and skateboarders' discussions of it provide skaters an opportunity to engage in a manner contradictory to dominant norms of masculinity, and as their passionately stated descriptions reveal, they place a high value on this opportunity.

One gets the sense, when talking to skaters, that skateboarding manifests as a self-actualizing practice: a time to express their "true selves," to escape the demands of work and family, to concentrate fully on their passion. Indeed, here we see the supposed promises of the entrepreneurial self: vigor and success, self-mastery in the form of demonstrated flexibility, the rejection of conformity, the very maximization of life itself (cf. Dardot and Laval 265–83).

But what we also see is what Sam Binkley calls "disembedding." He argues, "[n]eoliberalism fuels the work of neoliberal subjectification by exciting a disdain, even a disgust not just for the averageness of the average person or the abstract character of industrial labor, but for the general, undifferentiated docility of the social" (158–9). In other words, the neoliberal individual must disembed from the social in order to "develop those distinguishing capabilities that separate oneself from others" (153). Happiness, Binkley persuasively argues, operates as the "hinge" by which idealized neoliberal subjectivities are taken up, for the incitement to "tak[e] responsibility for one's emotional life" is a strategy for diffusing "the logics of power [...] to living subjects" (174).

Skateboarding may inspire individualized feelings of joy.

The freedoms of skateboarding that feel so much like self-actualization to the skaters are also a mode of disembedding, a tactic for removing oneself from the social and concentrating solely on the individualized experience of the self. Not a practice that inspires far-reaching social critique—or even much knowledge about the gendered world—skateboarding as escape or spiritual transcendence may inspire individualized feelings of joy, or even freedom from daily constraints, but it does so at the expense of connectedness and communality.

Conclusion: "You do it for the love of it"

I've argued throughout this essay that skateboarders' nascent critique of dominant masculinities takes shape in the neoliberal logics of the enterprising self. From this perspective, all of life—leisure, consumption, education, work—is reconfigured as a value-adding strategy. Skateboarders' alternative modes of inhabiting masculinity become strategies for building their worth and for articulating a highly individualized relationship to the world.

As Wendy Brown explains, the consequences for democracy of the suffusion of market values through the social order are not insignificant. She writes:

> When such economization configures the state as the manager of a firm and the subject as a unit of entrepreneurial and self-investing capital, the effect is not simply to narrow the functions of state and citizen or to enlarge the sphere of economically defined freedom at the expense of common investment in public life and public goods. Rather, it is to transpose the meaning and practice of democratic concerns with equality, freedom, and sovereignty from a political to an economic register [...] Liberty itself is narrowed to market conduct, divested of association with mastering the conditions of life, existential freedom, or securing the role of the demos. (41)

In brief, Brown is describing here nothing less than the neoliberal destruction of democracy. Read through this lens, skaters promising reimaginings of dominant masculinities register as just another move in the neoliberal marketing of identity politics. In other words, skateboarders' celebration of self-expression, difference, and even spiritual transcendence become a strategy for niche marketing, a tactic for affirming these young white men's individual value, and even worse, a means to negating—rather than strengthening—bonds with the broader social sphere.

But it is important to consider that, in so many of my conversations with skateboarders, they expressed a deep aversion to leveraging skateboarding itself as a value-adding practice. Indeed, as Iain Borden argues in *Skateboarding, Space, and the City*, street skating reimagines the commercialized spaces of urban streets as public playgrounds where the (male) body can be fully expressive. Skateboarding thus constantly and contradictorily traverses boundaries between private gain and public engagement and between marketized pleasures of consumption and resistance to selling subcultural practices.

As much as individuality pervades skateboarders' descriptions of their practice, a sense of true love, fun, joy, or devotion must motivate their participation in it in order for skaters to deem it authentic. Such emotional commitment to skateboarding—and the attendant devotion to feelings of pleasure—can be read as a renegotiation of masculine norms deeming pain, competition, and mastery to be paramount. Jack told me:

> You do it for the love of it, not to be cool, or not to be good at it, it's all the same thing, you know. It's like, the whole jock stereotype, usually you see it in sports, like the football jock, you know like some guy with slicked back hair you know, ladies' man or whatever, plays all these sports [...] A lot of them get caught up with skating, for whatever reason they see it and think, this'll be kind of fun. And they just skate to be like, skate to be good. They don't skate, they'll only do something really big and crazy if it's on film or if someone's taking a picture of it. Or if you know they just do it to be better than other people and not to have fun. That's not the way all of it is.

Alex told me:

> Right now, skateboarding, it just seems like, everybody's trying to start their own company and tryin' to make a lot of money and just trying to make their own impact on skateboarding and I think that, the companies who are really down for skateboarding since like, they've started and companies that are all about skateboarding sound fun, will survive. And skateboarding companies that are just all about the money will just die. So it kind of just separates out. Survival of the fittest I guess. Survival of the funnest, I would say.

How fitting that Alex slips from the Darwinian rhetoric of evolution through competition into a somewhat simple, even naïve, celebration of "authentic" fun. Crucially, "fun" here is still marketized, but it is branded with authenticity ("companies who are really down for skateboarding," as opposed to, I suppose, companies who are simply in the business of making money). But still, might we take seriously skaters' injunctions to cast off corporate demands in the name of fun? Without a doubt, survival of the funnest is hardly radical political stuff. And certainly, young men still have much more freedom to cast off the demands of neoliberalism than do young women, who supposedly must prove their worth in the neoliberal marketplace in order to "lean in" to personal success. Still, might it open doors for reimagining the contours of public life? Could skaters' nascent critiques of dominant cultures of masculinity be mobilized to reimagine democratic life?

References

Atencio, Matthew, Becky Beal, and Emily Chivers Yochim. "'It ain't just black kids and white kids': The Representation and Reproduction of Authentic 'Skurban' Masculinities." *Sociology of Sport Journal* 30.2 (2013): 153–72. Print.

Banet-Weiser, Sarah. *Authentic: The Politics of Ambivalence in a Brand Culture*. New York: New York University Press, 2012. Print.

Bellah, Robert N. et al. *Habits of the Heart: Individualism and Commitment in American Life*. Berkeley: University of California Press, 1985. Print.

Borden, Iain. *Skateboarding, Space, and the City: Architecture and the Body*. London: Bloomsbury Academic, 2001. Print.

Brown, Wendy. *Undoing the Demos: Neoliberalism's Stealth Revolution*. New York: Zone Books, 2015. Print.

Dardot, Pierre, and Christian Laval. *The New Way of the World: On Neo-Liberal Society*. London: Verso, 2013. Print.

Harvey, David. *A Brief History of Neoliberalism*. Oxford: Oxford University Press, 2005. Print.

Lipsitz, George. *The Possessive Investment in Whiteness: How White People Profit from Identity Politics*. Philadelphia, PA: Temple University Press, 1998. Print.

Yochim, Emily Chivers. *Skate Life: Re-imagining White Masculinity*. Ann Arbor: University of Michigan Press, 2010. Print.

Christian Peters

"Reclaim Your City!" *Skateboarding and Do-It-Yourself Urbanism*

Translated by Konstantin Butz

In cities around the globe, we witness new practices of a social "city-making": artists turn into *street* artists and rearrange and reconfigure streets, plazas, and overlooked wastelands that suddenly become artworks themselves (cf. Reinecke). Urban gardeners transform paved roadsides, roundabouts, and open spaces into chaotic and colorful flowerbeds and vegetable patches (cf. Müller, *Urban Gardening*). Activists of the crafting movement embellish traffic lights, street signs, and even whole junctions with bright knitwear (cf. Held). Citizens' initiatives engaged in local politics try to stop advancing gentrification wherever it occurs (cf. Dörfler 2010). Lovers attach padlocks to bridges (cf. Bund). Partygoers and party-organizers declare abandoned industrial areas new party locations (cf. Schwanhäußer). Ignoring city planners, architects, officials, and mayors—and thus acting outside the usual framework of civic involvement—this new "bottom-up urbanism" (Rauterberg 10) challenges traditional forms of city planning and urban development.[1] To whom does the city belong? How much value has the "right to the city" for citizens (Lefebvre, *Le droit à la ville*)? Where can we see new concepts of governance that enable individual citizens to actively participate in the configuration and design of the city?

Already today, it seems obvious that these idiosyncratic "informal city productions" à la Lefebvre (*The Production of Space*) and their ephemeral makeshift freestyle-spaces articulate a paradigmatic change of city planning: away from ideas of a city of participation in which citizens were at best halfheartedly involved in decision-making processes of the municipality without really being able to influence results that had already been finalized behind the scenes by investors, politicians, and the administration; toward a city of collaboration (cf. Terkessidis), a collaborative urbanism (cf. Fitz), which acknowledges citizens' initial competence to shape the city and to actively participate in its development at eye level with planning and construction experts. The city of Vienna constitutes an example of the new self-confidence and urban consciousness of citizens on the one hand, and on the other hand, the vision of a more and more astonished and insecure city administration. In 2016, for the second time, Vienna published a do-it-yourself city guide encouraging its people to become active as city-makers and participate in planning, shaping, and developing a livable city (cf. Magistrat der Stadt Wien).

This essay deals with the question of to what extent skateboarders—in addition to artists, creative folks, and "Commonists"[2] (cf. Baier, Müller, and Werner)—can also be regarded as city-makers and how the practice of skateboarding is involved in the production of urban space.

1 All quotations that were not taken from English publications have been translated by Konstantin Butz.

2 The term "commons" describes the collective attempt to socially decentralize the liberal market and the—apparently automatically—accompanying calculations of the homo oeconomicus by intentionally claiming public space for common utilization, by freely providing knowledge and know-how, and by collaboratively establishing economic projects (cf. Baier, Müller, and Werner 46–49). The internationally spreading phenomenon of DIY urbanism described in this essay can thus also be read as part of the "City of Commonists" as Baier, Müller, and Werner label it.

Three Different Urban Practices of Street Skateboarding

Street skateboarding is an urban practice. It always involves an active and intensive engagement with the materiality, forms, and social textures of the city. Ever since its emergence more than six decades ago, the cultural practice of skateboarding refers back to urban spaces. Following the evolution of this practice, the urban spaces it utilizes changed as well. While the "sidewalk surfing" of the early 1970s mainly started on the sidewalks of California, successive skateboarders first discovered the vertical (e.g. in empty swimming pools and halfpipes) and later, particularly at the beginning of the 1990s, exploited the urban space of the inner city as skate terrains. Currently, it is possible to discern three principal practices of street skateboarding according to their typical components, their required competences, their social significance, and the spaces the respective practice occupies: (1) classic street skateboarding, (2) indoor, outdoor, or plaza skateboarding, (3) DIY skateboarding.

Classic Street Skateboarding

Street skateboarding happens without the spatial and material framings that classic skate-specific spaces such as indoor and outdoor skate parks and street plazas designed for skateboarding provide. Its natural habitat is the street; it takes place in the public space of the city: in front of churches and theaters, in pedestrian zones, in marketplaces, on sidewalks, on playgrounds, and in the streets. Street skateboarding thus autonomously occupies its spaces and venues in the public realm and *in praxi* constitutes them as skate spots. The city thereby functions as a "land of opportunity" with boundless possibilities; it constitutes the unlimited playground of street skateboarding. Street skateboarding is therefore a practice of urban geography.

The city constitutes the unlimited playground of street skateboarding.

Within the skateboard community, street skating is regarded as the "royal road" among the different practices of skateboarding. There are several reasons for this: (1) street skateboarding playfully alters the basic rules and regulations embodied by the spaces it occupies. As it constantly challenges, overlooks, and defies the accustomed norms of public spaces, it often causes conflict and consequently is considered to represent the nonconformist, unconventional, undefined, and "true" way of skateboarding by the skateboard community. (2) Furthermore, street skateboarding—in contrast to DIY skateboarding and skateboarding in indoor and outdoor parks—finds its spaces in the form of "ready-mades" within the public sphere of the city. It uses the city as a stage where street skateboarders present their performative movements. Street skateboarding in public thus attracts much more attention than does skateboarding in the isolation of skate-specific spaces. Its spectacular presence in the everyday environments of the city and the bodily contestation of normative regulations inscribed in public spaces that becomes highly visible for bystanders and passersby make street skateboarding a highly controversial practice. Consequently, it dominates the overall image of skateboarding in the eyes of the public. (3) On top of that, street skateboarding combines all components that characterize the practice of skateboarding in general. While skateboarding in skate parks or skate plazas constitutes a special type of skating that works without the search for an appropriate skate spot, as the skateable terrain is artificially produced for skating, street skateboarding is organically implemented in urban practices and is only possible as an interaction that combines extensive searches on the board and the appropriation of situationally found skate spots.

Street skateboarding—which, as Iain Borden proposed in 2001, relies on Situationist tactics (cf. Coverley)—can be understood as an interplay of two practical components: (1) roaming in the city (*dérive*) and (2) the playful negotiation of space applied to a concrete skate spot (*détournement*) (Borden 173–228).[3] While the practice of nomadic roaming in the city is based and dependent on the elementary ability to ride that amalgamates body and board into an action unit, the negotiation of space at concrete skate spots requires a specific ability to perform tricks, i.e. the ability to couple the consistency and quality of a skate spot with the skater's own repertoire of movement(s).

On the level of social significance, street skateboarding is associated with emotions of wildness, lawlessness, and adventure, as well as an aura of rebelliousness. Similar to the street art scene and illegal spraying, illegal skating in the city is more prestigious than legal skating (cf. Reinecke 34). "Wild" street skateboarding in the city is more respected in the skateboard community than skating in spaces specifically designed for skateboarding. Street skating is regarded as more valuable and more creative. This additional value also becomes manifest in

3 The methods of *dérive* and *détournement* are used by the Situationist International (1957–1972) in their agenda to transform urban life. In their vocabulary, *dérive* describes an experimental technique of transient passage through varied ambiances, whereas *détournement* means the creation of new and unexpected meanings by disrupting the original and drawing it into new contexts (Coverley 92–94).

videos and photographs that preferably and primarily concentrate on the documentation of "wild" skateboarding. Filming in street plazas and in indoor and outdoor skate parks is very much characterized by an athletic and competitive approach. Its only function is to compare maneuvers and tricks, and thus only receives marginal attention within the medial representations of skateboard culture.

Indoor, Outdoor, and Plaza Skating

Skateboarding does not only take place in the public sphere of the street, but also in specifically constructed sites. Such constructed sites include indoor skate parks, outdoor skate parks, and so-called skate plazas. Throughout the history of skateboarding and in light of its growing popularity, these sites became necessary as more and more skateboarders populated public space and thereby articulated the need for their own spaces. Nowadays, many skate grounds are even operated and managed by the local city administration.

Constructed skateboarding sites are courses with obstacles made of wood or concrete that try to provide optimal opportunities for skateboarders to practice their activity. All of the three skate sites distinguished here (indoor park, outdoor park, skate plaza) are characterized by the fact that they were specifically and exclusively constructed for skateboarding; they are skate-specific sites. The practices that emerge within these three sites are thus very similar and can easily be compared. Consequently, in the following, they can be approached from a summarizing perspective.

There are a number of obvious differences between the three skate sites. For example, whereas indoor skate parks are roofed and thus sheltered, outdoor skate parks and plazas are exposed to all kinds of weather. Furthermore, there are usually entrance fees for indoor and outdoor skate parks, whereas plazas can be used free of charge. The latter constitute a relatively new type of skate site that is particularly distinct from skate parks as it simulates public space or, more precisely: the "natural street." Skate plazas are simulated street spots that would not be recognized as a skate site by nonskaters unless they saw someone actively skating there.

As a practice, park and plaza skating emphasize the component of a playful spatial negotiation of a concrete skate spot (*détournement*). While street skating is first of all dependent on the practice of *dérive* and the search for a skate spot that can be "played" with an applicable trick somewhere in the city, skate parks and street plazas already provide a whole variety of such spots for the skaters' convenience. Indoor and outdoor park and plaza skating are thus limited to merely one practice component regarded as constitutive for street skateboarding: *détournement*. As all skaters in parks and plazas use the same functionalized site that allows for optimal body-board activities through its architectural conception, the respective space is essentially neutralized as an active component in the playful activity of skating. Since park and plaza skating fix the potential of space as a coactor in skateboarding to a status quo, their practices become comparable: all skaters use the same obstacles and face the same conditions and difficulties. The skaters' actions and tricks—particularly as depicted in their medial representation in film and photography—become measurable in height and the respective degree of difficulty. As standardized and homogenized competition sites, skate parks and street plazas promote the achievement-oriented ideology of sports. According to Bale, they are "sportscapes" and crucially contribute to a "sportification" of skateboarding (67). Skating in skate parks and plazas comes closer to the training processes in high-performance sports.

Within skateboard culture, park and plaza skating are regarded as rather conformist because of their general focus on regulations and the disciplining of space that accompanies this:

> Skateboarding in the park is like walking through Central Park on the paths. One [street skating] is [that] you are making your own path, the other way is that you are making the path that urban planners say: "This is the path you should walk on." (Chiu 35)

Skate parks and plazas are officially approved sites with guidelines, standardizations, and directions so that skating in them does not presuppose a spotting of unknown spaces. It is thus not too surprising that many skaters regard it as less creative and less interesting to be represented medially. Standardized skating is considered the *sportified* version of skateboarding, and within the skateboard community people often experience it as artificial and inferior to the more creative street skating. The increasing construction of skate parks and plazas, however, hints at simultaneous tendencies to remove skateboarding from the public space of city centers and move it to specialized terrains. From the perspective of a critical reading, the municipal construction of skate sites could thus be viewed as a political instrument for the prosecution of skating. It disciplines, segregates, criminalizes, and *sportifies* skateboarding (cf. Vivoni, “Spots of spatial Desire”; *Contesting Public Space* and Howell, “The Poetics of Security”; “The Creative Class”; “Skatepark”).

DIY Skateboarding

DIY skateboarding constitutes the third of three practices of contemporary street skateboarding identified here. Within skateboard culture it is a relatively recent phenomenon that has not yet received much attention in academic analyses. It can be linked back to the current social relevance of the broader “do-it-yourself” movement. In order to adequately describe DIY skating within the frame of skateboard culture, it seems appropriate to start with a brief excursus examining this broader background. The slogan “do-it-yourself” (DIY) first appeared in a 1912 article in the magazine *Suburban Life* (Hornung, Nowak, and Kuni 8). It encouraged readers to paint the walls of their apartments themselves instead of hiring skilled professionals. In the years to follow, the idea of DIY was strongly politicized and extended from private basement hobby rooms to other social fields (e.g. design, work life, media). As a social movement, the idea of DIY has always carried alternative and subcultural as well as countercultural connotations. At least since the 1970s, when the hippie and punk movements found an anti-bourgeois expression in the “do-it-yourself” slogan, it has to be regarded as a form of creative protest and political resistance. Flyers and posters produced by political resistance groups such as the Edelweiss Pirates during the Nazi regime, as well as happenings and performances during the student protests of the 1960s and the antinuclear movement must therefore be seen as the historic precursors of the political DIY movement that still reverberate in current actions by “fun guerilla” groups such as the Critical Mass and their bike demonstrations, “hacking” activists, or “guerilla gardening” practitioners (cf. Hornung, Nowak, and Kuni 14).

The ideals of doing it yourself, of self-initiative, and of freedom from social and economic constraints flourished within the hippie, punk, and riot grrrl movements, and the DIY motto has recently taken on even greater significance. From a medial perspective, this trend becomes evident through a variety of TV shows, magazines, and advertisements that directly refer to the DIY ethos. In addition to the potential of protest, the driving forces behind the DIY boom thereby include the saving of expenses, aesthetic distinction, and the enjoyment of creativity and autonomy in the process of creation (cf. Honer 30).

The current boom of DIY as a form of autonomously producing things, of participation, and of cooperation can also be linked to a variety of social developments in the process of advancing technological modernization. It particularly corresponds with the possibilities of the Web 2.0, which is a platform for the transmission of knowledge (e.g. via the comment functions of online blogs), for the selling of one’s own goods, and the documentation of their production.

DIY skateboarding can be defined as the temporal and illegal appropriation and the physical and constructional modification of forgotten spaces in the city. While the playful negotiation of space, described as *détournement* before, particularly characterizes skate park and plaza skating, the constructional changes that skaters apply to their physical environment as determined by their own specific needs constitutes a distinctive characteristic of DIY skateboarding. German skateboarder Lennie Burmeister provides the following description of DIY skating:

> A DIY spot is built voluntarily and free of charge, out of pure self-motivation and in anticipation of enjoying the product. Creating a skateable space is often highly complex and sometimes illegal. These spots do, however, allow for more enjoyment because—as is the case for street skating—they have been given a new function. (quoted in Isenberg 44)

DIY skating has a strong physical-material dimension. It introduces a new component to the *détournement* of the practices of skateboarding: the skills for a hands-on modification of space. DIY skating is no longer only a practice of skateboarding in the narrower sense but also a manual modification of physical space and thus an active form of city-making. These constructional changes often happen at hidden and forgotten sites in the city. Skaters illegally appropriate them in order to create concrete landscapes they have designed themselves, often using building material (concrete, steel, padding) and tools they "found" in the direct vicinity.

DIY skating—similar to street skating—is initially based on the practical component of roaming in the city. Regardless of the extent of any necessary constructional measures, first of all, skaters have to find and discover a DIY spot. As such spots are seldom found on the public stages of urban centers, but rather need to be looked for in the hidden, secret, and overlooked sites of the city, skateboarders need to expose themselves to urban space in order to locate them. Such an approach is the only way to detect those neglected and forgotten wastelands, backyards, and abandoned properties that emerged after the postindustrial turn and have not been claimed by municipal revitalization programs or urban development projects and thus become possible DIY spots.

DIY skating depends on the possession of a DIY-specific "sense of place" (cf. Tuan). Skateboarders do not only need a sense for the physical and social qualities of an eventual spot but also have to imagine the latent skate-potential that can be activated by constructional interventions. After mastering the complex challenge of locating an adequate DIY spot, skaters have to develop a concrete idea and plan for its design and the accompanying building work. Such endeavors follow the rule: the more construction and manual labor necessary, the more careful the choice of spot must be. This choice is based on a consideration of any neighbors, the existence of water connections, and the availability of the required material. The building process itself then does not follow an architectural master plan, but rather relies on creative ideas and the spontaneous step-by-step solution of problems as they occur. In this context, it is possible to identify two forms of constructional interventions by skaters: "minimal-invasive-DIY" and the creation of so-called "homemade spots" (Peters, *Skateboarding* 160–62). In minimal-invasive-DIY skating, which bears great resemblance to customary street skateboarding, skaters only apply minor constructional changes to urban space. They might enhance a public bench with a metal ledge or fill a hole in the street with cement. The material intervention remains very small and hardly visible, so that it can easily occur in the public realm of the city. Minimal-invasive-DIY skating therefore differs from skating at so-called "self-made spots." These spots only become skateable after massive constructional changes that can take months or even years. Skateboarders illegally appropriate these hidden and forgotten urban sites in order to develop ideas and plans for their material transformation and their skate-specific valorization. This quite often results in the construction of entire DIY parks that become important attractions for the skaters of a whole city.

Skateboarders illegally appropriate hidden and forgotten urban sites.

An aura of authenticity, the allure of the adventurous, the thrill of the illegal, and the social coherence of the whole situation accompany the physical opportunities of DIY spots. One of Germany's best-known DIY spots was the so-called Ghettospot in Frankfurt. Tireless Frankfurt locals illegally built it on private property near the city center. Four years after its creation, however, much to the skaters' chagrin, the spot had to be vacated in 2011 due to the actions of its direct neighbors. Other popular "self-made spots" in Germany are Betonhausen in Berlin, 2er in Hannover, and Rote Flora in Hamburg (cf. Gilligan).

Ephemerality is a central characteristic of the "intentionally dilettante freestyle architecture" of DIY spots (Müller, "Informelles Gärtnern" 19). Regardless of how much effort and time the participating skaters invest in the construction of a spot, it usually remains illegal and thus temporary.

The frequent building of new spots as a component of the practice of DIY skating integrates an entirely new spectrum of manual and constructional competence into skateboard culture. In light of this development, skate magazines not only discuss kickflips and board designs, but also cover scoops, the drying times of concrete, cladding, and cement mixers.

Skate magazines meet the high demand for constructional knowhow by regularly publishing specific building instructions and plans. Furthermore, magazines constantly propagate creative suggestions of how to enhance the city as a skateboarding playground in line with the DIY idea.

Nowadays, the originally entirely informal DIY skating has become so established within the cosmos of skateboarding that even official sponsors support the phenomenon. Companies follow a strategy that tries to incorporate the authentic, pristine, and noncommercial DIY skating in order to associate the accompanying attributes with their own brand essence.

Although DIY skating has been discovered by the commercial skateboard industry (which is now exploiting its goals), it still maintains an important and authentic role within the skateboard community. Skaters regard it as "core," which means that DIY belongs to the very essence of skateboarding. This fact can certainly also be attributed to the informal spatial knowledge that is only available to those involved in the construction work and that regulates access to the partly secret DIY spots and their location in industrial areas, wastelands, and the urban periphery. Photographer and artist Richard Gilligan consequently faced enormous difficulties just trying to find his way to interesting locations for his book *DIY* that documents the building of several DIY spots (cf. Gilligan):

> I discovered most of my locations after many hours of research and after talking to friends and acquaintances. Usually, I knew where I wanted to go but there were also sites that you would only discover if you met the right person by chance. For such incidents, you permanently have to be open and willing to start an unknown adventure. I made most discoveries through blogs, friends, or in skateboard magazines. (quoted in Irvine, "Ray of Sunshine" 129)

As a broadly established culture of human motion, skateboarding has been enmeshed in the social field of DIY from its early beginnings onward. It is no wonder that the ideals of hippies, punks, and riot grrrls also found expression in skateboard culture (cf. Butz for comments on the social figure of the skate punk; cf. Pavlidis for remarks on the riot grrrl movement of the

1990s). The recent DIY boom in skateboard culture thus does not have to be interpreted as a new phenomenon of a hitherto completely hedonistic and solely pop-oriented youth culture, but rather as a perpetuation of an always-existing tendency within the extremely heterogeneous practice of skateboarding.

Today's DIY skating is affiliated with former traditions of skateboarding such as the construction of ramps and the popular idea of so-called "homemade ramps" or "no budget ramps" (Krosigk and Tscharn 115–37). But what exactly are the factors behind the current DIY boom within skateboard culture?

DIY-Skateboarding and City-Making

Because of its culturally and economically expanding relevance during the last decades, skateboarding has become more and more established within the cultural mainstream. Today, we can find skateboard communities and skate shops in almost any city of the "Western world" (i.e. any city that is influenced by the Western world). This development is accompanied by the emergence of municipal defense strategies against skateboarding that often lead to the construction of skate-specific sites. As a consequence, the socio-spatial segregation of skating and processes of social regulation parallel the cultural establishment of skateboarding. The practices of DIY skating react against these forms of control. They emphasize the individualism and originality of skateboarding. Thus, DIY skating, at least to a certain extent, constitutes a return of skateboarding from the cultural mainstream of skate parks and plazas to the social niche of a subculture. DIY skating virtually articulates the skateboard scene's desire for exclusive community formation and the reversion to the "traditional values" of skateboard culture.

The cultural establishment of skating went hand in hand with its constantly increasing commercialization. Older and more experienced skaters in particular started to comment on this development in a highly critical way: "Too much commerce, not enough skating," became the tenor of the scene after the turn of the millennium. Reacting to this lament, the nascent DIY skating movement started to convey and revitalize feelings of freedom and the authenticity of the street. It can be regarded as a disengagement of skating from the logics and mechanisms of the (skateboard) market (Peters, *Skateboarding* 166–68).

The increasing globalization of skateboarding—including travels to the ever-popular skate cities of Barcelona, Los Angeles, and New York City and the homogenizing media influence on the perpetuation of an ideal style—caused skaters to long for local experiences and autonomous aestheticizations of the immediate environment. DIY skating responds to this desire by providing local retreats that are exclusively reserved for the core scene and can be fully arranged and designed by the skaters themselves. Skaters have the opportunity to feel more exclusive, to define their subcultural affiliations more sharply, and to escape the arbitrariness of the mainstream.

The current DIY activities within skateboard culture can be seen as a countermovement to the ever-progressing culturalization, commercialization, and globalization of skateboarding; DIY basically represents the re-subculturalization of skateboarding. The spots that first come into being through skaters' constructional interventions are thus not merely skate spots; they also come to represent specific types of social institutions or, in other words, politico-performative spaces of an "idiosyncratic habitat" (Werner 54). The work undertaken by skateboarders at these spots can be read as (I) work in a physical space, (II) work on the self, and (III) work with/through a collective: (I) DIY spots are often obtained through the temporal occupation and development of wastelands. These sites, after gradual and improvised appropriation and cultivation, change from forgotten non-places to attractive and appealing spaces. They oscillate between public and private, between desolate and lively, between irrelevant and functional, between exclusion and inclusion. (II) The work done at a specific spot does not only change the physical site itself but also alters the working subjects. "Doing it yourself" thus also becomes a form of "doing self." The skaters' engagement with space always constitutes a practice of subjectification and of social location. (III) Additionally, the intensive joint work on a site that is integrated into the local everyday lifestyle of skaters also fosters personal relationships and social contacts. Building a spot together brings about a mutual identity that is directly associated with the physical space. Despite the fact that their social features can also

DIY represents the re-subculturalization of skateboarding.

promote mechanisms of exclusion, DIY spots are thus strong collective spaces.

With its remarkably clear parallels to the urban gardening movement and similar phenomena such as "bottom-up urbanism" and the "city of Commonists" (cf. Baier, Müller, and Werner; Rauterberg), DIY skating involves a more urbanistic approach, and it also represents a search for innovative forms of urban governance, including finding new modes of political participation for citizens. Especially in times of public debt and constantly shrinking resources for municipal administration and urban development, DIY skating generates promising potential. The self-initiative of skaters who want to help fashion their city by building skate sites and spots themselves appears particularly valuable. In view of popular models of urban planning such as the "sustainable city" (Dangschat) or the "creative city" (Florida), it could be economically advantageous for municipalities to enhance their planning processes by incorporating the ideas and willingness of skaters to actively and physically participate in the fashioning of urban space. The first legalized DIY spots in cities such as Liverpool in England, Hannover and Berlin in Germany, and Malmö in Sweden already point in that direction. Malmö, the home town of skateboarder and DIY activist Pontus Alv, became known as a skate city all over Europe because of the city administration's liberal attitude toward illegally built DIY spots (cf. Irvine, "Go to Town").

Malmö-style official recognition of the DIY competence of the skateboard community and its productive integration into the official planning processes of the city administration seems much more widespread and realistic now than it did only a few years ago. The positive experiences the city administration of Cologne had with the building of the street plaza Kap 686 or the realization of the skate sculpture 1000 Plateaus in Berlin support this estimation. They prove that informal sports can become relevant location factors that positively influence urban development within a city. The efforts of the city administration of Munich to legalize river surfing on the Eisbach in the Englischer Garten are exemplary in this respect; in recent years, the Eisbach surfers have become one of the most popular tourist attractions in the city (cf. Peters, "Großstadt-Surfen"). Despite such examples and although the cultural potential of skateboarding has been increasingly recognized during the recent past, its full and official approval and acceptance still seem a long way off.

Skateboarding as a Collaborative City Practice in DIY Urbanism
An increasing number of apologists of urban processes in the wake of the writings of theorist Richard Florida claim that creativity and its accompanying "magic ingredients" (Baurmann 28) of art, fashion, film, and music play a decisive role in the future economic development of cities. If they are right, urban movements such as skateboarding or street art represent a strong cultural avant-garde acknowledged by municipal and economic politics. Skateboarders, street artists, and urban gardening activists thus become trendsetters who generate the crucial impulses for the positive development of a city.

By using the city beyond the functions intended by architects, urban planners, and administrations, skaters educe cultural potential from urban spaces that would otherwise remain invisible and unused. In this sense, skaters are spatial pioneers of an urban creative economy that carefully explores overlooked vacancies and temporary wastelands in order to valorize them as "secondhand spaces." They are among the protagonists of the many movements that are currently employing various different methods to appropriate public space and claim a "right to the city" for everyone.

The cultural practice of DIY enhances skateboarding and its spatial and symbolic potential with a dimension that also directly challenges the physical structures of the city. Through DIY skateboarding, skaters actively, autonomously, and manually contribute to the fashioning of urban space. As artists and activists, skateboarders *make* the city. They are protagonists of a do-it-yourself urbanism that explores the conditions and relations between citizens, city administrations, and urban planning. Skateboarders thus become agents of a collaborative city development, and their four-wheeled movement gives rise to a far wider process of change.

References

Baier, Andrea, Christa Müller, and Karin Werner. *Stadt der Commonisten. Neue urbane Räume des Do it yourself*. Bielefeld: Transcript, 2011. Print.

Bale, John. "Sport and Landscape." *Sport and Space. New Challenges to Planning and Architecture. Proceedings of a European Conference*. Ed. Søren Riiskjaer. Copenhagen: Council of Europe, 1992. 64–71. Print.

Baurmann, Jana Gioia. "Bum Bum Bares." *Die Zeit*, August 27 (2015): 28. Print.

Borden, Iain. *Skateboarding, Space and the City: Architecture and the Body*. Oxford/New York: Berg, 2001. Print.

Bund, Kerstin. "Das Gewicht der Liebe." *Die Zeit* September 15 (2011): 20. Print.

Butz, Konstantin. *Grinding California. Culture and Corporeality in American Skate Punk*. Bielefeld: Transcript, 2012.

Chiu, Chihsin. "Contestation and Conformity: Street and Park Skateboarding in New York City Public Space." *Space and Culture* 12.1 (2009): 25–42. Print.

Coverley, Merlin. *Psychogeography*. Harpenden: Pocket Essentials, 2010.

Dangschat, Jens. "Sustainable City - Nachhaltige Zukunft für Stadtgesellschaften." *Nachhaltige Entwicklung. Eine Herausforderung an die Soziologie*. Ed. Karl-Werner Brand. Opladen: Leske & Budrich, 1997. 169–94. Print.

Dörfler, Thomas. *Gentrification in Prenzlauer Berg. Milieuwandel eines Berliner Sozialraums seit 1989*. Bielefeld: Transcript, 2010.

Fitz, Angelika. "Die Stadt sind wir? Positionen eines kollaborativen Urbanismus." *Kulturpolitische Mitteilungen* 152.1 (2016): 37–39. Print.

Florida, Richard. *The Rise of the Creative Class. And How It's Transforming Work, Leisure and Everyday Life*. New York: Basic Books, 2002. Print.

Gilligan, Richard. *DIY*. Paris: 19/80 Éditions, 2012. Print.

Held, Sarah. "Knit happens. Subversive Handarbeit als Aktivismus." *Design Quartier Ehrenfeld Akademie* 2011, www.d-q-e.net/akademie/akademie-sarah_held.pdf. Accessed September 12, 2012.

Honer, Anne. "Heimwerker-Typen." *Do It Yourself: Die Mitmach-Revolution*. Eds. Helmut Gold et al. Mainz: Ventil-Verlag, 2011. 26–30. Print.

Hornung, Annabelle, Tine Novak, and Verena Kuni. "'Do It Yourself: Die Mitmach-Revolution.' Eine Einführung in die Ausstellung." *Do It Yourself: Die Mitmach-Revolution*. Eds. Helmut Gold et al. Mainz: Ventil-Verlag, 2011. 8–18. Print.

Howell, Ocean. "The Poetics of Security: Skateboarding, Urban Design, and the New Public Space." *UrbanPolicy.net*, 2001, http://bss.sfsu.edu/urbanaction/ua2001/ps2.html. Accessed August 15, 2011.

Howell, Ocean. "The Creative Class and the Gentrifying City: Skateboarding in Philadelphia's Love Park." *Journal of Architectural Education* 59.2 (2005): 32–42. Print.

Howell, Ocean. "Skatepark as Neoliberal Playground: Urban Governance, Recreation Space, and the Cultivation of Personal Responsibility." *Space and Culture* 11.4 (2008): 475–96. Print.

Irvine, Alex. "Ray of Sunshine. Neues von Rich Gilligan." *Kingpin Skateboarding Europe* 98 (2012): 128–29. Print.

Irvine, Alex. "Go to Town. Pontus Alv in Malmö." *Kingpin Skateboarding Europe* 98 (2012): 104–11. Print.

Isenberg, Niklas. "Sicht der Dinge: Park oder Straße? Skateboarding quo vadis?" *Monster Skateboard Magazin* 309 (2012): 44. Print.

Krosigk, Holger von, and Helge Tscharn. *Elements of Street Skateboarding. Streetstyle Book 2*. Stuttgart: Tropen, 2003. Print.

Lange, Bastian. *Die Räume der Kreativszenen. Culturepreneurs und ihre Orte in Berlin*. Bielefeld: Transcript, 2007. Print.

Lefebvre, Henri. *The Production of Space*. Malden, MA: Blackwell, 1991. Print.

Lefebvre, Henri. *Le droit à la ville*. Paris: Anthropos, 2009. Print.

Magistrat der Stadt Wien. *Do it yourself Stadtanleitung*. Vienna, 2016. Print.

Müller, Christa, ed. *Urban Gardening.* Über *die Rückkehr der Gärten in die Stadt*. 2nd ed. Munich: Oekom, 2011. Print.

Müller, Christa. "Informelles Gärtnern. Zur Freestyle-Architektur des Urban Gardening." *Bauwelt* 103.39 (2012): 16–19. Print.

Pavlidis, Adele. "From Riot Grrrls to Roller Derby? Exploring the Relations Between Gender, Music and Sport." *Leisure Studies* 31.2 (2012): 165–76. Print.

Peters, Christian. "Großstadt-Surfen in München – Der Film 'Keep Surfing' illustriert den Strukturwandel des Sports." *sportunterricht* 60 (2011): 135–40. Print.

Peters, Christian. *Skateboarding. Ethnographie einer urbanen Praxis*. Münster: Waxmann, 2016. Print.

Rauterberg, Hanno. *Wir sind die Stadt! Urbanes Leben in der Digitalmoderne*. Berlin: Suhrkamp, 2013. Print.

Reinecke, Julia. *Street-Art. Eine Subkultur zwischen Kunst und Kommerz*. 2nd ed. Bielefeld: Transcript, 2012. Print.

Schwanhäußer, Anja. *Kosmonauten des Underground. Ethnographie einer Berliner Szene*. Frankfurt/Main: Campus-Verlag, 2010. Print.

Terkessidis, Mark. *Kollaboration*. Berlin: Suhrkamp, 2015. Print.

Tuan, Yi Fu. *Topophilia: A Study of Environmental Perception, Attitudes and Values*. New York: Columbia University, 1990. Print.

Vivoni, Francesco. "Spots of Spatial Desire – Skateparks, Skateplazas and Urban Politics." *Journal of Sport and Social Issues* 33.2 (2009): 130–49. Print.

Vivoni, Francisco. *Contesting Public Space: Skateboarding, Urban Development and the Politics of Play*. Dissertation, University of Illinois at Urbana-Champaign, 2010. Print.

Werner, Katrin. "Eigensinnige Beheimatungen. Gemeinschaftsgärten als Orte des Widerstands gegen die neoliberale Ordnung." *Urban Gardening.* Über *die Rückkehr der Gärten in die Stadt*. 2nd ed. Ed. Christa Müller. Munich: Oekom, 2011. 54–75. Print.

ZáNean McClain, E. Missy Wright, Becky Beal, and Matthew Atencio

Adult Stakeholders' Perceptions and Practices of Gender Inclusion in Skateboarding

Although skateboarding has a reputation as an alternative sport emphasizing participant control and democratic decision-making, it has been well documented that females are still greatly underrepresented in this activity. Several scholars have examined this phenomenon and identified various factors that impact female accessibility and acceptance in skateboarding. Many of these are based in deeply held sexist beliefs that males are more authentic participants because they are stronger, more athletic, and more inclined to take physical risks (Atencio et al. 3–9; Kelly et al., "You Can Break So Many More Rules" 119–27; Laurendeau 296–301). Several researchers have documented how female skateboarders negotiate this male-centered practice

(Bäckström 29–34; Kelly et al., "Skater Girlhood" 229–33; Porter 75–79; Young and Dallaire 235–39), while others have examined skateboarding's gendered media representations (Rinehart 241) as well as industry practices (Beal and Wilson 34).

We complement this existing research on the male-centeredness of skateboarding by examining the perceptions and practices of adult stakeholders who organize skateboard park activities in regard to women's place in skateboarding. Scholars have highlighted the prominent role that adult staff and coaches occupy in public recreation spaces, specifically in structuring codes of inclusion and identity (Cooky 264–66; Donnelly and Coakley 16). We concomitantly suggest that this line of inquiry is paramount because the vast majority of skateboarding in the United States takes place outside of formal educational institutions, and is therefore not necessarily under the auspices of Title IX, which reduces the role government has in overseeing gender equity within this activity. Unlike in Canada or in many European countries that have federal government programs that intentionally utilize sport for gender equity and inclusion (e.g., Kelly 138; Maxwell et al. 467), the United States leaves the role of inclusion in community sport largely up to local municipalities and private parties. In this latter context, Coakley suggests that prevailing neoliberal policies, aligned with global corporate capital, have now enabled private interests to greatly influence sport and recreation in public spaces (313–20). And while public skate parks in the United States are often operated by city or regional municipalities, there is an increasing trend whereby private and corporate interests influence their design, events, and policies (Howell 476–81). We thus argue that examining adults' roles in skate parks is crucial because these individuals operate as private interests who determine life in public recreation spaces.

Under this broader contextualization, we explore the micropolitics found within particular locations by examining how and why various adult stakeholders invest in specific local parks. Specifically, this chapter examines whether and in what ways adult stakeholders may have practiced gender inclusion within their conceptualization of individual and community development. We demonstrate how adult stakeholders have influenced the climate of skate parks in regard to the structuring of opportunities for girls and the implications of their practices.

In our project, we discerned that there were numerous skate park groups not officially affiliated with the community parks and recreation departments. These groups included volunteer neighborhood coalitions, not-for-profit groups, independent contractors, and multinational corporations that programmed, guided, and regulated the spaces and practices of public skate parks; this public-private mixture of urban youth sports stakeholders has been described elsewhere as the phenomenon of "social enterprise" which is currently prominent under neoliberal conditions (Atencio et al., *Moving Boarders*). This chapter specifically focuses on four key adult stakeholders representing those groups who had formal roles in running skateboard programs or overseeing skate parks in two different cities within the San Francisco Bay Area. We have been deeply immersed in these two skate parks for over three and a half years. Multiple formal and informal interviews were conducted with each of the four adults and jointly the researchers observed over 140 hours at these parks in order to ascertain key social dynamics as they pertained to gender inclusion and interaction.

It is important to note that the concept of social inclusion is complex and contested, frequently leading to different practices (Kelly 143; Ponic and Frisby 1523). For this analysis, we use Donnelly and Coakley's framework to help identify several facets and practices of gender inclusion (8–9 most specifically). Some of the key elements identified in their framework are: providing opportunities to display competence, creating viable social networks, creating a sense of acceptance, and ensuring that females have a position of power where their voices matter and can impact policy. Addressed below are the adult stakeholders' goals and motivations for being involved in skateboarding and promoting girls' participation. Furthermore, we reveal the strategies these adults used to promote female inclusion in skateboarding.

Findings

Bay City Skate Park: Jane, Mike, and the Bay City Skate Park Group (BCSPG)

The Bay City Skate Park[1] (BCSP) was recently constructed and is located in a large and solidly middle-class suburb of the San Francisco Bay Area. It was financed by municipal funds and is directly managed by the city's Parks and Recreation Department. Like many other newer iterations of skate parks in the United States, the impetus to build this spot came from community members who advocated for a safe place for their children to skate. These community members eventually formed a group, the Bay City Skate Park Group (BCSPG), and continue to be very active in developing the culture of the skate park. Their mission is clearly noted on their Facebook page: "The Bay City Skate Park Group is a group of skaters, parents and community members who work with the City [...] to ensure our free, public skate park is safe, welcoming, and inclusive for skaters and their families." The BCSP is located within a city that has a median income of $108,000, while only 6% of the population lives in poverty. The three largest ethnic groups in the city are Asians (about 50%), Whites (about 24%), and Hispanics (about 13%) (California Demographics). While the BCSP was always intended to be completely funded by the city, several residents who lived near the site of the park still resisted it and delayed construction for several years. The main concern of these residents was that the skate park would attract deviant young males and, perhaps, reduce the value of their homes.

1 The names of this park, the city, and the adult organizers have been changed to protect anonymity and therefore no direct web page has been provided for the key descriptions.

We talked with two of the leaders of this group: Jane, who is the coordinator of the group, and Mike who is a skateboard instructor. Jane became involved with the BCSPG because her son was a skater and she wanted to have a safe space for him to skate with his friends. She also runs the group's Facebook page where information about future events and public interest stories are shared. Mike is a former professional skateboarder, and is also a middle-aged father of a young boy. Mike became involved with the BCSPG because he wanted to help create both a "healthy" and a "family-friendly" skate environment.

Indeed, we have visited the Bay City Skate Park many times and have observed that the park is mainly used by males, even though there is a wide variety of ages (4–50+ years old), and usage appears to reflect the city's ethnic makeup, with White, Asian, and Hispanic individuals regularly frequenting the park. Jane and Mike are definitely committed to having females taking up a significant presence in the park. This appreciation of females translates into active programming for girls through regular events. Jane works with social activist groups such as the Girls Riders Organization (GRO) and Skate Like a Girl (SLAG), for instance, and Mike organizes skateboarding camps which girls frequently attend. In this regard, Jane once commented that "everybody's here [...] You have girls, that's something that's really important to me, having girls and women." Mike subsequently expressed his approval and pride in the Bay City Skate Park's female participation rates:

> There's definitely a great girl presence. We probably have about six to eight locals that are consistently at the park of girls and then we have maybe about twenty, twenty-five young teenage or a little older girls that come for the different events or different programs like GRO. (Girl Riders Organization)

While Jane and Mike suggest that there is a healthy presence of girls, our observations reveal a different reality. That is, we typically observe only three to four females skating regularly, unless there is a special event for girls; in these events we have seen up to twenty female participants. During these events, they tend to use the sections of the skate park near the front parking lot where beginners often congregate, as many of them are new skaters; they very rarely venture to the back of the skate park where older males and a few younger ones utilize the deep pool bowl. Our findings thus indicate that these adults' dedication to increasing gender inclusion has not completely translated into equitable participation for females within the skate park on a daily basis.

We typically observe only three to four females skating regularly.

Motivations for Including Females

The BCSPG primarily aims to create an inclusive "family-friendly" space, which translates into creating an environment in which newcomers of all ages feel welcomed. In this way, females are not singled out as the only traditionally excluded social group. Neither Jane nor Mike discussed their motivations for including girls as a direct response to sexism they had experienced or witnessed; instead, their motivation stemmed from their appreciation for skate culture's emphasis on an open community that fosters individuality and creativity. They were imbued with this desire to provide this type of physical activity experience to all children. For example, Jane noted:

> Yeah, well I gravitated toward skateboarding because I just really admire the culture, I guess. I do. It's about setting a goal and then just committing to it. I love the way they cheer each other on. When somebody does something really well, everybody's like "great, great, okay, great, now I'm going to figure out how to do that." It's just a great culture, I think. It's such an outlet for kids who maybe aren't as comfortable with organized sports.

Mike discussed the features of skateboarding that resonated strongly with him, stating that: "I think the elements of the creative aspects of it and the freedom and the challenges that are embedded in skateboarding is what kind of spoke to me." He subsequently expressed his desire to help mentor children to be healthy and committed to the positive aspects of skateboarding that he values from personal experience:

> Skateboarding culture in itself is broad. It is fragmented. It's not like we're all in it as one in one way in a culture. There's parts that I strongly disagree with in skateboard culture, like things that I don't like. I don't like anything that undermines a young person's healthy development, I don't like that [...] but the interest for me was how I could, I was always passionate about trying to mentor kids in such a way as to help them kind of avoid the pitfalls and mistakes I made in the past or others have made.

As noted in the next section, this motivation to be a positive mentor to youth, including girls, contributes to Bay City Skate Park's vision and even programming of a family-friendly space. In addition, we shall see below that maintaining a family-friendly skate park also meant controlling the perceived negative behaviors of young males that also used this space.

Goals and Strategies: Creating a Family Atmosphere, Programming for Girls, and Policing Males

One of the main issues the BCSPG faced while negotiating for the existence of the skate park was that local residents felt that a skate park would attract unruly (masculine) behavior. Skateboarders are typically positioned as rebellious young males (Brayton 363–65) and creating a park that is neither strictly regulated nor supervised increased concerns within the surrounding established neighborhood. Jane subsequently described how an underlying issue for many residents was the fear of young males congregating:

> [...] the main argument against building a public skate park is that people do not want too many young men gathered in one place for any reason, period. You're just scary. You can get past the noise and you can get past the traffic and the graffiti and it comes down to a fear [...] Maybe it's a primordial thing, but it's a fear of a lot of young 16 to 25-year-old males in one place, period, and so you've got to get past that.

To counter this underlying preconception, the BCSPG emphasized how the park would exist as a family-friendly environment while remaining inclusive, as noted by Jane in her interview with us: "We [Parks and Recreation] agreed to an open, free, public, family skate park. We're still working on that [and that] is what I'm saying." Consequently, one of the main strategies that has been enacted is the installment of "soft" control, which means having a range of community adults unofficially maintain the park culture, as noted below:

> People still smoke pot up on the hills and stuff like that, but the whole presence of parents, and more of a family atmosphere, just keeps those kinds of people out so we get serious skaters and people who just want to enjoy the park.

Mike also expressed his concern about the skate park when it was primarily inhabited and utilized by young males. He inferred that a more diverse demographic of users, including female clientele, would likely reduce unwanted behavior from young men.

More specifically, he identified the need for adult role models (rather than police) to control the park:

> Mike: When the girls are not there and when there's no one there, I think that's when there's our most challenging times.
>
> Interviewer: What do you mean when there's nobody there?
>
> Mike: When there's no one there, just the skaters there that are local that need that extra supervision, or they need to look up and see someone who they respect whether it's a ranger, or another professional, or an older skater.

Both Jane and Mike used the strategy of informal adult supervision to help create a social environment that would discourage behaviors such as bullying and drug use. In this way, they hoped to create a space that was "safe" and welcoming. The creation of an inviting environment by adult stakeholders has been discussed as a key social inclusion practice in the literature (Forde et al. 133), although a tension arises here because adults (instead of youths) set the standards of what constitutes acceptable behavior. This does not necessarily represent the inclusive practice of empowering youth by giving them responsibility to create codes of inclusion as well as to mitigate conflict, in their own ways. However, this type of adult intervention does open up space for girls to feel comfortable to learn skills that would sustain their skateboarding participation here and elsewhere. This tension was expressed by some parents of skateboarders at this park who sometimes shared concerns about how adults often set the standards for "appropriate" behavior. These parents were also concerned that some groups of kids could even become targeted and marginalized because of these standards.

Additionally, Jane and Mike noted that it was important to program activities specifically for girls in order to recruit them and maintain their involvement. As previously mentioned, Jane has worked with the local chapter of GRO to create girl sessions that focus on teaching skills and building camaraderie which are both key components of inclusion (Donnelly and Coakley 14). Mike has also developed skateboard camps solely for females.

He consequently highlighted the need to increase the female presence within this skate park, since he believed that individual girls in the park had a more difficult time engaging in skateboarding:

> [...] but I think once they get connected to the other girls in the park I think something special happens there where they kind of find their peer group amongst the girls, and it's pretty cool to see young little girls and the older girls come together and share skateboarding together and learn. So we need to do some more events there for girls. We need to do some more contests. We need to do some more programs to kind of celebrate that, but it's special.

In summary, the BCSPG supported a raft of adult-driven practices that were intended to create a family-friendly and healthy environment that was considered welcome to all parties. However, in practice, developing a family-friendly space meant that certain practices were utilized in order to identify and police young males' behaviors through consistent "soft" regulation. In our view, then, this regular focus on controlling masculine behaviors identified as negative becomes problematic because it privileges a specific type of acceptable skate identity and practice that could be marginalizing and exclusive to certain males that do not appear to "fit the mold." This facet of Bay City skateboarding therefore challenges the social inclusion concept. Overall, we believe that the most effective strategy implemented by the BCSPG was the development of girls' comfort and skill levels through event programming specifically aimed at increasing the presence and full participation of females. We will later highlight this type of regular female skate programming as utilized in another skate park we researched, Oakland's Town Park, which is described below.

Oakland's Town Park: Keith "K-Dub" Williams and Rob "Skate" Ferguson

Keith "K-Dub" Williams and Rob "Skate" Ferguson are two male adults within the local skateboarding scene who sometimes work with one another on skate park projects, as well as hosting various community events together across the Bay Area. Keith and Rob are dedicated to using skateboarding as a means of supporting youth development, as well as community organizing and engagement, often within communities such as Oakland where lower-income youth of color live and skate. Next, we discuss how both of these individuals seemed to utilize an open-door policy regarding the inclusion of females in skateboarding, although there were some differences in terms of how this occurred and even shifted over time. We also contend that more institutionalized and sustainable practices are required to overcome the barriers females face when entering the traditionally male activity of skateboarding, especially on an everyday basis.

Keith is a seasoned community organizer, who has a long history of skateboarding both as a practitioner and also as a leader dedicated to ensuring that youth of color have opportunities to grow and succeed through this activity. Keith was born and raised in Los Angeles, CA where he began skateboarding in the late 1970s. He is the cofounder and producer of Tha Hood Games, which originated in 2005–06 while he was head of a skateboard club, the O-High Playas, while teaching art at Oakland High School (Heckler). After noticing the diversity of the crowd at the X Games and not finding that same diversity represented in the participating skaters, Keith partnered with pro skater Karl Watson to create Tha Hood Games in order to bring quality community events to the inner city. Currently, Keith is closely associated with a skate park in de Fremery Park (this skate park is commonly known as Town Park) in Oakland, CA. The surrounding context of Oakland's Town Park skate park differs greatly from that of the Bay City Skate Park. Town Park is located in Oakland, where the median income is $54,000, with a poverty rate over three times as great as Bay City's, with nearly 20% of the population living in poverty. With respect to ethnic diversity in Oakland, the three largest groups, Hispanic, White, and Black, each represent about a quarter of the population (California Demographics).

Rob "Skate" Ferguson, known locally as "Rob Skate," is heavily involved in the local skateboarding scene. He can be found across various cities in the Bay Area, especially since his skate coaching company provides lessons in many local skate parks. He also sponsors competitions called the Cali Am Jam. As a self-proclaimed "industrialist," Rob consciously works to broaden his brand and thus is not directly committed to a particular city, although he does regularly support events and skateboarders at Oakland's Town Park.

Compared to the other leaders featured in this chapter, Rob has the most significant entrepreneurial history. As a teenager, he coached individuals in skateboarding and in his early twenties he founded his company, 4141Corp, an organization that fosters youth development through skateboarding. Rob views skateboarding as a valuable tool to keep young people active, and he also believes that this activity can teach them character values such as "perseverance and camaraderie." Rob told us that he is a mentor to youth in the local area, and that they ask him for various forms of advice. In this way, Rob says that he is viewed by the youth as a father figure or even a big brother. Rob further noted that he wanted to support the youth and their broader communities by providing skateboarding activities: "I'm pretty much the one that makes sure there's constant nourishment going on and there's constant events."

Motivations for Including Girls

Both Keith and Rob perceive that providing opportunities to children and youth is key. Meanwhile, they avoid "policing" activities which we saw with the BCSPG and other committed adults involved in regulating male behavior. Instead, both of these adult leaders follow more of an open-door or "build it and they will come" type of mentality. That is, both of these local adult males see skate parks as creating inclusive community skateboarding experience for *all* interested parties. As they seem to display an openness toward social inclusion, with an open-door approach, we also speculate below how they may or may not directly acknowledge the state or conditions of females within local skateboarding domains. While girl skaters were brought up in discussions about the local skate scene, the majority of their elaboration seemed to be geared toward supporting all local youth skateboarders, in a broader sense, as noted by Keith in this interview extract:

> This one (Town Park skate park) has a distinct culture and that's how, you know, I try to establish that culture because I'm the one that put it together so I might as well establish

> the culture. My whole thing is this is for the kids, you know. If they can't see themselves in it, then what? Because usually in skateboard culture you don't see yourself in it if you're from around here (Oakland, CA).

In addition, Keith and Rob further discussed the prevalence of girl and women skaters in the industries associated with skateboarding, acknowledging that girls can and do skate, and want to be a part of skate culture. Although skateboarding is typically seen as predominantly involving male participants and codes (Young and Dallaire 236), both men articulated that females were beginning to find their own space in skateboarding culture; they both discussed how the presence of females in skateboarding was increasing. Rob noted how things seemed to be changing at the local level: "There's a large following of girls in San Jose, CA. Then some other programs over in San Francisco, CA. It's just all-girl programs, too, as well. There's a whole club just for girls." Moreover, Keith stated how female skateboarding was especially increasing in other countries:

> Brazil, women skateboarders in Brazil are no joke. I mean they're winning everything around the world and they're just, you know, they're amazing. When you go to the X Games, in some of the bigger events they [women] seem to be pretty well represented around the world.

These comments signal how these two adult male organizers have taken notice of female skaters, and their presence from local to global levels. As well, both Rob and Keith understand that females are being incorporated into the skateboarding scene as beginners and even elite skaters.

In the next section, we will examine more closely the actual approaches used by Keith and Rob in order to include and benefit females through skateboarding. In essence, their strategies differed from one another, although both have had success in some ways. We suggest that both initially seemed to focus more broadly on providing opportunities for all youths (including both females and males) through their open-door approaches, foregoing explicit or systematic strategies for including females in local skate parks. This seemed to have limited impact on improving gender relations and inclusion. However, lately, there has been more explicit support for female skateboarders through regular social activist events and skate coaching programs, particularly as enacted by Keith in his role as the leader of Town Park.

Goals and Strategies: Situated and Strategic Approaches for Female Inclusion

Quite simply, we contend that these two leaders utilized different approaches when it came to female skateboarding. On the one hand, Keith exhibited what we consider to be a situated approach in creating opportunities for female skaters, whereas, on the other hand, Rob demonstrated a more strategic approach. This situated approach employed by Keith, particularly at the beginning of our study, involves an awareness of issues surrounding the inclusion of girls within the skate community whereby occasional efforts were made to include girls. In the quotation below, Keith makes reference to girl skaters in a male dominated space, suggesting that the industry does not market to female skaters, while females also made choices not to be involved in skateboarding:

The industry does not market to female skaters.

> You know, individually out here I've had girls come through for a minute and then they don't stay with it as long. Lately we're getting a lot of older girls, like ladies who are twenty-three to twenty-seven coming out. But for girls overall industry-wise it's just a market that's tough.

At the same time, Keith expressed the view that he did actually look for "shorties" in Town Park to be involved (Keith stated that "shorties" included young children, females, and those who were inexperienced). Early in our study, then, some of his comments and practices indicated that social inclusion occurred in a broader sense for all "shorties," rather than more specifically in terms of supporting the inclusion of girls. The following quote from Keith reflects this perspective.

> But I'm always going to look out for the shorties because I know how "aggro" some of the guys get. "Oh, you're in my way. You're in my run." I'm like, "Dude, tomorrow the contest won't be here, you can have the park all to yourself." Shorties get a chance to get out there.

Another example derived from a field observation further illustrates how Keith enacted a subjective and situational approach to supporting females in skateboarding. In one case, a fourteen-year-old female skater at a skateboarding event hosted in Town Park was noticed by Keith standing on the perimeter of the skate park and skating on the low ramps away from all the other participants in the skate park. When Keith noticed her he called the teenager over, pointed to a young woman skater on the other side of the skate park and told her to introduce herself to the young woman. From that point on, the teenager and the young woman skated the ramps, and it seemed that the teenager was being unofficially coached by this young woman. By the end of the event, the teenager was riding the large ramps and had built up her confidence to start showcasing her skills, demonstrating popular skate tricks. She eventually won a prize in the category of the most improved jump. This example highlights a preliminary instance of how Keith was gender inclusive, although this type of practice was not regularly observed until later on in our study, when he actually implemented some direct, systematic strategies to include females in a more sustained manner. Although the above case shows Keith's willingness to include girls in skateboarding, this earlier unsystematic approach could have had gaps when it came to incorporating female skaters, as seen in the next field note example:

> A young African-American woman was standing near the entrance of the skate park clearly nervous to move forward into the skate park. She was in plain sight to all people within the entrance area. Although visible to many organizers and participants, this young woman was not invited to enter into the skate park. Overall, just a few female skaters were at the skate park during this event, like at the last event we observed in Town Park, and Keith did not seek her out to involve her in any way (it is unknown if Keith was

aware of the young woman standing by the fence with a skateboard in her hand during the observation).

Taken together, these two key examples illustrate Keith's individualized approach to gender inclusion, which earlier in our study was unsystematic and dependent on the situation as well as his own subjective involvement. This contrasted with his later involvement with female skate activist groups such as the local SLAG chapter, an organization which regularly hosts skate sessions and other social events for females in order to promote a gender inclusive skate community. By 2016, Town Park was hosting regular SLAG female skate sessions which were promoted on social media and in the local skate scene by affiliate groups such as Mahfia.TV. This latter approach reflected a more institutionalized and sustainable approach that could be used to make structural changes for gender inclusion, at least during specified dates and times when events were held.

In comparison, Rob's approach to inclusion was systematic and strategic in the sense that he sought out females for his skate camps and lessons. However, this does not necessarily mean that these females could contest exclusive masculine practices, nor does it mean that females could skateboard without barriers on a more daily basis. We define this strategic approach as an approach whereby a person is aware that there are issues surrounding the inclusion of girls within the skate social community, which then leads to certain procedures being enacted to rectify this situation. Our definition here is predicated upon there being evidence of conscious effort in designing opportunities to enable knowledge and skill learning (Sheate and Parttidário 280–85). Indeed, during an interview, Rob pulled out his laptop to show the authors of this chapter various youth camps that he taught in which girls were often welcomed and present. The camp's promotional material featured skateboarding lessons involving both boys and girls. Rob expressed that he was intentionally creating a space for female skaters to learn and enjoy the skateboarding experience, which aligns with information provided on his skate academy website. Two further examples of this strategic approach can be seen in Rob's quotes below, regarding how he reaches out to girl skateboarders:

> Actually, I intentionally reach out to girls, but with the younger generation it is just becoming more and more popular amongst girls. I see a lot of girls that are definitely hungry to come out and skate. Every year, actually, I have tons of programs where it's almost 50/50 on having girls and guys.

Later in the interview, Rob talked about the practices he implemented when teaching kids in schools how to skateboard. On his laptop once again, Rob showed us a picture that highlighted his work in showcasing girl skaters, stating, "There was lots of girls and guys that were part of that program. It was good."

As demonstrated in the examples above, Keith's situated and Rob's strategic approaches may both work to allow for greater female inclusion within local skateboarding spaces, in some instances. Keith works in a "hands-on" manner and personally invites females into skate spaces, recognizing them when they are there. Yet this does not occur if he is oblivious to their presence or if he is engaged in other activities such as maintenance in the skate park, and so chooses not to approach females. This unsystematic practice could result in females being marginalized and excluded from skate parks without his direct knowledge or intervention. However, later on in our study, when SLAG began to host regular skate sessions for females in Town Park, led by female coaches, we could see the implementation of a more conscious and sustainable approach to female inclusion. This latter approach is without doubt more successful in promoting a state of gender inclusion when compared with Keith's earlier situated gender inclusion practices.

Rob's approach, offering camps and programs that recruit fee-paying children, is clearly strategic; both boys and girls are welcomed into these programs, and girls are acknowledged as a key demographic in the skate scene. At the same time, his Cali Am Jam skate event included no category addressing female competition specifically; indeed, one competition that we observed in a local skate park included only male skaters, and no girls skated even during the breaks. Given that gender was addressed only in the context of finite skate lessons and camps for girls (and boys, too), which of course led to financial gain, Rob's gender strategy seemed more market-oriented and came under his male presence and mentorship. This seems to indicate that dominant masculine codes, which often foster exclusive practices, were unaddressed both in everyday local skateboarding and in skate culture more generally. As Atencio and Beal have argued, the entrepreneurial motivation for capital gain in skateboarding does not necessarily address and foster sustainable socially inclusive practices, especially for females, as masculine codes remain in place ("Beautiful Losers" 2–13).

In summary, we have highlighted how Keith and Rob are both advocates in promoting skateboarding to positively engage their local communities and encourage the personal development of skaters, especially in youth of color. Their various gendered practices reflected limited situated and strategic approaches, as well as perhaps more substantial and interventionist ways of supporting female skateboarders, as we saw later with Keith's involvement in SLAG sessions at Town Park. We conclude this section by suggesting that without an explicit and sustainable strategy that directly addresses the needs of females and the barriers that they consistently encounter, regular inclusion of females can be inconsistent and short-lived. Meanwhile, the overarching masculine codes and exclusion mechanisms underpinning skateboarding remain in place.

Discussion

It is evident, from the interviews and observations, that the adults in our study were sincere and committed to using skateboarding to support youth and, by extension, their local communities. Without doubt, these adults expended significant time and energy to create environments in skate parks that would sustain this type of youth and community development. What we found compelling were their different assumptions about which groups of youth needed support and, accordingly, which forms this support eventually took in both of these skate parks. Below we will discuss how the agendas and practices of the adult stakeholders described above were profoundly influenced by their specific local contexts. We argue that the stakeholders' unique locations and socioeconomic contexts directly framed the scope of how females could be included within skate parks. In so doing, our work seeks to demonstrate the significant influence of local contextual factors that may provide for the proliferation of diverse gendered practices in youth cultures.

As noted previously, Jane and the BCSPG had to persuade local naysayers who were opposed to building the park due to fears about potential anti-social behaviors and reduction in housing values. Jane and her supporters thus had to demonstrate how their proposed skate park was in fact beneficial to the local community. As such, they explicitly proposed that they would create a seemingly socially inclusive "family-friendly" skate park. This meant that the BCSPG had to walk a fine line between targeting and perhaps problematizing young males as part of creating an inclusive and acceptable social environment. Instead of labeling all young male skateboarders as potentially criminal, which would have required a fenced-in and formally monitored park, they decided to simply enhance the local adult presence to dissuade what was considered unruly behavior. Simultaneously, the BCSPG purposefully created programs to cater to girls and newcomers in order to promote their vision of a "family-friendly" environment.

On the other hand, Town Park was created with very little formal support from the city of Oakland. The Parks and Recreation department provided Keith the blacktop space to operate. Yet, in fact, it was Keith, some local skateboarders, and private individuals and companies who built the wooden elements of the first iteration of the park. Levi Strauss and Company, makers of Levi's Jeans, funded the second iteration of Town Park, a permanent cement park, with a huge cash donation. Unlike BCSP, there was little or no concern from the local West Oakland community about Town Park negatively impacting the value of the neighborhood. Instead, it is Keith's contention that the skate park can add value to the local neighborhood, an idea that has been supported by the city of Oakland, as well as by local neighborhood supporters and businesses. Importantly, Keith believes the park can add local value by providing young people of color a space in which they have access to mentorship and can learn a variety of skills. Thus, in the context of Oakland and the socioeconomic realities facing its youth, it is understandable that Keith's focus is to bring young people of color, who often tend to be males, together in a supportive mentoring environment. This context is quite different from the community conditions and needs of the BCSP, and we can see this divergence in the subsequent actions of Jane and Mike.

We also see differences pertaining to perceptions of what keeps a skate park from being inclusive. In the case of the BCSP, it appears that an individual's "deviant" behavior was identified as the key barrier to inclusive skateboarding, and therefore adults needed to be present in order to help regulate youth in that space. In a different skate context, Rob spoke regarding the development of an inclusive skateboarding community as it relates to youths' sense of self-ownership and regulation within the skate park: "If you are engaged with your community then you know what's going on and you're only going to want positive reinforcement within it."

Ideas pertaining to structural inequalities were mentioned more by Keith than by any of the other adults that we interviewed. Keith felt that the lack of infrastructure and opportunities in Oakland was a key problem for youths, a structural issue so to speak, and thus he focused on creating and maintaining a space that provided not just recreational opportunities, but also skills that would be useful within the local economy. Likewise, Rob noted that, through his coaching programs and community events, he took on a mentorship role primarily for young men of color. While he extends his mentorship to females who participate in his private lessons and camps, he does not proactively involve them in the broader skateboarding scene in a more fundamental way. Doing so would require more structural practices such as ensuring that his skate competition series, which overwhelmingly end up showcasing urban males of color and their abilities, include girl divisions and award winners, and not just age brackets open to all. This approach to gendered inclusion is more hands-off and puts the onus to participate on individual females, as indicated by Keith in this next statement: "The little girl with the scooter coming right there. If they want to go in, if she wants to go in then she can." However, Keith's vision seems to have shifted over the past two years, as Town Park has been much more proactive in promoting youth development for females, particularly through the use of SLAG skate sessions that are now promoted and hosted on a regular basis. We discuss the implications of this type of regular female skate event below, as this type of environment was also present in BCSP.

The BCSPG, as a community organization of local adults, has always been influential in the operation of BCSP. And this group has always been systematic and purposeful about its inclusion of females as part of its family-friendly mission. These adults thus intentionally promoted and recruited girls to special events, providing regular skill-learning opportunities designed for females. This provided females with a sense of empowerment and ownership of the park, and also fostered a temporary environment in which social relationships and friendships amongst women and girls were developed.

Adult leaders in skateboarding should identify mechanisms of exclusion.

Overall, we believe that the female-centered opportunities created by Jane and Mike by utilizing groups such as GRO and SLAG are vital for nurturing inclusive spaces for females, even on a short-term basis. As noted by Cooky, this practice of directly targeting and recruiting girls is critical in addressing females' engagement in sport and physical activity (268). We argue that creating an open environment in which females can skateboard without any other explicit or institutionalized strategies to involve them equates to a problematic open-door policy that has been described before by Cooky (259–78). In her study of Los Angeles area community sport programs designed to attract young women of color, she acknowledged that this policy of simply providing an open space for them to participate is not enough to attract and retain them.

Knowing about the societal contexts in which exclusionary practices lead to barriers for those underrepresented in youth sports is key for adult leaders (Hayes and Killingley 69). In their chapter on promoting inclusive practices for sport coaches, these authors noted the impact coaches can have on youth engagement by challenging barriers and stereotypes related to gender. We therefore suggest that adult leaders in skateboarding should identify mechanisms of exclusion that impact upon female skateboarders, and subsequently implement targeted gendered practices that would benefit them. Indeed, as many scholars have noted (e.g. Coakley 310; Cooky 263; Bean et al. 4; Hartmann and Kwauk 286), creating inclusive sport spaces for females goes beyond simply providing structural opportunities, as it also requires targeted strategies within these structures to consistently develop sustainable and supportive spaces for females so that they are empowered to participate in, and eventually influence, their youth sport contexts. Yet looking ahead, it still remains to be seen how regular event programming for females, which we saw in both BCSP and Town Park, will actually translate into everyday changes in masculine skate culture.

Conclusion

The four adults that we observed leading these two skate parks had diverse views with regard to general practices of social inclusion. While these adult leaders were seemingly invested in a vision of inclusive youth sport, their practices took on many different forms with varying degrees of effectiveness. A broader concern here is that these attempts to install inclusive practices in skateboarding may not be sustainable, given that public parks are primarily relying on private groups or individuals to facilitate activities and programs. Indeed, we observed that many of the private individuals who have been supporting the skate parks do this work for free or for as long as their own child remains interested in skateboarding. And these leaders often stand alone as the sole champion of their skate program. It is thus not surprising that the burnout rate among these individuals can be high, as we witnessed, with constant turnover leading to disruption in the continuity of inclusive programs and practices. One key member of the BCSPG revealed to us that she is leaving due to the significant time and effort required. This supports Forde and colleagues' findings on the importance of inclusive programming having *numerous* staff champions, so that programs can remain viable in terms of leadership and program identity when key members leave (134).

At this stage, we argue that relying solely upon private individuals with good intentions is insufficient. Enhancing gender inclusion in skateboarding will also require educated and professional staff with appropriate awareness and expertise in this type of inclusion practice (Donnelly and Coakley 16). Furthermore, as Coakley has noted, inclusion is an ongoing process that needs to be contextualized and grounded in the community's needs (Coakley personal communication), with inclusive programs that demonstrate a willingness to adapt based on the needs of those involved (Forde et al. 127). Essentially, creating ongoing dialogue with all constituencies involved and sustaining processes of democratic decision-making is a continual, necessary, and perhaps messy process; this can be problematic for private stakeholders who are often volunteers or entrepreneurs and thus not specifically trained in these areas. And, looking ahead, we agree with Donnelly and Coakley that systematic, reproductive mechanisms are required in order to locate and train more leaders who will support a vision of inclusive youth sport practice (15).

We conclude by drawing upon Rauscher and Cooky, who argue that youth sport focusing on positive development still tends to emphasize "the individual and the immediate context of girls' lives" which may serve to obscure "larger systems of inequality and privilege" (288). They further suggest that ignoring the broader contexts of social exclusion allows entrenched systems of oppression to remain in place. The upshot here is that girls in skateboarding (or any marginalized youth sport group) need to be educated and aware of social constraints such as patriarchy and sexism that filter down to daily practice. If these constraints are not addressed, then the default is the neoliberal assumption that individuals alone are responsible for leveraging their own skills in order to successfully participate in skateboarding. By contrast, we argue that it is the responsibility of communities and a range of public and private actors to develop institutionalized practices and programs that will support the inclusion of young women and men in skateboarding.

References

4141Corp. *About 4141Corp*. January 1, 2014, http://www.4141corp.com/about.html. Accessed July 28, 2014.

Atencio, Matthew, and Becky Beal. "Beautiful Losers: The Symbolic Exhibition and Legitimization of Outsider Masculinity." *Sport in Society: Cultures, Commerce, Media, Politics* 14.1 (2011): 1–16. Print.

Atencio, Matthew, Becky Beal, and Charlene Wilson. "Distinction of Risk: Urban Skateboarding, Street Habitus, and the Construction of Hierarchical Gender Relations." *Qualitative Research in Sport and Exercise* 1 (2009): 3–20. Print.

Atencio, Matthew, Becky Beal, Missy Wright, and ZáNean McClain. *Moving Boarders: The Changing Landscape of Urban Youth Sports.* Fayetteville, AR: University of Arkansas Press. 2018. Print.

Bäckström, Asa. "Gender Manoeuvring in Swedish Skateboarding: Negotiations of Femininities and the Hierarchical Gender Structure." *Young* 21 (2013): 29–53. Print.

Beal, Becky, and Charlene Wilson. "'Chicks Dig Scars': Transformations in the Subculture of Skateboarding." *Understanding Lifestyle Sports: Consumption. Identity, and Difference*. Ed. Belinda Wheaton. London: Routledge Press, 2004. 31–54. Print.

Bean, Corliss, Tanya Forneris, and Tanya Halsall. "Girls Just Wanna Have Fun: A Process Evaluation of a Female Youth-Driven Physical Activity-Based Life Skills Program." *SpringerPlus* 3.401 (2014): 1–15. Print.

Brayton, Sean. "'Black-lash': Revisiting the 'White Negro' Through Skateboarding." *Sociology of Sport Journal* 22 (2005): 356–72. Print.

California demographics. 2014, http://www.california-demographics.com/. Accessed July 15, 2015.

Coakley, Jay. "Youth Sports: What Counts as 'Positive Development'?" *Journal of Sport and Social Issues* 35.3 (2011): 306–24. Print.

Cooky, Cheryl. "'Girls Just Aren't Interested': The Social Construction of Interest in Girls' Sport." *Sociological Perspectives* 52.2 (2009): 259–83. Print.

Donnelly, Peter, and Jay Coakley. *The Role of Recreation in Promoting Social Inclusion*. Toronto: Laidlaw Foundation, 2002. Print.

Forde, Shawn D., Donna S. Lee, Cathy Mills, and Wendy Frisby. "Moving Towards Social Inclusion: Manager and Staff Perspectives on Award Winning Community Sport and Recreation Program for Immigrants." *Sport Management Review* 18 (2015): 126–38. Print.

Girls Riders Organization. *About GRO. Inspire, Educate & Support Girls Through Action Sports*. 4 March (2013), http://girlsriders.org/?page_id=2. Accessed September 12, 2014.

Hartmann, Doug, and Christina Kwauk. "Sport and Development: An Overview, Critique, and Reconstruction." *Journal of Sport and Exercise Psychology* 35.3 (2011): 284–305. Print.

Hayes, Sid, and Tracy Killingley. "Inclusive Practice in Sport Coaching." *Becoming a Sports Coach*. Eds. James Wallis and John Lambert. Abindgon, UK: Routledge, 2015. 69–82. Print.

Heckler. "Town Park in Oakland." *Heckler Magazine*, October 27, 2012, http://www.heckler.com/town-park-in-oakland. Accessed August 15, 2014.

Howell, Ocean. "Skatepark as Neoliberal Playground: Urban Governance, Recreation, Space, and the Cultivation of Personal Responsibility." *Space and Culture* 11.4 (2008): 475–96. Print.

Kelly, Deidre, Shauna Pomerantz, and Dawn Currie. "Skater Girlhood and Emphasized Femininity: 'You Can't Land an Ollie Properly in Heels'." *Gender and Education* 17.3 (2005): 229–48. Print.

Kelly, Deidre, Shauna Pomerantz, and Dawn Currie. "'You Can Break So Many More Rules': The Identity Work and Play of Becoming Skater Girls." *Youth Culture and Sport: Identity, Power, and Politics*. Eds. Michael Giardina and Michelle Donnelly. New York: Routledge, 2008. 113–43. Print.

Kelly, Laura. "Social Inclusion Through Sports-Based Interventions?" *Critical Social Policy* 31.1 (2011): 126–50. Print.

Laurendeau, Jason. "Gendered Risk Regimes: A Theoretical Consideration of Edgework and Gender." *Sociology of Sport Journal* 25 (2008): 294–309. Print.

Ponic, Pamela, and Wendy Frisby. "Unpacking Assumptions about Inclusion in Community-Based Health Promotion: Perspectives of Women Living in Poverty." *Qualitative Health Research* 20.11 (2010): 1519–31. Print.

Porter, Natalie. "Female Skateboarders and Their Negotiation of Space and Identity." *Journal for Arts, Sciences, and Technology* 1 (2003): 75–80. Print.

Rauscher, Lauren, and Cheryl Cooky. "Ready for Anything the World Gives Her?: A Critical Look at Sports-Based Positive Youth Development for Girls." *Sex Roles* 7-8 (2016): 288–98. Print.

Rinehart, Robert. "'Babes & Boards: Opportunities in New Millennium Sport?" *Journal of Sport & Social Issues* 29 (2005): 232–55. Print.

Sheate, William, and Maria Rosário Partidário. "Strategic Approaches and Assessment Techniques: Potential for Knowledge Brokerage Towards Sustainability." *Environmental Impact Assessment Review* 30.4 (2010): 278–88. Print.

Skate Like A Girl. *About Skate Like a Girl: Vision, Mission & Values.* August 1, 2013, http://www.skatelikeagirl.com/about-us.html. Accessed September 12, 2014.

Young, Alana, and Christine Dallaire. "Beware*#! Sk8 at Your Own Risk: The Discourses of Young Females Skateboarders." *Tribal Play: Subcultural Journeys Through Sport*. Eds. Michael Atkinson and Kevin Young. Bingley: Emerald Group Publishing, 2008. 235–54. Print.

Iain Borden

Another Pavement, Another Beach *Skateboarding and the Performative Critique of Architecture*[1]

"Transform the world"—all well and good. It is being transformed. But into what? Here, at your feet, is one small but crucial element in that mutation. (Lefebvre, *Introduction to Modernity* 126)

Considering the city means not only thinking about ways of knowing it, but also contemplating the fact that the city will always in part remain unknown to us. One such zone of the unknown is not geographic or social, but temporal: the future. Given that we can barely begin to understand the present, and that our world is full of hesitancies and contradictions, how can we even begin to know how the urban will be constituted next year, next decade, or next millennium? While the answer is, of course, that we cannot know such things, we can still try to glimpse, prefigure or even affect the way the future unknown city might operate. Such actions should then not project into the future a finite and

1 This essay was first published in *The Unknown City: Contesting Architecture and Social Space*. Eds. Iain Borden et al. Massachusetts and London: MIT Press, 2002. 178–99. [The editors]

definitive model, a kind of *a priori* decision taken on behalf of our future selves, but should be, following Lefebvre above, a direction, a tendency and, above all, at once theoretical and practical. Furthermore, this combination of the theoretical and the practical does not necessarily mean a schism between the two, a juncture in which each term ultimately remains separate from the other. On the contrary, we must invoke a dialectic of the two such that "[l]anguage and the living word are components of a praxis," resisting the fetishization of language in order to "go beyond the active word, to find, to discover—to create—what is yet to be said" (5).

This chapter explores a particular urban practice—that of skateboarding—for its implicit yet continuous tendency to critique contemporary cities for their meanings and modes of operation, and to prefigure what a future unknown city might be.

> Skating is a continual search for the unknown. (Gayle)

The abstract space of capitalism harbors many contradictions, not the least being the simultaneous dissolution of old relations and generation of new relations; as such, abstract space is destined not to last forever, and already contains the birth of a new space within itself, Lefebvre's putative *differential space* in which socio-spatial differences are emphasized and celebrated (Lefebvre, *Production of Space* 52, 352–400). Skateboarding, I propose, is a critical practice, challenging of both the form and political mechanics of urban life, and so in its own small way is part of this birth of differential space. Through an everyday practice—neither a conscious theorization nor a codified political program—skateboarding suggests that pleasure rather than work, use values rather than exchange values, activity rather than passivity are potential components of the future, as yet unknown city.

Zero-Degree Architecture

During the 1970s and early 1980s, skateboarders first undertook a series of spatial appropriations, rethinking the suburban drive as ocean surf, taking over schoolyards and drained swimming pools, and, in the purpose-built skate parks, producing a super-architectural space in which body, skateboard, and terrain were brought together and recomposed in an extraordinary encounter. And skateboarders relived photographic and video images of themselves, making the body into a mediated entity and, conversely, the image into a lived representation. But starting from the early 1980s onward, skateboarding's focus has shifted, becoming more urban in character, directly confrontational not only with architecture but also with the economic logic of capitalist abstract space. It is on this street skating that I focus here.

Around 1984, Los Angeles skaters began the first radical extensions of skateboarding into the most quotidian and conventional elements of the urban landscape. Using the ollie as their basic move, the impact-adhesion-ascension procedure by which the skater unweights the front of the skateboard to make it pop up seemingly unaided into the air, they rode up onto the walls, steps, and street furniture of the Santa Monica strand and Venice Boardwalk. In the words of Stacy Peralta, skateboard manufacturer, filmmaker, and ex-professional skater:

> Skaters can exist on the essentials of what is out there. Anything is part of the run. For urban skaters the city is the hardware on their trip.

For example, *Public Domain* and *Ban This*, the videos Peralta produced and directed in 1988–89, show skaters in the streets of Los Angeles and Santa Barbara jumping over cars, riding onto the walls of buildings, over hydrants and planters, onto benches, flying over steps, and sliding down the freestanding handrails in front of a bank.

The first thing to note about this new kind of skateboarding is that it is no longer situated in the undulating, semi-suburban terrain of the Hollywood Hills and Santa Monica canyon, among the moneyed detached villas and swimming pools, and has instead come downtown, to the inner city.

> I realized that I would have to leave the hills and open countryside to progress in skating. Towards the urban jungle I headed [...] Bigger and more varied types of terrain were my driving force. (Bowman)

And this is a process which has continued; today it is not only the downtown streets of New York, Washington, San Francisco, and Philadelphia which are the most intense skate scenes, but also those of London, Prague, Melbourne, Mexico City, and other cities worldwide. The new skateboarding sites are not private houses or suburban roads, hidden from public view, but university campuses, urban squares, public institutions and buildings, national theatres, commercial office plazas, as well as the more quotidian spaces of streets, sidewalks, and parking lots; they range from specific sites such as, for example, the Annenberg Center for Performing Arts in Philadelphia, to any parking lot or bus bench in any city worldwide. All these are appropriations of places, not dissimilar to the 1970s appropriations of schoolyard banks and backyard pools, but here, like Paul Virilio's call for an inhabitation of the "critical spaces" of hospitals, theatres, universities, factories, and so on, skaters undertake a "counter-habitation" of habitually uninhabited but nonetheless public spaces (cited in Said). Skaters exploit the ambiguity of the ownership and function of public and semipublic space, displaying their actions to the public at large. But why is this, and what does it mean for the experience of urban architecture?

Cities offer more opportunities for those who live in their cores and concentrated heterogeneous social spaces than for those who live in the suburbs; the rich architectural and social fabric of the city offers skateboarders a plethora of building types, social relations, times and spaces, many of which do not necessarily require money to be accessed or at least visited. As a result, city dwellers have more choice than suburbanists and are potentially more adaptive, even when lacking in economic privilege.

> [E]ven when he is not wealthy the city dweller reaps the benefits of past glories and enjoys a considerable latitude of initiative, the make-believe existence of his environment is less fictitious and unsatisfactory than that of his suburban or new-town counterpart; it is enlivened by monuments, chance encounters and the various occupations and distractions forming part of his everyday experience; city make-believe favors the adaptation of time and space. (Lefebvre, *Everyday Life in the Modern World* 123)

But making a decision about which spaces and relations to enter into is not an easy one, and for any metropolitan dweller is ultimately conditioned by a whole range of not only locational and financial conditions, but also those of time, friendship, gender, race, age, culture, and ideology. In particular, it is difficult to make such decisions based on any sense of urban *style*, for while industrialization and commercialization pervades into every aspect of urban life, we have little language or style of experience beyond the formal "styles" of architectural physicality and the commodified "lifestyles" of fashion, food, and such like. Analytically, this is in part due to a theoretical inheritance from Marx, who tended to reduce urbanization to organization and the demands of production, and so ignored the possibilities of adaptation to the city (134–5). Socially, it means that we have no *language* of urban living, and instead we are surrounded by an emptiness filled by signs. In contrast, skateboarding, as we shall see, offers a partial glimpse of a counter-future to this condition, a creation of the city by those engaging directly with its everyday spaces.

> The productive potential expressed and realized in industrial production might have been diverted towards that most essential of productions, the City, urban society. In such a city, creation of creations, everyday life would become a creation of which each citizen and each community would be capable. (135)

As part of their own participation in the realization of this "productive potential," skaters recognize that architecture has no innate or fixed meaning, and they are thus free to reinterpret it as they will.

> The corporate types see their structures as powerful and strong. I see them as something I can enjoy, something I can manipulate to my advantage. (Jesse Neuhaus in Garchik)

It is sometimes argued that the most effectively appropriated spaces are those occupied by symbols (such as gardens, parks, religious buildings), because this appropriation offers the chance to invert social relations and meanings and so create a kind of heterotopic space (Lefebvre, *Production of Space* 366; Foucault, "Of Other Spaces"). To this end, skaters and other subversive or countercultural urbanists like graffiti artists certainly do occasionally work against highly symbolic monuments—for example, one of the favored highly visible locations for Norwegian skaters since the mid-1990s has been along the raised walkways and outside the central doorway of the immense Rådhus in Oslo. Similarly, Czech skaters have utilized the space around the National Theatre in Prague, London skaters have since the 1970s done the same around the high-cultural Southbank Centre, while Parisian skaters are often to be seen in and around the high architecture follies of Parc La Villette, designed by Bernard Tschumi (Papadakis, Broadbent, and Toy).

Skateboarders implicitly realize the importance of the streets as a place to act.

But it is in the open, public space of streets and squares that countercultural and counter-spatial activities most readily take place, as these are the spaces that are not yet dominated by the high ideologies and powers of the state—a point which Lefebvre notes in his little-read yet highly informative study of the events of Paris in 1968.

> It was in the streets that the demonstrations took place. It was in the streets that spontaneity expressed itself [...] The streets have become politicized—this fact points up the political void prevailing in the specialized areas. Social space has assumed new meaning. This entails new meaning. This entails new risks. Political practice transferred to the streets sidesteps the (economic and social) practice which emanates from identifiable places. (Lefebvre, *The Explosion* 71–72)

Skateboarders implicitly realize the importance of the streets as a place to act; rather than ideologically frontal or monumental architecture, skateboarders usually prefer the lack of meaning and symbolism of more everyday spaces—the space of the street, the urban plaza, the mini-mall—just as graffiti artists tend to write on out-of-the-way (not always very visible) sites.

In part, this is to prevent social conflict, but it is also an attempt to write anew, not to change meaning but to insert a meaning where previously there was none.

What then are these other kinds of spaces, those without explicit meaning or symbolism? Most obviously, they are the leftover spaces of modernist town planning, or the spaces of decision-making (typically the urban plaza) which symbolize not through overt iconography but predominantly through their expansivity of space. Lefebvre characterizes these, after Roland Barthes, as a kind of spatial degree zero: zero points of language (everyday speech), objects (functional objects), spaces (traffic circulation, deserted spaces in the heart of the city), needs (predicted, satisfied in advance), and time (programmed, organized according to a preexisting space).

> Zero point is a transparency interrupting communication and relationships just at the moment when everything seems communicable because everything seems both rational and real; and then there is nothing to communicate! (Lefebvre, *Everyday Life in the Modern World* 184)

Architecturally, the city is reduced to the status and form of an instrument, passed over by a capitalist and state rationality which prefers to operate on a national or international scale.

> The statutes of urban "zones" and "areas" are reduced to a juxtaposition of spaces, of functions, of elements on the ground. Sectors and functions are tightly subordinated to centers of decision-making. Homogeneity overwhelms the differences originating from nature (the site), from peasant surroundings (territory and the soil), from history. The city, or what remains of it, is built or is rearranged, in the likeness of a sum or combination of elements. (Lefebvre, *Writings on Cities* 127)

The new town and the reconstructed old city alike are reduced to the legibility of signs, their spaces optimized for the function of decision-making.

For the experience of such architecture, there is a similarly reductive effect. In Barthes' concept of "zero point" elaborated in *Le degré zéro de l'écriture/Writing Degree Zero* (1953/1967), the neutralization and disappearance of symbols is justified by the writer claiming to state simply and coldly what is, acting purely as a witness (Lefebvre, *Everyday Life in the Modern World* 183–84). In terms of architecture, the lack of discernible qualitative differences, and the corresponding surfeit of instructions and signals, is rendered as a feeling of monotony and lack of diversity, the urban having lost the characteristics of the creative *oeuvre* and of appropriation.

> There is a poverty of daily life as nothing has replaced the symbols, the appropriations, the styles, the monuments, the times and rhythms, the different and qualified spaces of the traditional city. Urban society, because of the dissolution of this city submitted to pressures which it cannot withstand, tends on the one hand to blend with the planned land use of the territory into the "urban fabric" determined by the constraints of traffic, and on the other hand, into dwelling units such as those of the detached house and the housing estates. (Lefebvre, *Writings on Cities* 128)

The metropolitan dweller and architect alike become mere witnesses to the functioning of the city, in which exchanges of decisions and commodities dominate over social relations and uses. The experience of urban space is reduced to that of the modern museum, where constraints on the bodies of visitors create a kind of "organized walking" in which route, speed, gestures, speaking, and sound are all controlled (Bennett).

This does not mean, however, that passivity and ennui are the only possible responses to such reductive architecture. Resistance to zero-degree architecture takes place outside of the buildings themselves, in the streets, countering the everyday, routinized phenomena of privatized urban space and the commodification and pacification of urban experience by enacting a different space and time for the city.

> Formerly abstract and incomplete, the dissociations now become complete. Projected onto the terrain, it is here that

> they can transcend themselves—in the streets. It is here that student meets worker, and reason reduced to a function again recovers speech. (Lefebvre, *The Explosion* 98)

Skateboarders target the spaces and times of the urban degree zero, reinscribing themselves onto functional everyday spaces and objects.

> [Skateboarding] is a challenge to our everyday concepts of the functions of buildings, and to the closed world we create for ourselves out of this massively unlimited city. (Hodgkinson)

For example, a handrail is a highly functional object, for which both the time and nature of use is fully programmed. If there is a meaning at all in a handrail, then it is directly related to function: that of safety. The surprise of the skateboarder's reuse of the handrail—ollieing up onto the rail, and sliding down its length sideways, weighted perilously on the skateboard deck as it at once balances and moves along the fulcrum line of the metal bar—is that it targets something to do with safety, to do with everyday security, and turns it into an object of risk, where previously it was precisely risk that was being erased. The whole logic of the handrail is turned on its head. More usually, however, such an object has no apparent history or wider cultural or social meaning outside of the use for which it is intentionally designed and provided. In place or on top of this absence of meaning, skateboarding inscribes a new one; where previously there was only the most banal of uses, skateboarders create not just a change of use but an *ex novo* act. The "meaning" of the skateboard move then in part takes its power and vitality from the fact that it comes out of the blue, an unexpected and sudden eruption of meaning where society had previously been content to say nothing. Skateboarding is a critique of the emptiness of meaning.

> Empty of cars, car parks have only form and no function. ("Searching, Finding, Living, Sharing")

Rhythm and Urban Senses

If the meaning of the architecture of the new town and reconstructed postwar city is at zero point, what then does skateboarding address? What is the ground on which it acts? The answer lies less in the realm of culture of meaning, and more in that of physical and sensory rhythms.

While cities are made from social relations as conceived and constructed by thought, they are not, and cannot be, purely ideational. The "urban is not a soul, a spirit, a philosophical entity" (Lefebvre, *Writings on Cities* 103), so the city is the immediate reality, the practico-material of the urban; it is the architectural fact with which the urban cannot dispense. And of course, this "architectural fact" necessarily takes on a certain form, which in turn poses certain constraints and conditions, but also specific opportunities in time and space. Lefebvre notes, for example, the remarkable architecture of stairs in Mediterranean cities, which link spaces and times, and so provide the rhythm for space and time of walking in the city (237).

What then if we applied the same "rhythmanalysis" (Lefebvre, *Éléments de rythmanalyse*; Lefebvre, *Production of Space* 205–7) to modern cities, to the architecture of the zero-degree city? What kind of rhythm and experience do they presuppose? This is exactly the condition for urban skateboarders, being both presented with, and exploitative of, the physical space-times of modernist urban space. Firstly, it is the spaces of the modern metropolis that skateboarders address: the spaces of the square and the street, the campus and semipublic buildings. Beyond these spaces being functional spaces, each corresponding to a particular activity or ideological purpose, they are also conceived of primarily as objects in space, as dispositions of three-dimensional form (each modulated according to its own programmatic and aesthetic concerns) in a universal, abstract space. Space here then is at once homogeneous, and—subjected to the various technical forces and resources available—more or less capable of being fragmented into any subdivision, plot, or architectural component that might be wished of it.

> What then is the principal contradiction to be found? Between the capacity to conceive of and treat space on a global (or worldwide) scale on the one hand, and its frag-

> mentation by a multiplicity of procedures or processes, all fragmentary themselves, on the other. (Lefebvre, *Production of Space* 355)

Skateboarders treat space exactly as conceived and presented in this form of architectural urbanism. Firstly, space becomes a uniform entity, a constant layer through the city that can be utilized, in this case, as a surface on which to skate. All elements of the city are thus reduced to the homogeneous level of skateable terrain, for "[a]nything is part of the run" (Peralta).

> Buildings are building blocks for the open minded. ("Searching, Finding, Living, Sharing")

Secondly, skaters follow the homogeneity-fragmentation contradiction of abstract space by oscillating from this macro conception of space to the micro one of the architectural element; they move from the open canvas of the urban realm to the close focus of a specific wall, bench, fire hydrant, curb, or rail.

> Bumps, curbs and gaps. The street is really universal. (Rodriguez)

> From a perfect bank, to a smooth marble step, to a lamp post: movement around lines and shadows. An unusual arrangement of street furniture can be inspiration for radness. ("Searching, Finding, Living, Sharing")

The spatial rhythm adopted is then that of a passage or journey from one element to another, the run across the city spaces interspersed with moments and momentary settlings on specific sites. This is not an activity which could take place in a medieval, renaissance, or early industrial city. It requires the smooth surfaces and running spaces of the paved, concrete city—"the polished marble planes of [Mies] van der Rohe's plazas are Mecca to Chicago's skateboarders" (Garchik)—and, above all, it requires the object-space-object-space rhythm born from a fragmentation of objects within a homogeneous space. For the skateboarder, the "primary relationships are not with his fellow man, but with the earth beneath his feet, concrete and all" (Mulshine).

Rhythmanalysis does not only refer to space, however, and also involves the rhythm of time. The temporal rhythms—the various routines, cyclical patterns, speeds, durations, precisions, repetitions—of the city, as well as its spaces, offer a frame for skateboarders. Here it is the essentially fragmentary temporal use of urban space that skateboarders respond to, exploiting the streets, urban plazas, and street furniture that others rarely use in any constant manner for long periods. For the zero-point architecture of the new town and decision-making center, the skater interweaves their own composition of time into that of regular temporal patterns, such as waging a fast assault on a handrail outside a bank, adding a speeding skateboard to the slower pattern of those walking on the sidewalk— "skating past all the business-suit lames that slog gloomily down the sidewalk, barely lifting their feet, like they're kicking shit with every step" (Brian Casey in Mulshine)—or staying longer in an urban plaza as others hurry through. (I saw this last kind of temporal tactic most evenings in the mid-1990s outside Euston Station in London, where a few skaters often spent an hour or so riding over its planters, benches, and low walls, while commuters rushed through to their transport connections.) For the more contested terrains of postmodernity—such as the shopping mall or privatized public space—a different temporal tactic has to be used. In particular, skaters exploit the highly bounded temporality of, for example, a privatized office district by stepping outside of its normal patterns of use. In places in London like Canary Wharf or Broadgate—both versions of privatized urban space, with very precise patterns of usage—skaters use the hours of the weekend or evening to conduct their own activities, separate from the conventional times kept by office workers. This appropriation of the unused time of a particular urban element is also applied to smaller, less spectacular parts of the urban street; the bus bench out of rush hour, or the department store parking lot outside of shopping hours, can also be the focus of skateboarders who take advantage of the few minutes or hours in which it otherwise lies dormant.

All elements of the city are reduced to the homogeneous level of skateable terrain.

Micro experience is also part of rhythmanalysis—the relation of the self to the physical minutiae of the city that are not always obvious to, or considered by, the dominant visualization of the city upon which we most commonly depend.

> These are my streets. I know every crack of every sidewalk there is down here. (Alva)

For skaters, this involves hearing; when travelling at speed the skater, like a cyclist, responds to the more obvious sounds of the city, such as a car accelerating up from behind or a police siren, and to the noises of a car door, people talking, and footsteps. In particular, the sound of the skateboard over the ground yields much information about the conditions of the surface, such as its speed, grip, and predictability. More importantly, micro rhythmanalysis involves a sense of touch, generated either from direct contact with the terrain—hand on building, foot on wall—or from the smoothness and textual rhythms of the surface underneath, passed up through the wheels, trucks, and deck up into the skater's feet and body. Here such things as the smoothness of pure tarmac or concrete, the roughness of metaled road, or the intermittent counter rhythm of paving slab cracks all combine to create a textual pattern bound into the skateboarder's experience of urban space. The compositional sound rhythms—the monotonal constancy of the subtle roar of tarmac, the silence-click-silence-click of paving slabs, combined with the intermittent pure silences when the skateboard leaves the ground through an ollie, and the sudden cracks as it once again hits terrain and elements—are a feature of this urban space.

The skateboard run, with its patterned moves, junctures, noises, and silences is then at once an exploitation and denial of zero-degree architecture, exploiting its surfaces and smoothness, while using its roughness and objectival qualities to create a new appropriative rhythm quite distinct from the routinized, passive experiences which it usually enforces; street skateboarding is "a total focus of mind, body and environment to a level way beyond that of the dead consumers interested at best in money, beer, and 'the lads'" (Powell). The "new school" skateboard—with its light deck, small wheels, and equal front-back orientation specifically designed for street skating—is a tool in hand for this rhythm, a tool that is also absorbed into the new rhythmic production of super-architectural space.

As this last point suggests, it is not only the city that is reengaged with in the intersection of skateboard, body, and architecture. The construction of the body too is changed. In terms that recall Georg Simmel's identification in the modern metropolis of a fundamental reorientation of the physiology and psychological of its inhabitants, an "intensification of nervous stimulation which results from the swift and uninterrupted change of outer and inner stimuli," or what David Frisby calls "neurasthenia." Lefebvre notes that:

> The physiological functions of the "modern" man's nervous and cerebral systems seem to have fallen victim to an excessively demanding regime, to a kind of hypertension and exhaustion. He has not yet "adapted" to the conditions of his life, to the speed of its sequences and rhythms, to the (momentarily) excessive abstraction of the frequently erroneous concepts he has so recently acquired. His nerves and senses have not yet been adequately trained by the urban and technical life he leads. (*Critique of Everyday Life* 120)

For skateboarders, like all metropolitan dwellers, modern urban conditions produce new kinds of socio-spatial conditions, impacting at psychological and formal as well as social levels. In Lefebvre's consideration of events, unlike Simmel's, the new kind of person this creates is not yet fully evolved, not fully adapted. In particular, the modern individual cannot abstract out the concept from the thing, for these are mixed together in their perception, creating a confused unity in which relations, order, and hierarchy are lost. This is a state of "deliberate semi-neurosis," partly playacting, and "often little more than an ambivalent infantilism" (Lefebvre, *Critique of Everyday Life* 120).

We might speculate then that this "ambivalent infantilism" is exactly the condition of skateboarders, faced with the intense conditions of the modern city. And in terms of epistemology, or more precisely in the context of the absence of codified socio-political awareness on the part of many skaters, this would be largely correct. But the very same condition also contains the seeds of resistance, critique, and creative production. As Lefebvre notes, the fact that the modern individual is not yet "fully adapted" suggests that a process of evolution is underway. He examines this process more explicitly elsewhere, seeing it as involving a transformation and development of our senses. It is then in lived experience, rather than abstract theoretical knowledge, that the skateboarder's adaptation can initially be seen.

> The activity which gives the external world and its "phenomena" shape is not a "mental" activity, theoretical and formal, but a practical, concrete one. Practical tools, not simple concepts, are the means by which social man has shaped his perceptible world. As regards the processes of knowledge by means of which we understand this "world" [...] they are our senses. But our senses have been transformed by action [...] Thus it is that our senses, organs, vital needs, instincts, feelings have been permeated with consciousness, with human reason, since they too have been shaped by social life. (163)

Such concerns directly raise the question of spatiality, as Fredric Jameson does in his identification of the alarming disjunction of body and built environment in the Westin Bonaventure Hotel in Los Angeles, where postmodern hyperspace "has finally succeeded in transcending the capacities of the individual human body to locate itself, to organize its immediate surrounding perceptually, and cognitively to map its position in a mappable external world" (38–45).

The skateboarder's highly developed integrated sense of balance, speed, hearing, sight, touch, and responsivity is then a product of the modern metropolis, a newly evolved sensory and cognitive mapping; the aim is not only to receive the city but to return it to itself, to change through movement and physical energy the nature of the experience of the urban realm.

> A feel of rhythm and an aroma of sweat overcome my senses on this Wednesday evening as the popping sound of wooden tails and the connection of metal trucks to metal coping takes place. (Carnel)

> One step ahead of the pedestrian or static eye, the architects and the artists, the people who look at shapes and patterns around themselves and see beauty in these things people have created from pattern and relationships of shapes to shapes and people to shapes. To us these things are more. These things have purpose because we have movement as well as vision. ("Searching, Finding, Living, Sharing")

Skateboarding is thus part of the untheorized element of praxis (Lefebvre, *Sociology of Marx* 38–9), that which focuses on the development of a sensuous enjoyment of the object (rehabilitating the world of senses as practical-sensuous, through the immediate sensing of art, cities, buildings, objects of common use, landscapes, and relationships) and on the recognition of particular needs (here the need for activity, muscular extension, direct engagement with objects).

> It's better than drugs. You won't believe the adrenalin. The feeling of accomplishment is insane. (Ben Powell in Evans)

The skateboarder's senses are then historically produced, both as products of the historical constraints of the city, and as agents of engagement with the present and future opportunities of the city. These senses are not then a basic need, the satisfaction of which brings simply "momentary relief to constant struggle" (Lefebvre, *Sociology of Marx* 41), but a historically produced capacity to enjoy and reproduce the city. They are a sensory and spatialized version of the Althusserian concept of ideology as the imaginary representation of the subject's relationship to their real conditions of existence.

It would be wrong then to see skateboarding as a nostalgic return to the physicality of enjoyment; rather it is a new physicality of enjoyment latent in the possibilities of modern architecture. Whereas, for example, the oldest towns of England are, due to their medieval architecture and urban fabric, "crap to skate" ("Fire and Friends"), the modern architecture of the new town offers surface (concrete not cobbles), expansivity (squares not alleys), urban elements (fragments in space, not modulations of space), and above all, the appropriativity of public space, semipublic space, and certain private spaces. To give one precise example of skateboarding's engagement with this architectural possibility, the small wheels of new-school skateboards are an attempt to exploit the smoothness of terrains while increasing the height of the ollie move, and as such are born from the level horizontality of the pavement and, simultaneously, aimed at a denial of that horizontality. The city offers at once precise hard-faced objects, a precise delineation of where particular functions take place, and, simultaneously, an ambiguity of meaning, circulation patterns, control, and ownership. It is this modern city that skateboarding is at once born from and works against.

Performative Critique

Many questions are raised by all this, not least as to how skateboarding, by virtue of using architecture without participating in its productive or exchange functions, might pose a reassertion of use values over exchange values and so, implicitly, mount a critique of labor and consumption in capitalism. How does this relate to the subcultural values of skateboarding, through which its practitioners construct a kind of romanticist generalized opposition to society and so create a social world in which self-identifying values and appearances are formed in distinction to conventional codes of behavior? What of skateboarders' attitudes and constructions of race, age, class, gender, sexuality, and, above all, masculinity? What of the global dispersion of skateboarding, and its spatially generalized activity through millions of skateboarders in just about every major and minor city throughout the world? Conversely, what of the extremely localized physical marks and striations created by skateboarding on the urban realm—the aggressive grinds of truck against concrete, board against wood, and their destructive assault on the micro-boundaries of architecture? What of appropriations of time and not just space, and what of skateboarders' attitudes to history, politics, and the material constructions of the urban? What of spontaneity? What of the city as *oeuvre*, as the production of human beings and the richly significant play of collective creation (Lefebvre, *Writings on Cities* 101), and of the city as the place of love, desire, turmoil, and

Skateboarding is antagonistic toward the urban environment.

uncertainty? And what of spatial, temporal, and social censorship on the part of safety experts, urban legislators, and managers, who have tried to invoke laws of trespass, criminal damage, and curfew to control skateboarding?

These questions must remain unanswered here, but suffice to say that skateboarding is antagonistic toward the urban environment—"a skateboard is the one thing you can use as a weapon in the street that you don't get patted down for" (Craig Steyck in Gabriel). But beyond simple accusations that skaters cause physical damage to persons and to property, in redefining space for themselves skateboarders threaten accepted definitions of space, confronting the social, spatial, and temporal logic of capitalist space; skateboarders take over space conceptually as well as physically and so strike at the very heart of what everyone else understands by the city.

> Around 37th, there is a quiet garden spot where students can relax in the shade of some flowering trees and enjoy a restful moment. Be sure to do some grinds on the edge of the steps down to this place, or just drop right down them (there are only two). Do a slide or something before you go. They're in a city. Don't let them forget it. (Brian Casey in Mulshine)

Skateboarders are part of a long process in the history of cities, a fight by the disempowered and disenfranchised for a distinctive social space of their own. They bring time, space, and social being together through a confrontation of the body and board with the architectural surface, and, as a result, they redefine the city and its architecture, their own social identity and bodies, the production/reproduction nexus of architecture, the emphasis on production, exchange, and consumption, and the lived nature of representations. This is the most overt political space produced by skateboarders, a pleasure ground carved out of the city as a kind of continuous reaffirmation of one of the central maxims of the 1968 Paris revolts, that *sous les pavés, la plage*—beneath the pavement, the beach (Shields).

Above all, it is in the continual performance of skateboarding—which rather than reading or writing the city, *speaks* the city through utterance as bodily engagement—that its meaning and actions are manifested. This performance cannot be seen or understood through pure abstraction; like rhythms, skateboarding requires a multiplicity of senses, thoughts, and activities to be enacted, represented, and comprehended.

> Rhythms. Rhythms. They reveal and hide, being much more varied than in music or the so-called civil code of successions, relatively simple texts in relation to the city. Rhythms: music of the City, a picture which listens to itself, image in the present of a discontinuous sum. (Lefebvre, *Writings on Cities* 227)

Rhythms then disclose things, not through explanation or codified interpretation, but through lived experience. For Lefebvre, locating and understanding rhythms is to find a truly social time-space that is at once a practice, conception, and experience. Above all, because the experiencer relates the fundamental conditions of their own temporality to that of the world outside, they create an engagement between subject and object that is ultimately a lived form of dialectical thought.

> Here is found that old philosophical question (the subject and the object and their relationships) posed in non-speculative terms, close to practice. The observer at the window knows that he takes as first reference *his time*, but that the first impression displaces itself and includes the most diverse rhythms, as long as they remain *to scale*. The passage from the *subject* to the *object* requires neither a leap over an abyss, nor the crossing of the desert. (Lefebvre, *Writings on Cities* 227)

Skateboarding is then a kind of unconscious dialectical thought, an engagement with the spatial and temporal rhythms of the city, wherein skateboarders use themselves as reference to rethink the city through the practice of skateboarding. Skateboarding is not the ignorance of "unthinking and unknowingness," but rather an activity in which a certain newness is born from knowledge, representation, and lived experience enacted together. It is also an activity which refutes architecture as domination of the self.

> Skateboarding is my only identity for better or worse. (Cates)

Rather than allowing architecture and the city to dictate what they are, and to demand who urban dwellers are, the skateboarder poses the unanswerable questions of "what are you?" and "who am I?" Ultimately, these are not questions for the past or present, but for the future construction of the as yet unknown city. All this occurs not as metatheory or political program, but through bodily action performed on everyday streets, spaces, and times—far from being the diminution of its importance, this is the very source of skateboarding's historical relevance and being.

References

Alva, Tony. "Interview." *Heckler* (1996), http://heckler.com. Accessed May 5, 1996.

Barthes, Roland. *Writing Degree Zero*. London: Cape, 1967. Print.

Bennett, Tony. *The Birth of the Museum: History, Theory, Politics*. London: Routledge, 1995. Print.

Bowman, Ewan. "Comment." *Sidewalk Surfer* 13 (1997): unpaginated. Print.

Carnel, Chris. "Interview with Bryce Kanights," *Heckler* (1996), http://heckler.com. Accessed May 5, 1996.

Cates, Dan. "Comment." *Sidewalk Surfer* 13 (1997), unpaginated. Print.

Evans, Siân Liz. "Young, Gifted and Board Stupid." *The Big Issue* 126 (1995): 18. Print.

"Fire and Friends," *Sidewalk Surfer* 3 (1996): unpaginated. Print.

Foucault, Michel. "Of Other Spaces: Utopias and Heterotopias." *Architecture Culture 1943–1968: A Documentary Anthology.* Ed. Joan Ockman. New York: Rizzoli, 1993. 422–23. Print.

Frisby, David. *Fragments of Modernity: Theories of Modernity in the Work of Simmel, Kracauer and Benjamin*. Cambridge, Mass.: MIT, 1986. Print.

Garchik, Leah. "The Urban Landscape." *San Francisco Chronicle* (1994). www.dansworld.com/urban.html. Accessed April 11, 2000.

Gayle, Caine. "Multiple Choice Through Words and Pictures." *Slap* 4.9 (1995): 33. Print.

Hodgkinson, Tom. "Rad, Mad and Dangerous to Know?" *Midweek*, January 18, 1990: 10.

Lefebvre, Henri. *The Explosion: Marxism and the French Revolution.* New York: Monthly Review, 1969. Print.

Lefebvre, Henri. *The Sociology of Marx*. New York: Columbia University Press, 1982. Print.

Lefebvre, Henri. *Everyday Life in the Modern World*. London: Transaction, 1984. Print.

Lefebvre, Henri. *The Production of Space*. Oxford: Blackwell, 1991. Print.

Lefebvre, Henri. *Critique of Everyday Life. Volume 1: Introduction*. London: Verso, 1991. Print.

Lefebvre, Henri. *Introduction to Modernity: Twelve Preludes September 1959–May 1961*. London: Verso, 1995. Print.

Lefebvre, Henri. *Writings on Cities*. Eds. Eleonore Kofman and Elizabeth Lebas. Oxford: Blackwell, 1996. Print.

Mulshine, Paul. "Wild in the Streets." *Philadelphia Magazine* 78.4 (1987): 120. Print.

Papadakis, Andreas, Geoffrey Broadbent, and Maggie Toy, eds. *Free Spirit in Architecture: Omnibus Volume*. London: Academy Editions, 1992.

Peralta, Stacy. "Interview." *Interview* 17 July (1987): 102–03. Print.

Powell, Ben. "Not a Toy." *Sidewalk Surfer* 3 (1996): unpaginated. Print.

Rodriguez, Matt. "Interview." *Heckler* (1996), http://heckler.com. Accessed May 5, 1996.

Said, Edward. "Culture and Imperialism." *Design Book Review* 29–30 (1993): 6–13. Print.

"Searching, Finding, Living, Sharing." *R.A.D. Magazine* 79, September (1989): 16. Print.

Shields, Rob. *An English Précis of Henri Lefebvre's "La Production de l'espace"*. University of Sussex: Urban and Regional Studies Working Paper no. 63, 1988. Print.

Simmel, Georg. "The Metropolis and Mental Life." *Cities and Society: The Revised Reader in Urban Sociology*. Eds. Paul K. Hatt and Albert J. Reiss. New York: Free Press, 1951. Print.

Authors

Iain Borden is a professor of architecture and urban culture at The Bartlett, University College London. Iain's research focuses on social and cultural experiences of cities and architecture, and his most recent book, *Skateboarding and the City: A Complete History*, is being published by Bloomsbury in 2019.

Konstantin Butz is a researcher and lecturer at the Academy of Media Arts Cologne, Germany. He completed his studies in American studies and cultural studies with a dissertation on the American subculture of skate punk (published in 2012). His research interests include subcultures, youth cultures, and (un-) popular literature and music.

Ocean Howell is a retired professional skateboarder and an associate professor of history at the Clark Honors College at the University of Oregon. He received his PhD from the University of California, Berkeley in 2010. He is the author of *Making the Mission: Planning and Ethnicity in San Francisco* (University of Chicago Press, 2015).

Kyle Kusz is an associate professor at the University of Rhode Island. Author of *Revolt of the White Athlete: Race, Media, and the Emergence of Extreme Athletes in America* (Peter Lang, 2007), his work examines the role of American sports media narratives in contemporary racial formations and politics.

ZáNean McClain is an associate professor. She researches instructional effectiveness and inclusive physical activity.
E. Missy Wright is an assistant professor. She teaches research methods, sport sociology, and psychology, and conducts community-engaged research.
Becky Beal is a professor of sociology and philosophy of sport. She researches the cultural politics of sport.
Matthew Atencio is an associate professor. He researches youth studies and sociocultural pedagogies in sports and physical activity. They all work in the department of kinesiology at California State University, East Bay (CSUEB).

Christian Peters is a geographer and sports scientist. He works as a teacher and journalist in Cologne, Germany. His research interests include sports geographies, city development, and urban and youth cultures.

Kai Reinhart is a researcher and lecturer at the Institute of Sports Science of the University of Münster. He completed his studies in history, German philology, and sports science with a dissertation on official sport and informal sport scenes in the GDR (published in 2010). His research interests include skateboarding, mountaineering, football, the body, and philosophy.

Eckehart Velten Schäfer works as a journalist, sociologist, and historian in Berlin. In 2017, he completed his dissertation on the history of body, space, and signification in the practice of skateboarding since the 1960s at the Carl von Ossietzky Universität Oldenburg. He intends to publish it as a book in 2018 or 2019. His interests include social theory, the relation of sport and society, the city and urbanism, as well as political and cultural movements in the twentieth century.

Francisco Vivoni is an assistant professor in the department of sociology at Worcester State University. His current research centers on built environments, social control, and struggles over public space.

Emily Chivers Yochim is an associate professor in the department of communication arts and theatre at Allegheny College, where she teaches feminist media and cultural studies. She is the author of *Skate Life: Re-Imagining White Masculinity* (University of Michigan Press, 2010) and *Mothering Through Precarity: Women's Work and Digital Media*, with Julie A. Wilson (Duke University Press, 2017).

The editors would like to thank all contributing authors as well as Alexander Butz, Sylee Gore, Moritz Ingwersen, Franz König, Mischa Kuball, Hanna Schmandin, and Johannes Wohnseifer.

Editors: Konstantin Butz and Christian Peters
Design: Alexander Butz, hej@alxbtz.com
Photos: Johannes Wohnseifer, courtesy of Galerie Gisela Capitain, Cologne & König Galerie, Berlin
Print: Livonia Print Ltd.

First published by Koenig Books, London

Koenig Books Ltd
At the Serpentine Gallery
Kensington Gardens
London W2 3XA
www.koenigbooks.co.uk

Printed in Latvia

Distribution

Germany, Austria, Switzerland / Europe
Buchhandlung Walther König
Ehrenstr. 4,
D - 50672 Köln
Tel: +49 (0) 221 / 20 59 6 53
verlag@buchhandlung-walther-koenig.de

UK & Ireland
Cornerhouse Publications Ltd. - HOME
2 Tony Wilson Place
UK - Manchester M15 4FN
Tel: +44 (0) 161 212 3466
publications@cornerhouse.org

Outside Europe
D.A.P. / Distributed Art Publishers, Inc.
75 Broad Street, Suite 630
USA - New York, NY 10004
Tel: +1 (0) 212 627 1999
enadel@dapinc.com

ISBN 978-3-96098-341-5